LORDS OF FEAR

Stan Lee, Gerry Conway, Scott Edelman, Chris Cl
Roy Thomas & Dann Thomas with Bill Mantlo & .

WRITERS

Steve Ditko, Jack Kirby, Rich Buckler, Rico Rival, Ruben Yandoc,
Ron Wilson, John Byrne, Al Milgrom, Larry Alexander & Geof Isherwood

PENCILERS

Steve Ditko, Vince Colletta, Chic Stone, Joe Sinnott, Rico Rival,
Ruben Yandoc, Bob Wiacek, Al Milgrom & Jim Sanders III with
Jim Mooney, Dan Adkins, Tony DeZuniga & Tim Dzon

INKERS

Linda Lessmann, Stan Goldberg, Glynis Wein,
Petra Goldberg, Hugh Paley, Phil Rachelson,
Gregory Wright & George Roussos

COLORISTS

Artie Simek, John Costanza, Marcus Pelayo,
San José, Ray Holloway, Bruce Patterson,
Jim Novak & Pat Brosseau with Terry Szenics,
Charlotte Jetter & Clem Robins

LETTERERS

Mike Rockwitz & Barry Dutter

ASSISTANT EDITORS

Stan Lee, Roy Thomas, Len Wein, Marv Wolfman, Archie Goodwin,
Terry Kavanagh & Mike Rockwitz with Michael Higgins

EDITORS

Front Cover Artists: Geof Isherwood & Veronica Gandini
Back Cover Artists: Gil Kane & Bernie Wrightson

Doctor Strange created by Stan Lee & Steve Ditko

Collection Editor: Mark D. Beazley
Assistant Editor: Caitlin O'Connell
Associate Managing Editor: Kateri Woody
Associate Manager, Digital Assets: Joe Hochstein
Masterworks Editor: Cory Sedlmeier
Senior Editor, Special Projects: Jennifer Grünwald

VP Production & Special Projects: Jeff Youngquist
Research & Layout: Jeph York
Manager, Special Projects: Brian Overton
Production: ColorTek, Ryan Devall, Romie Jeffers, Digikore & Joe Frontirre
Book Designer: Adam Del Re
SVP Print, Sales & Marketing: David Gabriel

Editor In Chief: Axel Alonso
Chief Creative Officer: Joe Quesada
President: Dan Buckley
Executive Producer: Alan Fine

DOCTOR STRANGE: LORDS OF FEAR. Contains material originally published in magazine form as THOR #136 and #229-230; DEAD OF NIGHT #11; MARVEL SPOTLIGHT #26; MARVEL TWO-IN-ONE #18; MARVEL TEAM-UP #68; DOCTOR STRANGE, SORCERER SUPREME #31-33 and #38-40; STRANGE TALES #110 and #116; and MARVEL COMICS PRESENTS (1988) #1-4. First printing 2017. ISBN# 978-1-302-90786-0. Published by MARVEL WORLDWIDE, INC., a subsidiary of MARVEL ENTERTAINMENT, LLC. OFFICE OF PUBLICATION: 135 West 50th Street, New York, NY 10020. **Printed in the U.S.A.** DAN BUCKLEY, President, Marvel Entertainment; JOE QUESADA, Chief Creative Officer; TOM BREVOORT, SVP of Publishing; DAVID BOGART, SVP of Business Affairs & Operations, Publishing & Partnership; C.B. CEBULSKI, VP of Brand Management & Development, Asia; DAVID GABRIEL, SVP of Sales & Marketing, Publishing; JEFF YOUNGQUIST, VP of Production & Special Projects; DAN CARR, Executive Director of Publishing Technology; ALEX MORALES, Director of Publishing Operations; SUSAN CRESPI, Production Manager; STAN LEE, Chairman Emeritus. For information regarding advertising in Marvel Comics or on Marvel.com, please contact Jonathan Parkhideh, VP of Digital Media & Marketing Solutions, at jparkhideh@marvel.com. For Marvel subscription inquiries, please call 888-511-5480. **Manufactured between 11/3/2017 and 12/5/2017 by LSC COMMUNICATIONS INC., KENDALLVILLE, IN, USA.**

10 9 8 7 6 5 4 3 2 1

10 THINGS ONLY SCARECROW SUPER-FANS WILL KNOW (AND MAYBE NOT EVEN THEM) by Scott Edelman

As all True Believers know, many decades ago, in the final issue of a weird anthology comic book that boasted shorts drawn by the likes of Jack Kirby, Steve Ditko and Don Heck, Marvel decided that as a send-off it would take a chance on launching a new character, one that seemed quite bizarre at the time, but which all these years later we're still talking about. And that strange, untested hero was —

The Scarecrow!

Wait, what?

Oh, you thought I was referring to *Amazing Fantasy #15*, and Spider-Man's surprise appearance therein?

Nope. I was talking about *Dead of Night #11*, the last issue of a completely different anthology title featuring short pieces by those greats (although that time around they were reprints), which as a last gasp before cancelation published the initial adventure of a character described on the cover as "Marveldom's #1 Shock-Star."

Quite a claim to be making the first time the Scarecrow was revealed to the world — and from this vantage point I no longer remember whether I suggested that blurb or whether it was written by then editor in chief Len Wein — but of one thing I am certain: Twenty-year-old me wanted those words to be true. And while the character first seen in *Dead of Night #11* didn't rock the comics world as much as that other curious character in *Amazing Fantasy #15*, hey — we're still talking about him more than 40 years later, and you're holding this massive *Doctor Strange: The Fear Lords* volume in your hands, so that must count for something, right?

And the fact that you're reading these words right now rather than leaping right over them to look at all the colorful pictures tells me there's something about this supernatural super hero that continues to intrigue. Let me tell you the untold history of the Scarecrow by sharing 10 things even his super-fans might not know.

1. If the Grim Reaper had lived, the Scarecrow might never have been born. Back in 1974, when I was working as an assistant editor in the Marvel Bullpen, the editors were hungry for regular ongoing characters to appear in the black-and-white line, which featured such oversized comic magazines as *Monsters Unleashed* and *Tales of the Zombie*. Cocky kid that I was, I was sure I could fill that need, and so I pitched a pulp-era vigilante who somehow gets propelled into modern times and takes out gruesome vengeance on modern-day criminals. He was to be called the Grim Reaper, and he didn't get very far. All that exists of him today is a concept sketch penciled by P. Craig Russell of Killraven fame. Though the Grim Reaper's failure to thrive was disappointing, his death paved the way for the Scarecrow, who took his own forms of gruesome vengeance on evildoers.

2. Long before *Uncanny X-Men* and *Alpha Flight* made John Byrne famous, he drew a very different Scarecrow. With the Grim Reaper stillborn, I leapt on fellow new comics pro Roger Slifer's casual comment that no one had ever called a hero the Scarecrow before, and decided that since no one had, it was up to me to be the one to do it. Why had no one ever done it before? Why did Rog not run with the idea himself? I don't have the answer to either of those questions. All I know is that with the editors of the black-and-white books still hungry for content, I intended to deliver. And while I cooked up many possible origin stories and sought a home for my man made of straw, John Byrne sent in a drawing — whether meant solely as a gift for a friend, or instead as a pitch from a fellow newbie for a shot at drawing the book, I no longer remember — one showing the Scarecrow not with the head you've come to know and dread, but with a carved pumpkin as a noggin, its eyes, nose and mouth aglow. That design didn't survive, and Byrne's image was only seen in a rare 1975 fundraising portfolio for the now-defunct professional organization the Academy of Comic Book Arts.

3. Before closing out *Dead of Night*, the Scarecrow killed two other Marvel titles. Once the Scarecrow concept was approved, he almost made his debut in two other books before finally landing in *Dead of Night #11*. First, editor Tony Isabella okayed him to appear in the pages of *Monsters Unleashed*, that same magazine that might have housed the Grim Reaper, meaning for him to alternate with such other supernatural characters as Tigra and Frankenstein's Monster. (In fact, his debut there was even announced in 1974 in the pages of fanzines.) But before he could appear, that title died and the Scarecrow was once more... unleashed. Next, with Len Wein looking for new backups to feature in *Giant-Size Werewolf by Night*, that's where he ended up. Well... not really. For that title, too, was canceled before my hero could appear, and so he was finally put before the public in *Dead of Night*, where it turned out he took that title down with him, too. Not many characters have had the honor of killing not one, not two, but three different comic books! Was the Scarecrow cursed?

4. My first Marvel comic book wasn't written Marvel-style. I always loved hearing tales of Stan Lee leaping atop his desk to act out stories during the creation of the comics I loved at the beginning of the Silver Age (tales I later learned were not at all apocryphal), and I looked forward to replicating that process with whomever was chosen to draw the Scarecrow's first appearance, once it was finally going to happen. But Rico Rival, chosen to draw the Scarecrow's debut, was one of the many artists Marvel was working with long-distance at the time from the Philippines, which meant I was required to do a full script, the way things tended to be done over at what we used to call the Distinguished Competition. I can remember waiting nervously for the art to arrive in the Bullpen, wondering whether Rival would be able to pull off my vision. Was I happy with the result? I was. He did an amazing job bringing the Scarecrow to...life? Though that wasn't the first readers would see of the character, as the cover was penciled by Gil Kane and inked by Bernie Wrightson.

5. The painting that the Cult of Kalumai struggled to steal in the Scarecrow's origin story belongs to me. If you've already read the initial Scarecrow adventure, you know that his debut begins with cult members attempting to steal a painting, which later appears not only as an object being auctioned, but also as a full-page splash on page 5. Amazingly, that painting currently hangs in my house. How was I able to achieve what Gregor Rovik could not, either by money or by stealth? Thank friend Duffy Vohland, without whom I'd never have gotten my staff job at Marvel in the first place (which is a story for another time).

He commissioned a huge replica of that Scarecrow painting as a gift, drawn by Paty Cockrum. I wish I could remember whether the occasion was my birthday, or Christmas, or to celebrate the publication of my first comic, but whatever the reason, it's now a vivid reminder of both my debut and the character. And in case you're wondering — no, I've never seen the Scarecrow attempt to escape from the confines of the frame...yet.

6. The Scarecrow was meant to have his own bimonthly title...until he wasn't. Buyers of certain Marvel comics in 1975 would have found *The Scarecrow* listed in subscription ads at a price of 12 issues for $3.50. (Oh, but that it were 1975 again!) Before the first issue of his own bimonthly magazine could appear, though, Marvel underwent a horror implosion, and mine was one of the titles that died before it could be born. Which meant that what was intended to be *The Scarecrow #1* was instead published in *Marvel Spotlight #26*, wedged between issues starring Sinbad and the Sub-Mariner. What should have been the third solo adventure, or second issue of the character's own title, was never to be. But, ah, that issue was begun, as you shall soon see...

7. Before writing the Scarecrow's second adventure, I had a chat with Andy Kaufman. During the summer of 1975, I was a frequent visitor to New York's Improv Comedy Club, which meant I spent many nights marveling at the bizarre antics of comedian Andy Kaufman. At that time, his fame was still in the future, as he hadn't yet made appearances on *Saturday Night Live* (which debuted the same year as the Scarecrow) and his star-making role on *Taxi* was still a few years away. I chatted with him at the bar one night after a performance, explained who I was, and asked whether it would be okay with him if I were to mention him in that second issue. And so, with his permission, I had Jess and Harmony enter a scene debating whether Kaufman was funny or a faker. Kaufman's career soon took off, which made his appearances on the comedy club circuit more irregular, so I never learned what he thought of the mention. I hope he would have liked it.

8. Before the Scarecrow's own title was canceled, an artist had already begun drawing what was supposed to have been issue #2. Once the Scarecrow's own book was added to the schedule, when we all still thought the story would be *The Scarecrow #1*, we were hard at work on the second issue of the character's solo title. I was thrilled to hear that I'd be working with Don Perlin, who'd been doing such an amazing job on the *Werewolf by Night* title. I was also thrilled that since Don was local, I'd be able to work on our stories Marvel-style, because that would complete the circle to the Marvel Comics I loved as a kid. But we never got that far, for first there was going to be an issue drawn by Ruben Yandoc, with Don providing a splash page before he took over the full art job with issue #3. Alas, before anything but that splash page could be drawn, the book was killed. No story notes survive for either of those two issues, but that splash page does exist, letting us all see what the comics world lost when Don couldn't bring the Scarecrow to life on a regular basis.

9. Had the title continued, the Scarecrow was going to be a little less supernatural, a little more super heroic. Scarecrow didn't continue, though in the pages of *F.O.O.M.*, Marvel's official fan magazine (which I edited for many issues), news about the Scarecrow did. To promote what was coming, I wrote that "as Don Perlin takes over the art with the third issue, supernatural turns super hero." Though I never got the chance to fulfill that promise, here's what it was all about: Once the plot arc of the Cult of Kalumai was completed, the plan was for the Scarecrow to use his supernatural abilities to become more of an avenger for the ills of the world, the same way a character such as Morbius the Living Vampire was more than just a, well, vampire, but rather a part of the larger Marvel Universe. Alas, due to the book's cancelation, that was never to be.

10. With the Scarecrow solo title canceled, I had plans to wrap up his arc in a seven-page back-up feature. During my time freelancing for Marvel, I'd written a ton of five- and six-page back-up stories, which existed not just to give new writers and artists a shot, but also to let the regular creators of a title catch up with their deadlines by allowing them some breathing space to come up with shorter lead stories in certain months. I'd written these sorts of shorts about Spider-Man, Nick Fury, Rick Jones, the Falcon, Drax the Destroyer and many other characters. Another one I'd planned to script, assuming Archie Goodwin, who was editor by then, okayed my plot, was going to be about the Scarecrow, as only the readers of a 1976 fanzine for which I was interviewed ever knew. But then I left comics to focus on my science fiction and horror short stories, and it never came to pass. Would I have been able to bring the Scarecrow to a satisfactory conclusion in a mere seven pages? I have no idea. But I sure would have loved a chance to find out!

Finally, now that I've shared 10 things you may not have known about the Scarecrow, let me share some things I never knew and never suspected —

That the Scarecrow would have life beyond those early issues, and Roy Thomas would conscript him as one of the Fear Lords, teaming him up with Nightmare, a character that scared the heck out of me when I first encountered him during his debut appearance in *Strange Tales* when I was 8.

That anyone would still be talking about my character more than 40 years later.

That there'd be an audience for an essay about what I was doing when I was 20 and wandering the Marvel Bullpen with wide eyes, printed alongside those original books, now looking more beautiful than ever.

But maybe I shouldn't be so surprised.

After all, as the cover to *Dead of Night #11* proclaimed, the Scarecrow is "Marveldom's #1 Shock-Star"!

---

*Some of **Scott Edelman**'s work appeared throughout Marvel's now-defunct black-and-white magazine imprint — including* Deadly Hands of Kung Fu, Marvel Preview *and* Monsters Unleashed. *He also wrote several issues of the original* Captain Marvel (Mar-Vell) *and introduced the rarely seen but memorable Scarecrow (a.k.a. Straw Man) for* Dead of Night. *At DC, he worked primarily in war and horror. For TV, he wrote for* Tales from the Darkside *and various Hanna-Barbera productions. Edelman edits* SCI FI Magazine *and* Science Fiction Weekly, *official magazines of the Syfy channel. His prose novel,* The Gift, *was nominated for a Lambda Award.*

"Dr. STRANGE MASTER OF BLACK MAGIC!"

MEN CALL HIM *DR. STRANGE!*

NEVER HAVE YOU KNOWN HIS LIKE!

IT IS A GREAT PLEASURE AND PRIVILEGE FOR THE EDITORS OF ***STRANGE TALES*** TO PRESENT, QUIETLY AND WITHOUT FANFARE, THE FIRST OF A NEW SERIES, BASED UPON A *DIFFERENT* KIND OF SUPER-HERO---

DR. STRANGE MASTER OF BLACK MAGIC!

STORY: STAN LEE
ART: STEVE DITKO
LETTERING: TERRY SZENICS

SOMEWHERE IN THE CITY, BETWEEN DARKNESS AND DAWN, A TORTURED MAN TOSSES FITFULLY IN HIS BED, VAINLY SEEKING PEACE THAT WILL NOT COME...
NO! NO!! GO AWAY! PLEASE-- PLEASE GO AWAY!

IT'S NO USE! I CAN'T SLEEP! I DARE NOT SLEEP! IT'S THAT SAME DREAM! EVERY NIGHT THE SAME! BUT WHY? WHAT CAN IT MEAN??

I CAN'T FIGHT IT ALONE! I NEED HELP! I'VE HEARD A NAME--- SPOKEN IN WHISPERS--- DR. STRANGE! HE DABBLES IN BLACK MAGIC! PERHAPS HE CAN HELP ME!

THE NEXT MORNING, ON A QUIET SIDE STREET IN NEW YORK'S COLORFUL GREENWICH VILLAGE...

I'M HERE TO SEE DR. STRANGE! HE DOESN'T KNOW ME, BUT---
DOCTOR STRANGE KNOWS ALL! ENTER!

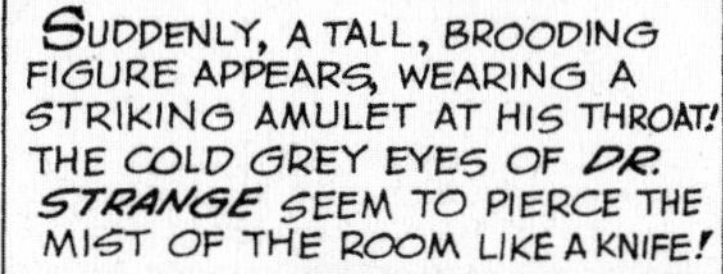
SUDDENLY, A TALL, BROODING FIGURE APPEARS, WEARING A STRIKING AMULET AT HIS THROAT! THE COLD GREY EYES OF DR. STRANGE SEEM TO PIERCE THE MIST OF THE ROOM LIKE A KNIFE!

I-I HAD TO COME! I'M IN TROUBLE!
NATURALLY! ALL WHO COME TO ME ARE! SPEAK...

IT'S MY DREAMS! EVERY NIGHT I HAVE THE SAME DREAM---OVER AND OVER!! IT'S TERRIBLE! I CAN'T STAND IT!
CONTINUE...

IT'S ALWAYS THE SAME! A HAUNTING FIGURE, BOUND IN CHAINS APPEARS... IT STARES AT ME! IT NEVER STOPS! NEVER!
ENOUGH!

TONIGHT I SHALL VISIT YOU! I SHALL FIND THE ANSWER TO YOUR DREAM! NOW GO!
BUT HOW?? HOW WILL YOU DO IT?

...BY ENTERING YOUR DREAM!!!
!!!

LATER, ALONE IN HIS ROOM, DR. STRANGE SITS SILENTLY IN FRONT OF AN ANCIENT INCENSE BURNER, AS HIS PHYSICAL BODY GOES INTO AN EERIE TRANCE...
IT IS TIME FOR ME TO VISIT THE MASTER, FROM WHOM ALL MY POWERS STEM...

LIKE A FLEETING GHOST, HIS METAPHYSICAL SPIRIT LEAVES HIS MOTIONLESS BODY AND DRIFTS AWAY...

...BEING WITHOUT FORM OR SUBSTANCE, NOTHING CAN IMPEDE ITS FLIGHT! IT DRIFTS EFFORTLESSLY THRU THE BUILDING WALL..

...HIGH INTO THE SKY... ACROSS THE VAST OCEAN ...ACROSS THE CONTINENTS... CONQUERING ALL OF TIME AND SPACE IN ITS SILENT FLIGHT...
2.

...UNTIL FINALLY, AT A HIDDEN TEMPLE SOMEWHERE IN THE REMOTE VASTNESS OF ASIA...

IT IS GOOD THAT YOU HAVE COME, MY SON! I SENSE DANGER SURROUNDING YOU! YOU MUST BE CAUTIOUS, FOR MY DAYS ARE NUMBERED, AND IT IS YOU WHO WILL SOME DAY TAKE MY PLACE IN THE BATTLE AGAINST THE FORCES OF DARKNESS AND EVIL!

I SHALL HEED YOUR WORDS, RESPECTED MASTER! I SHALL TRY TO PROVE WORTHY OF YOUR TRUST IN ME!
SO BE IT! NOW GO, FOR I AM WEARY! BUT MARK YOU WELL---SHOULD DANGER THREATEN, DEPEND UPON YOUR MAGIC AMULET!

THAT NIGHT, THOUSANDS OF MILES TO THE WEST, DR. STRANGE, IN HIS MORTAL FORM AGAIN, VISITS THE MAN WHO HAS SOUGHT HIS HELP!
YOU MUST SLEEP NOW---AND HAVE NO FEAR! I SHALL BE NEARBY!
I DON'T KNOW WHAT THERE IS ABOUT YOU, BUT IT GIVES A MAN A FEELING OF---CONFIDENCE!

MINUTES LATER...
SLEEP HAS OVERCOME HIM! HE BEGINS TO DREAM! IT IS TIME FOR ME TO ENTER MY TRANCE!

AND, AS HIS BODY GOES RIGID AND COLD, THE METAPHYSICAL SPIRIT OF DR. STRANGE DRIFTS UPWARD, INTO THE VERY DREAM ITSELF WHICH UNFURLS BEFORE IT!

IT IS DESOLATE HERE--LONELY AND FORBODING! WAIT! SOMEONE BEGINS TO APPEAR!

NO! NO!! STAY AWAY! PLEASE--- STAY AWAY!

YOU! WHOEVER--- WHATEVER YOU ARE---WHY DO YOU TORMENT HIM SO??
HE WELL KNOWS THE REASON WHY!
3.

I AM THE SYMBOL OF EVIL! THE EVIL HE HAS DONE! THAT IS WHY I AM CHAINED SO! IF YOU DO NOT BELIEVE---ASK MR. CRANG!

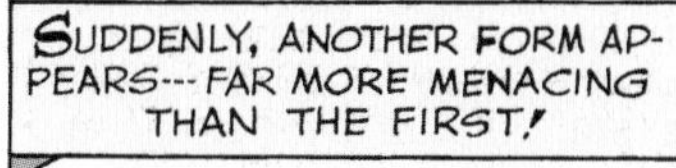
SUDDENLY, ANOTHER FORM APPEARS---FAR MORE MENACING THAN THE FIRST!

SO! IT IS DR. STRANGE! YOU HAVE ENTERED THE DIMENSION OF DREAMS FOR THE LAST TIME! NEVER AGAIN SHALL YOU THWART ME!
NIGHTMARE---MY ANCIENT FOE!

YOU KNOW THE RULES OF SORCERY, DR. STRANGE! THOSE WHO ENTER A HOSTILE DIMENSION MUST BE PREPARED TO PAY FOR IT---WITH THEIR LIVES!

MEANWHILE, IN THE SEMI-DARK BEDROOM, THE SLEEPER AWAKES!
HE MENTIONED MR. CRANG! SO THAT'S WHAT IT'S ALL ABOUT! THERE'S DR. STRANGE! HE MUST HAVE HEARD IT ALL!

HE IS IN A TRANCE---HELPLESS! IT'S JUST AS WELL! HE MUSTN'T BE ALLOWED TO LIVE WITH WHAT HE HAS LEARNED!

BEHOLD, DR. STRANGE---YOU MAY WITNESS YOUR OWN DESTRUCTION! YOUR MORTAL BODY IS UNPROTECTED---ITS LIFE IS ABOUT TO BE SNUFFED OUT!

NOTHING CAN SAVE YOU NOW!
THERE IS YET ONE WHO CAN! MASTER! HEAR ME! I NEED THEE, MASTER!!

AND, ACROSS THE LIMITLESS VOID OF TIME AND SPACE, TWO ANCIENT EARS HEAR THE DESPERATE CRY OF DR. STRANGE!

HE CALLS!

THERE IS ONLY ONE WAY TO HELP HIM---THRU THE ENCHANTED AMULET! I MUST CONCENTRATE----CONCENTRATE---
4.

AND, HALFWAY ACROSS THE WORLD, THE MYSTERIOUS GOLD AMULET ON DR. STRANGE'S CHEST BEGINS TO GLOW----- BRIGHTER, EVER BRIGHTER...

...UNTIL IT SLOWLY OPENS, REVEALING A FANTASTIC METAL EYE WITHIN...

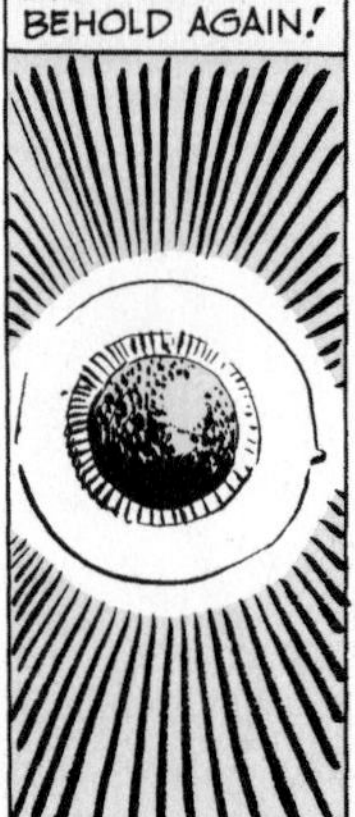

AN EYE SUCH AS NO MORTAL HAS EVER BEHELD ...SUCH AS NO MORTAL WOULD EVER WANT TO BEHOLD AGAIN!

AND SUDDENLY, FROM THAT UNBLINKING ORB, A BLINDING HYPNOTIC RAY SHOOTS OUT, FREEZING THE AMAZED HUMAN TO THE SPOT, AS HIS LIMBS GROW STRANGELY RIGID!

AND, IN THAT SPLIT-SECOND, TAKING ADVANTAGE OF THE SUDDEN INTERRUPTION, DR. STRANGE DARTS PAST HIS ENEMY IN THE DREAM DIMENSION...

I MADE IT! I'M SAFE IN MY OWN DIMENSION!
YOU'VE ELUDED ME THIS TIME, BUT I'LL GET YOU YET!

AND, AS THE AWESOME AMULET LOSES ITS BLINDING RADIANCE, THE METAPHYSICAL SPIRIT OF DR. STRANGE ONCE AGAIN ENTERS HIS EARTHLY BODY!

I SHALL RELIEVE YOU OF BOTH YOUR WEAPON, AND YOUR HYPNOTIC SPELL! NOW SPEAK-- AND SPEAK ONLY THE TRUTH, I COMMAND YOU!
IT'S OVER! YOU'RE STILL ALIVE! THAT MEANS I'VE LOST!

I WAS A FOOL TO COME TO YOU -I DIDN'T SUSPECT MY DREAMS WERE CAUSED BY THE MANY MEN I'D RUINED IN BUSINESS! CRANG WAS THE LAST OF THEM! I ROBBED HIM--- BUT HE COULDN'T PROVE IT! NOW---NOW I'LL CONFESS...
IT WILL BE THE ONLY WAY YOU CAN EVER SLEEP AGAIN!

NEXT ISSUE:

EXPLORE THE MYSTIC WORLD OF BLACK MAGIC ONCE AGAIN WITH DOCTOR STRANGE AS YOUR GUIDE!

-THE END-

DOCTOR STRANGE, MASTER OF BLACK MAGIC!
"RETURN TO THE NIGHTMARE WORLD!"
THE FIRST SAGA OF DOCTOR STRANGE (WHICH APPEARED IN STRANGE TALES #110) WAS A FAR GREATER SUCCESS THAN WE HAD EXPECTED! YOUR LETTERS DEMANDED MORE SUCH STORIES-- WITH MORE PAGES FOR EACH TALE! WELL, AS ALWAYS, YOU ARE THE REAL EDITORS OF THE MARVEL MAGS! AND SO, HERE ONCE AGAIN IS DOCTOR STRANGE AS YOU LIKE HIM-- IN A FEATURE-LENGTH SPELLBINDER WHICH TAKES YOU TO THE WONDERFUL WORLD OF THE MYSTIC ARTS! WE HAVE A HUNCH YOU'RE GOING TO LIKE THIS ONE--
WRITTEN BY.......STAN LEE
ILLUSTRATED BY...STEVE DITKO
LETTERED BY......ART SIMEK
ANOTHER SUPERNATURAL SENSATION PRESENTED BY THE MIGHTY MARVEL GROUP!
X-517
1

IF YOU ARE AN ORDINARY HUMAN MORTAL, THIS SCENE YOUR UNCOMPREHENDING EYES ARE GAZING UPON IS AN UNFAMILIAR, STARTLING SIGHT! FOR IT IS NOT OF OUR DIMENSION-- IT IS A SEGMENT OF THE DREAM DIMENSION, RULED OVER BY THE TYRANT KNOWN AS... NIGHTMARE!

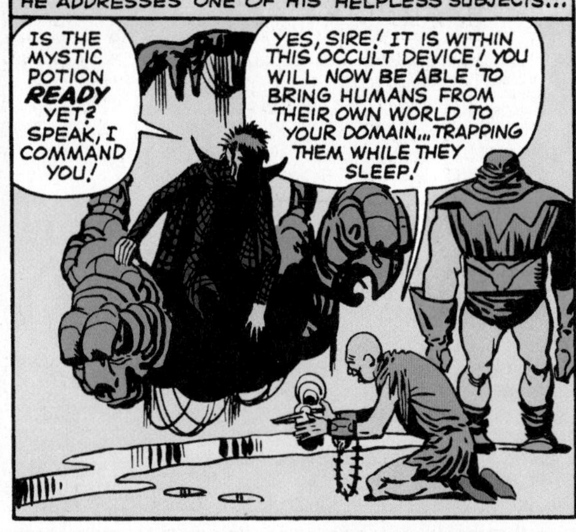
NIGHTMARE, THE POWERFUL! NIGHTMARE, THE CRUEL! NIGHTMARE, THE EVIL! LET US LISTEN AS HE ADDRESSES ONE OF HIS HELPLESS SUBJECTS...
IS THE MYSTIC POTION READY YET? SPEAK, I COMMAND YOU!
YES, SIRE! IT IS WITHIN THIS OCCULT DEVICE! YOU WILL NOW BE ABLE TO BRING HUMANS FROM THEIR OWN WORLD TO YOUR DOMAIN... TRAPPING THEM WHILE THEY SLEEP!

GOOD! WE MUST BRING HUMANS HERE, SO THAT I MAY STUDY THEM AND LEARN HOW TO DEFEAT THEM! FOR THE TIME HAS COME FOR ME TO CONQUER THEIR DIMENSION AS WELL AS MY OWN!

THERE ARE ONLY TWO MORTALS ON EARTH WITH THE POWER TO COMBAT ME--ONE IS THE ACCURSED DOCTOR STRANGE...
...AND THE OTHER IS HIS AGED TUTOR, THE ANCIENT ONE! BUT SOON I SHALL BE STRONG ENOUGH TO CONQUER THEM BOTH!

AND SO, OUR STAGE IS SET--AS THE SINISTER CREATURE FROM THE DREAM DIMENSION-- THE ONE KNOWN ONLY AS NIGHTMARE, PREPARES TO LAUNCH HIS MAGICAL ATTACK UPON OUR UNSUSPECTING WORLD!

MEANTIME, IN A SHADOWY, CANDLELIT APARTMENT IN A BACK STREET OF GREENWICH VILLAGE...
WHO DISTURBS DOCTOR STRANGE?
FORGIVE, MASTER! OFFICER OF THE LAW WISHES TO SEE YOU!
FORGIVE THE INTRUSION, SIR, BUT THIS IS AN IMPORTANT MATTER!
IN FACT, I SEE YOU HAVE BEEN READING ABOUT IT!
Daily Globe
EXTRA
ANOTHER "SLEEP VICTIM" REPORTED! MAN CANNOT BE AWAKENED AFTER TWO-DAYS OF SLEEP!
2

THE POLICE ARE CONCERNED ABOUT THE NUMBER OF PEOPLE WHO CANNOT BE AWAKENED AFTER THEY HAVE FALLEN ASLEEP! WHILE WE HAVE NO EVIDENCE OF A CRIME BEING COMMITTED, WE SUSPECT IT IS PART OF SOME EVIL DESIGN!
I AM DR. WARREN! THE MEDICAL PROFESSION CAN FIND NO WAY TO AWAKEN THE SLEEPERS! AS A LAST RESORT, WE ARE TURNING TO YOU, ON THE CHANCE THAT A FORM OF MYSTIC SPELL MAY BE INVOLVED!
YOU ARE WISE, GENTLEMEN! I FEAR THIS IS A PHENOMENOM WHICH INVOLVES THE DARK AND MYSTIC ARTS!

OF COURSE OFFICIALLY WE FIND IT HARD TO ACCEPT SUCH AN EXPLANATION! STILL, YOU HAVE AN AMAZING RECORD OF SUCCESS WITH OTHER OFF-BEAT CASES!
YOUR FAME IS WORLD WIDE, DOCTOR STRANGE! EVEN OUR LEADING SCIENTISTS HAVE DEEP RESPECT FOR YOUR REPUTATION!
SO! ENOUGH TALK! IF A SUPERNATURAL FORCE IS AT WORK, EVERY MOMENT COUNTS! YOU MUST BRING ME TO THE LATEST VICTIM AT ONCE!

MOMENTS LATER...
THIS MAN HAS BEEN ASLEEP WITH HIS EYES OPEN FOR OVER FORTY HOURS, DR. STRANGE! WE HAVE FOUND IT COMPLETELY IMPOSSIBLE TO AWAKEN HIM!
HMMM, I SEE BY THIS CHART THAT YOU HAVE TRIED EVERY MEANS AVAILABLE TO SCIENCE! THERE CAN BE ONLY ONE ANSWER...

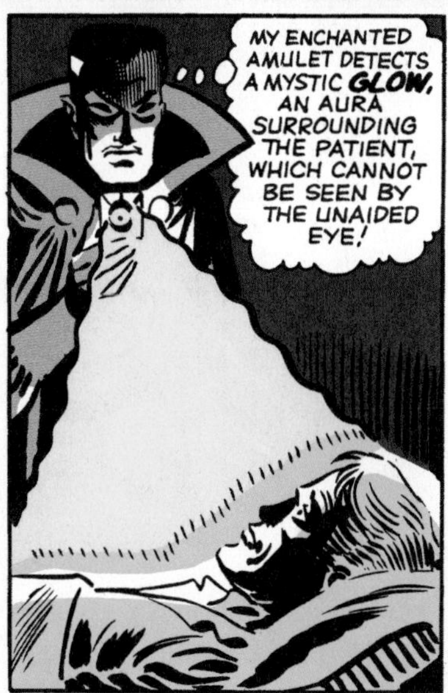
MY ENCHANTED AMULET DETECTS A MYSTIC GLOW, AN AURA SURROUNDING THE PATIENT, WHICH CANNOT BE SEEN BY THE UNAIDED EYE!

BEYOND A DOUBT THERE IS A SUPERNATURAL FORCE AT WORK HERE! THIS MAN IS NEITHER ASLEEP NOR AWAKE-- BUT RATHER IN A MAGICALLY-INDUCED SPELL!
I SHALL RETURN TO MY STUDY AND MEDITATE UPON WHAT MUST BE DONE!

AND SO, AFTER RETURNING TO HIS SILENT, SHADOWY SANCTUM...
I POSSESS THE ONLY KNOWN COPY OF THE BOOK OF VISHANTI! EVERY COUNTER-SPELL KNOWN TO THE MYSTIC ARTS IS INSCRIBED WITHIN THESE TIME-WORN PAGES!

AHHH, THIS IS THE INCANTATION I SEEK...

BUT THE SYMBOLS ARE FADED--DIFFICULT TO READ-- IF I INTERPRET THEM WRONGLY, ANYTHING CAN HAPPEN! DARE I UTTER THE CHANT???
3

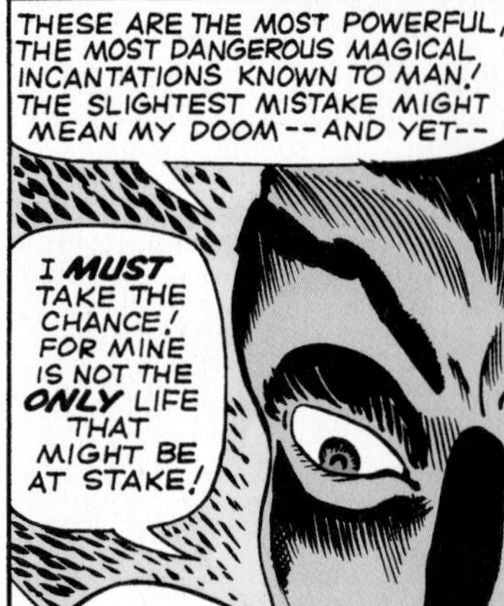

THESE ARE THE MOST POWERFUL, THE MOST DANGEROUS MAGICAL INCANTATIONS KNOWN TO MAN! THE SLIGHTEST MISTAKE MIGHT MEAN MY DOOM -- AND YET--
I MUST TAKE THE CHANCE! FOR MINE IS NOT THE ONLY LIFE THAT MIGHT BE AT STAKE!

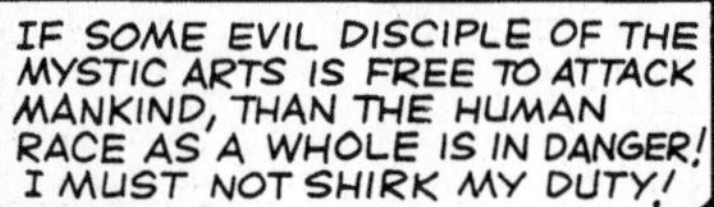

IF SOME EVIL DISCIPLE OF THE MYSTIC ARTS IS FREE TO ATTACK MANKIND, THAN THE HUMAN RACE AS A WHOLE IS IN DANGER! I MUST NOT SHIRK MY DUTY!

I SHALL RECITE THE CHANT SLOWLY-- CAREFULLY-- AND LEAVE THE REST TO FATE!

IN A LOW, SONOROUS TONE, DOCTOR STRANGE BEGINS THE POWERFUL SPELL...
IN THE NAME OF THE DREAD DORMAMMU... IN THE NAME OF THE ALL-SEEING AGAMOTTO... BY THE POWERS THAT DWELL IN THE DARKNESS...

...I SUMMON THE HOSTS OF HOGGOTH! LEAD ME TO THE SOURCE OF EVIL! OBEY THE WORDS OF DR. STRANGE!
I'VE SUCCEEDED! THE MIST OF HOGGOTH IS APPEARING! IT SHALL BE MY ENTRANCE TO THE SHADOW WORLD!

SILENTLY, THERE IN THE GLOOM, THE MORTAL FIGURE OF DOCTOR STRANGE ENTERS A STATE OF TRANCE, WHILE HIS ETHEREAL SELF RISES, AND DARES TO PIERCE THE MIST OF HOGGOTH!
AND NOW TO FIND THE ANSWERS I SEEK!

I MIGHT HAVE KNOWN THAT THE SOURCE OF DANGER WOULD BE HERE-- DEEP WITHIN THE NIGHTMARE WORLD!

I MUST REMAIN ON THIS NARROW PATH WHICH WAS FURNISHED BY THE POWER OF HOGGOTH!

SO LONG AS I STAND UPON THIS ENCHANTED PATH I AM SAFE-- THE SPELL OF HOGGOTH WILL PROTECT ME!
BUT, IF I STEP OFF-- THEN I AM VULNERABLE TO ANY DANGER!

BUT, A SHORT DISTANCE AWAY, A PAIR OF COLD, UNBLINKING EYES WATCH EVERY MOVE OF DR. STRANGE!
IT IS HE! THE ONE WE HATE THE MOST OF ALL LIVING CREATURES!
THIS IS OUR CHANCE TO UTTERLY DESTROY HIM! WE MUST NOT FAIL!
4

MASTER! THE HATED ONE COMES! IT IS DOCTOR STRANGE!
THE FOOL! NO MATTER HOW STRONG HE IS, I SHALL FIND A WAY TO SLAY HIM! FOR THIS IS MY WORLD--HERE NIGHT-MARE IS SUPREME!

THAT DOOR! IT SUDDENLY MATERIALIZED OUT OF NOWHERE! IT CAN MEAN ONLY ONE THING!
NIGHTMARE KNOWS I AM HERE! HE IS SETTING HIS TRAPS FOR ME! BUT I DARE NOT TURN BACK NOW!

THE DOOR IS SLOWLY OPEN-ING! I MUST ENTER!
SO LONG AS I REMAIN ON THE PATH, THE SPELL OF HOGGOTH WILL PROTECT ME!

AH! THIS IS NIGHTMARE'S FIRST TRAP! HE HAS CREATED TWO OTHER PATHS!
NOW I MUST CHOOSE THE CORRECT ONE, OR MY LIFE WILL BE FORFEIT!

ONCE AGAIN, THE ENCHANTED AMULET, GIVEN TO HIM BY THE ANCIENT ONE, SERVES TO DEFEAT THE FORCES OF EVIL...
THE POWER OF MY AMULET REVEALS THE TRUE PATH TO ME... FOR NOTHING EVIL CAN BASK FOR LONG IN ITS GLOW!

THE PATHS OF NIGHTMARE HAVE CRUMBLED AND FALLEN AWAY! AS FOR ME, I MUST CONTINUE ONWARD-- NO MATTER WHERE THE ENDLESS ROAD MAY LEAD!

AT LAST! MY ENEMY SHOWS HIMSELF! IT IS NIGHT-MARE!
SO, DOCTOR STRANGE, WE MEET AGAIN! BUT THIS SHALL BE THE LAST TIME -- FOR YOU SHALL NEVER LEAVE MY NIGHTMARE WORLD--ALIVE!
5

NO MATTER WHAT EVIL ENCHANTMENT YOU TURN MY WAY, IT CANNOT HARM ME SO LONG AS I REMAIN ON THE PATH OF HOGGOTH!
SO I SEE! BUT DO NOT GLOAT TOO SOON, HATED ONE! FOR I SHALL FIND A WAY TO DRIVE YOU FROM THAT PATH!

BUT FIRST, LOOK AHEAD OF YOU! THERE ARE THE HUMANS FROM YOUR OWN DIMENSION!
I HAVE CAPTURED THEIR ETHEREAL SELVES, AS YOU CAN SEE! IF YOU CAN REACH THEM, THEN THEY ARE FREE TO GO! BUT IF YOU DO NOT REACH THEM--ALL YOUR LIVES ARE FORFEIT!

I CANNOT AFFECT THE THE PATH YOU HAVE ALREADY TROD UPON!
...BUT I CAN DESTROY THE PATH WHICH LIES AHEAD--LIKE THIS!

NOW, DR. STRANGE, THE PROBLEM IS YOURS! HOW DO YOU REACH THOSE YOU WOULD SAVE, WITHOUT YOUR ENCHANTED PATH TO PROTECT YOU?

YOU HAVE FORGOTTEN, NIGHTMARE--I AM MASTER OF ALL MYSTIC ARTS! ONE FAMOUS FEAT OF MAGIC I CAN DUPLICATE IS THE ANCIENT INDIAN ROPE TRICK...

SURELY YOU ARE FAMILIAR WITH IT! AN INDIAN MAGICIAN UNROLLS A STRAND OF ROPE, JUST AS I UNROLL MY SASH--AND, AT A COMMAND, IT STIFFENS, AND RISES INTO THE AIR, AS MY SASH IS NOW DOING!

THEN, IN INDIA, THE MAGICIAN CLIMBS TO THE TOP OF THE ROPE AND VANISHES! BUT, FOR MY PART, I SHALL MERELY WALK ON MY SASH UNTIL I REACH YOUR CAPTIVES!

AND, WHILE MY SASH IS JOINED TO THE ENCHANTED PATH OF HOGGOTH, YOU ARE POWERLESS TO PREVENT ME FROM REACHING MY GOAL!
NOT SO, DOCTOR STRANGE! I SHALL MERELY BIDE MY TIME, TO MAKE MY EVENTUAL VICTORY EVEN SWEETER!
6

DO NOT FEAR THE HOLLOW WORDS OF NIGHTMARE! YOU ARE UNDER THE PROTECTION OF DOCTOR STRANGE NOW! AND SO YOU MAY WALK--TAKING CARE NOT TO STRAY FROM THE ENCHANTED PATH OF HOGGOTH!

HAH! I CAUGHT YOU NAPPING, STRANGE, JUST AS I HOPED I WOULD!
YOU FORGOT YOURSELF AND STEPPED ONTO MY PLATFORM, THEREBY LOSING THE PROTECTION OF HOGGOTH!

HE'S RIGHT! I WAS CARELESS! HE CAUSED HIS PLATFORM TO CRUMBLE AWAY BENEATH ME!
NOW I MUST REACH MY FALLING SASH, BEFORE IT IS TOO LATE!

TOO LATE! HE HAS MATERIALIZED A BARRIER! I CANNOT PASS!

AT LONG LAST, STRANGE, YOU ARE MY PRISONER! I HAVE VANQUISHED YOU!
THE OTHERS ARE FREE TO GO... THEIR FATE DOES NOT MATTER SO LONG AS YOU ARE MINE TO DESTROY!

THIS IS THE SPINYBEAST, WHOSE TOUCH MEANS DEATH! HE SEEMS TO WANT TO MEET YOU, STRANGE... TO TOUCH YOU!
OR IS IT BECAUSE OF THIS MYSTIC PROD, WITH WHICH I COMMAND HIM??

HOW I HAVE HUNGERED FOR THIS TRIUMPHANT MOMENT! HOW I HAVE DREAMED OF TASTING THE FRUITS OF MY VICTORY OVER YOU!
WHY DO YOU KEEP RETREATING, STRANGE? SURELY YOU MUST REALIZE MY SPINYBEAST WILL REACH YOU SOONER OR LATER!
AS THE ANCIENT ONE TAUGHT--THE BATTLE IS NEVER LOST WHILE LIFE REMAINS! I SHALL NOT GIVE UP!

BUT I CAN RETREAT NO FURTHER! A STILL MORE SINISTER THREAT AWAITS ME AT THE BOTTOM OF THE CREVICE BEHIND ME! IF I AM EVER TO MAKE A STAND, IT MUST BE HERE --AND NOW!
7

FOR THE SPACE OF TWO HEARTBEATS, DR. STRANGE WAITS, AND THEN-- AT A MENTAL COMMAND, HIS AMULET BEGINS TO GLEAM...

TEMPORARILY BLINDED BY THE UNEXPECTED GLOW, NIGHTMARE LOWERS HIS PROD-WAND SO THAT IT STRIKES HIS SPINYBEAST, KILLING IT INSTANTLY!

MY **EYES!** CAN'T SEE!

IT IS THAT ACCURSED **AMULET** OF HIS!

AND THEN, AFTER HIS SIGHT HAS RETURNED TO HIM AGAIN...

MY **SPINYBEAST**-- DEAD! THIS IS **STRANGE'S** DOING! HE **KNEW** MY ROD-WAND WOULD STRIKE IT!

FOR THAT, HE SHALL PAY A THOUSAND TIMES OVER-- BUT **WAIT!** WHERE **IS** THE HATED SORCERER??!

WHERE INDEED?? THAT ONE INSTANT'S RESPITE IS ALL DOCTOR STRANGE NEEDS TO ENABLE HIM TO SEIZE HIS FLOATING SASH AND REACH HIS PROTECTIVE, ENCHANTED ROAD AGAIN!

AND, AS THE SMALL GROUP OF MEN WALK TOWARDS THE MYSTIC MIST THRU WHICH THEY MAY ENTER THEIR NORMAL WORLD, A SHRILL, VINDICTIVE CRY FOLLOWS THEM, RINGING SHARPLY IN THEIR EARS...

YOU WILL NOT HAVE TIME TO **ENJOY** YOUR ILL-BEGOTTEN TRIUMPH, STRANGE! WE SHALL MEET AGAIN--SOONER THAN YOU THINK! AND, NEXT TIME, THE VICTORY SHALL BE **MINE!**

BUT, THE NEXT MEETING OF NIGHTMARE AND DR. STRANGE IS ANOTHER TALE FOR ANOTHER TIME! AND NOW, UNTIL NEXT ISSUE, MAY THE HOSTS OF THE VISHANTI SMILE UPON YOU--MAY THE MIGHTY DORMAMMU BE YOUR SLAVE!

THE END

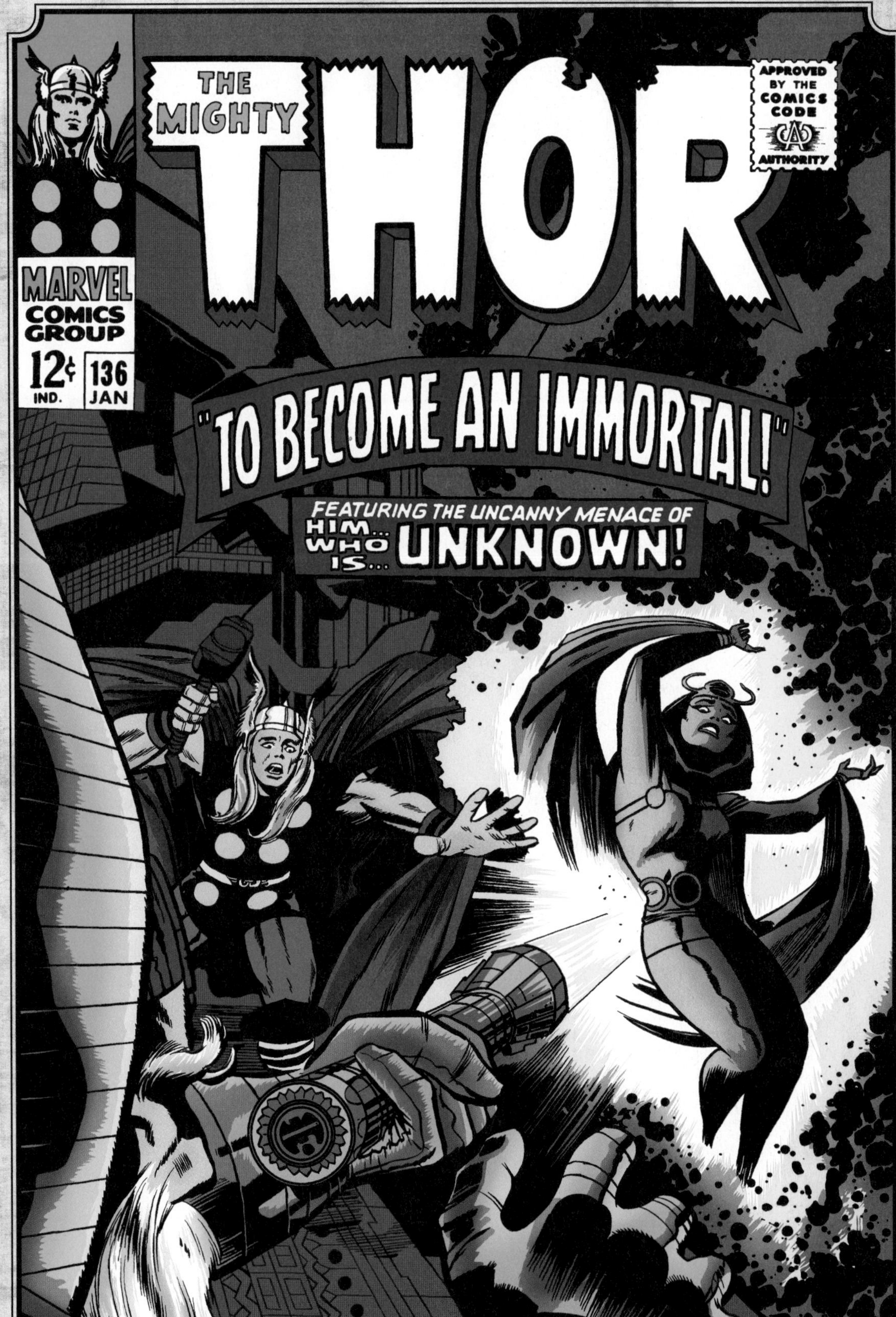
THE MIGHTY
THOR
APPROVED BY THE COMICS CODE AUTHORITY
MARVEL COMICS GROUP
12¢ IND.
136 JAN
"TO BECOME AN IMMORTAL!"
FEATURING THE UNCANNY MENACE OF
HIM... WHO IS... UNKNOWN!

THE MIGHTY THOR!
"TO BECOME AN IMMORTAL!"
THE TIME IS COME, BELOVED!
I MUST TAKE THEE--TO ASGARD!
THERE, THOU SHALT STAND BEFORE MY FATHER--THE OMNIPOTENT ODIN--WHO HATH PLEDGED THAT WE MAY BE WED!
WITH YOU BESIDE ME, MY DARLING--I FEAR NOTHING!
--NOT EVEN THE INCREDIBLE PROSPECT OF SEEING--THE HOME OF THE GODS!
ATOP A TOWERING MOUNTAIN PEAK SOMEWHERE IN EUROPE, THE MIGHTY THOR AND LOVELY JANE FOSTER, THE MORTAL WHO HAS WON HIS HEART, PREPARE FOR WHAT IS DESTINED TO BE THE MOST FATEFUL JOURNEY THEY HAVE EVER TAKEN--
A PROUD PHANTASMAGORIA OF PAGEANTRY, PRESENTED BY: STAN LEE and JACK KIRBY
DELINEATED BY VINCE COLLETTA
LETTERED BY ARTIE SIMEK
AND NOW, BE THOU PREPARED FOR THRILLS AND WONDERMENT BEYOND MORTAL KEN--
1

NEVER AGAIN, MY LOVE, SHALT THOU HAVE CAUSE FOR FEAR!
NEVER AGAIN SHALL THE GOD OF THUNDER FORSAKE THEE!
MY LIFE SHALL BE THINE-- FOREVERMORE!

AND NOW-- PLACE THINE ARMS AROUND ME --SO!
BY THE POWER OF MY ENCHANTED MALLET, WE NOW DEPART THIS MORTAL SPHERE!

LET THINE EYELIDS BE CLOSED, BELOVED--

FOR, WHEN NEXT THEY ARE OPENED--

THEY SHALL BEHOLD THE SIGHT OF ALL SIGHTS--
NOW, JANE FOSTER! NOW SHALT THOU LOOK--
THE COLORS-- THE BRIGHTNESS THE SHEER BEAUTY --IT'S ALMOST UNBEARABLE!

'TIS BUT THE SHIMMERING SPLENDOR OF THE FABLED RAINBOW BRIDGE, UPON WHICH WE DO STAND!
THOR! THAT NOISE! THOSE MEN--!
2

HAIL TO THEE, MOST NOBLE PRINCE!
HAIL TO THE MIGHTY GOD OF THUNDER!
'TIS BUT THE LOYAL CAVALRY OF ASGARD!
BUT, UPON WHAT MISSION DO THEY RIDE?
WE RIDE INTO BATTLE, O SON OF ODIN!
THE POWERFUL AND SINISTER KINGDOM OF THE TROLLS HATH RISEN AGAINST US!
EVEN NOW THEY DO CHALLENGE THE ROYAL RULE OF THY FATHER-- THE ALL-WISE!
ONWARD-- FOR IMMORTAL ASGARD!

MAKE WAY! WE HAVE CAPTURED A PRISONER--FOR INTERROGATION!
HOW MONSTROUS! THAT UNSPEAKABLE CREATURE-- IS HE-- A TROLL?
DO NOT AVERT THINE EYES, BELOVED!
THOU MUST BECOME ACCUSTOMED TO SUCH SIGHTS--
FOR, WITHIN THIS FABLED REALM, THE FORCE OF EVIL HATH MANY FACES!
3

SOMEHOW I-- I NEVER THOUGHT IT WOULD BE-- LIKE THIS--!
I GREET THEE, HEIMDALL!
BY RIGHT OF BIRTH DO I CLAIM THY LEAVE TO PASS!

LEAVE GRANTED-- FOR THEE AND THY COMPANION, MIGHTY ONE!
WHA--?!! THAT MAN! THAT SWORD! THAT HORNED HELMET--!

TREMBLE THOU NOT! 'TWAS ONLY HEIMDALL-- MATCHLESS, GRIZZLED GUARDIAN OF BIFROST, THE RAINBOW BRIDGE!
FORGIVE ME, DARLING! IT'S ALL SO NEW-- SO TERRIBLY STARTLING TO ME--!
FORGIVE THEE? ANYTHING THOU WOULDST DO REQUIRES NO FORGIVING, BELOVED!
COULD I ASK FORGIVENESS OF MY HEART--MY VERY SOUL?

BUT, THE TIME IS COME TO PREPARE THYSELF--
FOR, THE GLORY AND THE GRANDEUR OF ASGARD NOW AWAIT THEE!
4

BEHOLD THE WAR COUNCIL OF REGAL ODIN, WITHIN HIS ROYAL PALACE--!
WE HAVE CHARTED THE TROLL BATTLE-GROUND FOR THY ROYAL OBSERVATION, SIRE!
OUR WARRIORS AWAIT THY SUPREME COMMAND!
ASSEMBLE YE MY LEGIONS AT THE FAR PERIMETER! 'TIS THERE THE FOE IS WEAKEST!
A THOUSAND PARDONS, SIRE!
THE ROYAL DOOR DOTH OPEN BEHIND THEE!
WHO DARES BREACH THE PRIVACY OF IMPERIAL ODIN?!!

HAIL TO THEE, SOVEREIGN MOST SUPREME! HAIL, LORDLY MONARCH OF THE REALM!
THY SON MOST DUTIFUL HATH RETURNED-- TO PRESENT TO THEE --HIS BELOVED!
THOU MAYEST ENTER THE PRESENCE, THUNDER GOD!

ADVANCE, AND BE RECOGNIZED! I WOULDST FAIN SPEAK WITH YON MORTAL FEMALE!

ON EARTH, MY LORD, SHE DOTH POSSESS THE NAME JANE FOSTER!
I-CAN'T BELIEVE IT! I'M ACTUALLY --FACE-TO-FACE--WITH ODIN--THE ALL-FATHER!
FORGIVE ME, SIR--I-I'M AT A LOSS FOR WORDS--!

THOU MUST NOT TREMBLE, MY CHILD!
GIVE ME THY HAND-- THAT I MAY PLACE IT ON MINE!
MAYHAP THOU WILT DRAW CONFIDENCE, AND SERENITY, FROM THE STRENGTH WHICH IS MINE OWN!
5

MANY DAYS AGO, HONORED FATHER, THOU DIDST AFFIRM THAT WE MIGHT BE WED!
THE WORD OF ODIN IS A BOND ETERNAL!
MORTAL FEMALE --STAND FORTH! I SHALL MAKE THEE RAIMENT FIT FOR A GODDESS!
FOR GODDESS SHALT THOU BE!

SO BE IT!
WHAT-- WHAT HAS HAPPENED TO ME?

'TIS THE MOMENT WE HAVE LONG AWAITED! MY FATHER PREPARES TO MAKE THEE--AN IMMORTAL!
FOR, NONE BUT A TRUE GODDESS MAY WED A GOD!
I HAVE A GIFT TO BESTOW! STAND THEE BACK, FLESH OF MY FLESH!

I GRANT THEE A GIFT WORTHY OF A THUNDER GOD'S BRIDE...
THE ENCHANTED GIFT OF--- UNLIMITED FLIGHT!
NO LONGER ART THOU EARTHBOUND, JANE FOSTER! THUS SPEAKS ODIN!
I-I'M SOARING --INTO THE SKY!
MERELY THINK OF A DESTINATION --AND THOU SHALT FLY THERE FORTHWITH!
6

AS A CHILD, I OFTEN DAY-DREAMED--THOUGHT HOW WONDERFUL IT WOULD BE TO FLY LIKE A BIRD!
BUT, I NEVER DREAMT IT COULD BE SO TERRIFYING--SUCH AN ALIEN, UNNATURAL SENSATION!
SUDDENLY, THE TENSE, STARTLED GIRL GROWS PANICKY--OVERWHELMED BY HER NEW POWER--UNABLE TO ADJUST TO IT IN TIME--
IT-IT ISN'T POSSIBLE... TO FLY --BY THOUGHT ALONE! WHAT IF SOMETHING GOES WRONG?
WHAT IF--THE POWER VANISHES--?
OHHH!
SHE FALLS! SHE WAS NOT YET READY FOR SUCH A GIFT!

FATHER--BY THY LEAVE--I MUST FLY TO HER SIDE!

MY BREAST IS SORELY TROUBLED!
DOTH MY TRULY BELOVED HAVE SO LITTLE FAITH?
DID SHE DEIGN TO DOUBT THE WORD OF ODIN--THE PLEDGE OF THOR?

MY DARLING! THANK HEAVEN YOU REACHED ME IN TIME!
THOU MUST PUT ASIDE THINE EARTHLY FEARS!
THOU MUST LEARN THE UNQUESTIONING COURAGE OF AN IMMORTAL BORN!
7

SIRE, THE EARTH FEMALE SEEMS TO HAVE LITTLE TASTE FOR IMMORTALITY!
YET, SHE MUST LEARN TO AQUIT HERSELF LIKE A GODDESS! THERE IS NO OTHER WAY!
I SHALL AFFORD HER THE OPPORTUNITY TO MAKE AMENDS FOR WHAT HAS GONE BEFORE--!
SUMMON YE-- THE UNKNOWN!

SIRE! HAST THOU CONSIDERED THE AWESOME CONSEQUENCES?
THE UNKNOWN IS TOO FEAR-SOME--TOO POWERFUL FOR ANY SAVE THEE!
TRUE! BUT GODHOOD IS NOT LIGHTLY WON! LET THE TEST CONTINUE!
BRING THEE FORTH THE UNKNOWN! I HAVE SPOKEN!

SO TOTALLY FEARED-- SO UNIVERSALLY DREADED IS THE UNKNOWN, THAT NONE SAVE ODIN KNOW THE FULL EXTENT OF HIS POWER--
AND, IT HATH BEEN WHISPERED THAT EVEN THE ALL-WISE KNOWETH NOT FROM WHENCE THE MONSTER COMES!

ONLY A SOUND CAN SUMMON THE UNKNOWN!
A SOUND SUCH AS THE ONE WHICH WILL OCCUR WHEN I STRIKE YON ENCHANTED TUNING FORK--!

IT IS DONE!
THYONNNG!

THE PULSATING ECHOES FILL MY VERY SOUL WITH DREAD!
I MUST FLEE THIS ACCURSED CHAMBER BEFORE IT IS TOO LATE--BEFORE THE UNKNOWN APPEARS!
8

BY YOUR LEAVE, SIRE--THINE EMISSARY IS TRULY NUMB WITH FEAR! MAY I BRING HIM TO THE CHAMBER OF SILENT REPOSE?
AY! HE HATH FAITHFULLY FULFILLED HIS MACABRE MISSION! AWAY WITH HIM!
NOW, 'TIS TIME FOR THE BELOVED OF THOR TO PROVE WORTHY OF THAT WHICH IS TO BE!
HAVE COURAGE, MY LOVE! WHATEVER BEFALLS THEE, THOU MUST FACE IT LIKE ONE TO THE MANNER BORN!

FACE IT? FACE WHAT?? THOR! DON'T LEAVE ME! I-I'M AFRAID--!
I SHALL NOT BE FAR FROM THEE, BELOVED!
REMEMBER--THY NEWLY-GRANTED POWERS MAY AID THEE IN WHAT IS TO COME!
HAVE THEE FAITH, MY LOVE! THE PRIZE IS WORTH THE RISK!

THE DOOR IS CLOSED BEHIND ME! I'M ALONE--BUT WHERE? WAIT--MY EYES ARE GROWING ACCUSTOMED TO THE GLOOM--!
THERE IS--SOMEONE ELSE HERE! A PRESENCE I CANNOT CLEARLY SEE--BUT, I CAN SENSE ITS MONSTROUS FORM!

IT'S DRAWING CLOSER--CLOSER--I CAN HEAR IT BREATHING--HEAR ITS HEAVY LUMBERING FOOTFALLS--!

AND THEN, THE DESPERATE EARTH GIRL SEES--
A HAND--FROM OUT OF SOME UNSPEAKABLE NIGHTMARE--!

IN HER PANIC--HER NAMELESS, INDESCRIBABLE FEAR--THE HAPLESS GIRL FORGETS HER POWER OF FLIGHT--FORGETS HER PURPOSE IN THE GRIM RITUAL--FORGETS ALL, SAVE THE NAME OF--
THOR! THOR--HELP ME, MY DARLING--THOR!
9

I CANNOT FAIL MY LOVE WHEN SHE CALLS!
THE THUNDER GOD IS HERE!

I-I'M SORRY, DEAREST! I FAILED YOU! BUT-- I WAS SO FRIGHTENED--!
THOU SHALT NEVER BE FRIGHTENED AGAIN!
NOT WHILST THOR DOTH LIVE!

BUT THEN, BEFORE ANOTHER WORD CAN BE UTTERED--BEFORE ANOTHER MOVE CAN BE MADE--THE MYSTERIOUS, INDESCRIBABLE UNKNOWN STRIKES--!

BACK, THOU FOUL, INHUMAN BRUTE! BACK--BEFORE THE AVENGING HAMMER OF THE SON OF ODIN!! BACK--TO THE SLIME FROM WHENCE THOU COMEST!

THROOOM!
10

HE IS GONE! THE FURY OF MY MALLET HATH DRIVEN HIM BEYOND THIS IMMORTAL SPHERE!
I MUST GET OUT! I MUST LEAVE--RUN AWAY--ESCAPE THIS WORLD OF FEAR AND MADNESS!
I CAN STAND NO MORE! IF I STAY --I'LL GO MAD!

OMNIPOTENT ONE! WITH ALL DUE RESPECT, ART THOU NOT CAUSING JANE FOSTER TO UNDERGO MORE THAN MORTAL FEMALE CAN ENDURE?
I SAY THEE NAY! IF THOU WOULDST HAVE HER A GODDESS BE, THEN A GODDESS' HEART MUST SHE POSSESS!

HAST THOU SO SOON FORGOTTEN?
ON FEAR DOTH THE UNKNOWN FEED! IT IS FOR THAT REASON HE HATH NEVER INVADED THE GOLDEN REALM--
FOR THE GODS OF ASGARD KNOW NOT THE MEANING OF FEAR!

BUT--HEAR ME, FATHER! SHE IS NO WARRIOR! SHE IS NO VALKYRIE BORN! SHE IS BUT MY BELOVED--GENTLE--AND KIND--AND TRUE!
IS THERE NO PLACE FOR ONE SUCH AS SHE IN THE HOME OF THE GODS??
NO! DON'T ASK HIM! I DON'T WANT IT! I WON'T BE A GODDESS! I WON'T STAY IN ASGARD!
IT'S TOO HORRIBLE! TOO UNENDURABLE! DON'T YOU REALIZE HOW MAD IT IS?!!

SHE HATH MORE WISDOM THAN THEE, MY SON! THOUGH ASGARD BE HEAVEN ENOW--HER PLACE IS ON EARTH--BELOW!
NO, FATHER--
NO!

I HAVE SPOKEN!
11

'TIS CLEAR TO ME NOW! THOU DIDST PLAN THE ENTIRE THING!
IT WAS NEVER INTENDED THAT JANE FOSTER SHOULD BECOME AN IMMORTAL!
STAND THEE BACK, THUNDER GOD! NONE MAY APPROACH THE PRESENCE IN ANGER!
LET HIM BE! MY SON HATH THE RIGHT!
MOST NOBLE THOR-- I UNDERSTAND THY RAGE, THY DISAPPOINTMENT --BUT, 'TIS NOT AS THOU HAST STATED!

MY HEART DOTH GRIEVE FOR THEE! BUT, THOU MUST ENDURE THIS HAPPENSTANCE IN GODLY MANNER!
I SHALL ENDURE NOTHING! I SHALL FOLLOW HER--!
WHAT?!! YOU DARE DISPUTE THE WILL OF ODIN!

THOUGH MY MERCY BE WITHOUT PEER--KNOW YOU MY WRATH IS ALL-CONSUMING!

THOU BE THE SON OF MY HEART--THE FLESH OF MY FLESH!
THOU ART BRAVEST --MOST FAITHFUL-- MOST HEROIC IN ALL THE COSMOS!
BUT STILL AM I LORD ODIN! STILL IS MY WORD SUPREME-- MY WILL UNQUESTIONED!

NOW RISE, GOD OF THUNDER! IN THY HEART OF HEARTS THOU KNOWEST GODHOOD WAS NOT FOR ONE SUCH AS SHE!
STILL DO I LOVE HER, MY FATHER! THOUGH SHE BE FRAIL, AND WEAK--HAVE I NOT STRENGTH ENOW FOR THE TWO?
12

MY POWER IS BEYOND ALL MEASURE--BEYOND ALL COMPREHENSION--AND YET, I CANNOT ALTER AN EMOTION OF THE HEART!
BUT, WE SHALL SPEAK OF THIS NO MORE!
SINCE THE UNKNOWN IS NOW AT LARGE, I ORDER THEE ON TO GUNDERSHELM, TO GUARD THE GLADE OF CRYSTALS FROM HIS ATTACK!
'TIS JUST AS WELL! IF FORTUNE LOOKS UPON ME WITH FAVOR, MAYHAP I SHALL FALL IN BATTLE!

WONDROUS IS THE POWER OF ODIN! NO SOONER DO I RAISE MY HEAD, THAN I AM IN THE LAND OF GUNDERSHELM--
ONLY HERE, AT THE EDGE OF THE GLADE OF CRYSTALS, CAN THE UNKNOWN ENTER ASGARD!
I MUST DEVOTE MYSELF TO MY TASK WITH A MIGHTY VENGEANCE--!
FOR, IF I SHOULD DWELL UPON WHAT HATH BEFALLEN, THEN SURELY SHALL I LOSE THE VERY WILL TO LIVE!

NO! THERE IS ONLY ONE REMEDY! ONLY ONE BALM FOR MY ACHING HEART!
I MUST HURL MYSELF INTO BATTLE--FIGHT AS NEVER BEFORE--FIGHT AS ONLY THE GOD OF THUNDER CAN!
TLANNNG!
THAT SOUND! THE CRYSTALS RING! 'TIS THE OMINOUS NOTE WHICH HATH THE POWER TO SUMMON--THE UNKNOWN!

AN EVIL TROLL! 'TIS THOU WHO HAST DARED GIVE THE FORBIDDEN SIGNAL!
TLANNG!
IT IS DONE! NOT EVEN THE HAMMER OF THOR CAN STOP HIM NOW!
13

AND, EVEN AS MIGHTY THOR HEARS THE THUNDEROUS APPROACH OF THE UNKNOWN, A MYSTIFIED JANE FOSTER FINDS HERSELF IN A BUSTLING HOSPITAL CORRIDOR, SOMEWHERE ON THE WEST COAST--
STRANGE--I SEEM TO HAVE FORGOTTEN WHY I CAME HERE!
AND YET, I KNOW THAT THIS IS WHERE I BELONG! I FEEL AS THOUGH FATE IS GUIDING MY FOOTSTEPS!
YOUNG LADY--!

ARE YOU THE NEW RESIDENT NURSE WHO WAS DUE TO ARRIVE TODAY?
ALL OF A SUDDEN IT'S CRYSTAL CLEAR TO ME! HOW FOOLISH I WAS TO HAVE FORGOTTEN!
WHY YES, I AM! MY NAME IS JANE FOSTER! I HOPE I'M NOT TOO LATE!
NO--YOU'RE RIGHT ON TIME, MY DEAR!

DR. KINCAID, THIS IS NURSE FOSTER--OUR NEW RESIDENT!
THANK YOU, NURSE PARKWELL!
I FEEL SO--SECURE! AS IF--I'VE COME HOME--AT LAST!
PLEASE COME IN, YOUNG LADY!

I'M DR. KINCAID! IT'S MY CUSTOM TO WELCOME THE NEW NURSES AND EXPLAIN THEIR DUTIES TO THEM!
HE'S SO--HANDSOME! I FEEL AS THOUGH I'VE--KNOWN HIM--BEFORE! OR--IS IT JUST THAT I'VE SEEN HIM SO OFTEN--IN MY DREAMS?
I HOPE YOU WILL BE HAPPY HERE WITH US, NURSE FOSTER!
OH, I WILL, DOCTOR! I JUST KNOW I WILL!

THUS, WE BID ADIEU TO LOVELY JANE FOSTER, THE MORTAL GIRL WHOM ODIN, IN HIS INFINITE WISDOM, HAS GIVEN A SECOND CHANCE AT LIFE--AND LOVE--AND ULTIMATE HAPPINESS!
BUT, WHAT OF THE HEART-SICK THUNDER GOD? LET US RETURN TO THE BATTLING THOR, AS HE WHEELS ABOUT TO CHALLENGE--THE UNKNOWN--!
BACK, THOU NAMELESS, SOULLESS THING OF EVIL! BACK, TO THE STYGIAN NOWHERE FROM WHENCE THOU CAME!
14

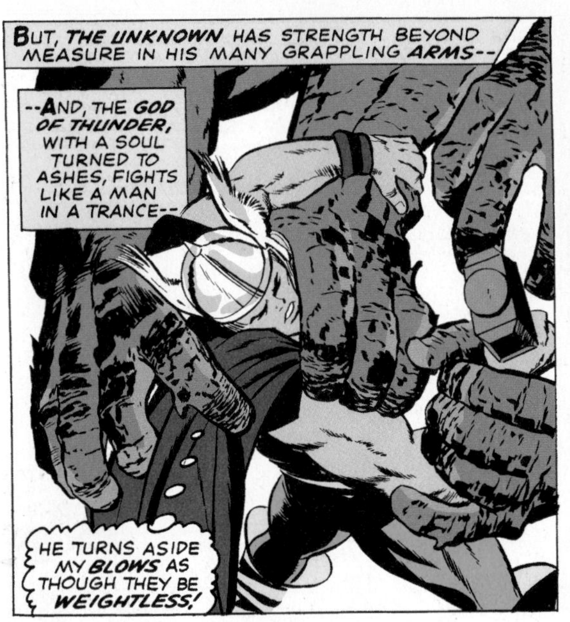
BUT, THE UNKNOWN HAS STRENGTH BEYOND MEASURE IN HIS MANY GRAPPLING ARMS--
--AND, THE GOD OF THUNDER, WITH A SOUL TURNED TO ASHES, FIGHTS LIKE A MAN IN A TRANCE--
HE TURNS ASIDE MY BLOWS AS THOUGH THEY BE WEIGHTLESS!

BUT, HE DOTH STRIKE AT ME WITH A FORCE BEYOND COMPREHENSION--!
FTAM!

HE FEELS MY DEFEAT IS COME! HE GIRDS HIMSELF --FOR THE FINAL KILL!
IF THIS THEN IS THE END WHICH FATE HATH ORDAINED FOR THE LUCKLESS THOR--SO BE IT!

SUDDENLY, AS THE GOLDEN-HAIRED GLADIATOR--SEEMINGLY LACKING THE WILL TO FIGHT ON--WATCHES HIS FOE WITH HYPNOTIC FASCINATION, ANOTHER ARM IS RAISED AGAINST THE UNKNOWN--
RISE AND FIGHT, THUNDER GOD!
CLANG!

FIGHT, SON OF ODIN! FIGHT, AS YOU HAVE FOUGHT SO GALLANTLY IN DAYS OF YORE!
FOR, IF YOU SHOULD FAIL NOW--THEN MY LIFE, TOO, IS SURELY FORFEIT!
I SAY THEE NAY! NONE OTHER SHALL PERISH THRU FAULT OF THOR!

THEN, WITH A BLOOD-CURDLING BATTLE CRY RINGING FROM HIS LIPS, THE MIGHTIEST WARRIOR OF ALL TIME ONCE AGAIN ENTERS THE FRAY-- HIS SMASHING HAMMER DRIVING THE UNKNOWN BACK AS DAYLIGHT SHATTERS THE GLOOM OF NIGHT--!
THOOM!
CLANG!
15

FINALLY, WHEN THE HAZE OF WHITE-HOT FURY CLEARS FROM THE TORTURED BRAIN OF THE IMMORTAL AVENGER, HIS STEELY-BLUE EYES BLINK IN ASTONISHMENT--FOR, THE UNKNOWN IS--GONE!
HE HATH BEEN VANQUISHED!
BUT, WHAT OF MY NEW-FOUND ALLY?
THOUGH I HAVE HEARD OF YOUR PROWESS SINCE MY BIRTH--NEVER HAVE I BEHELD SO MAGNIFICENT A SIGHT AS--THOR IN BATTLE!
LET ME NOW BEHOLD THE ONE WHOSE BLADE HATH BEEN UNSHEATHED IN THOR'S BEHALF!

BY THE BRISTLING BEARD OF ODIN--'TIS A FEMALE! --SO BEAUTEOUS AS TO STAGGER EVEN A GOD!
ART THOU TRULY REAL--OR MERELY A VISION OF LOVELINESS, CONJURED IN DESPERATION BY THE AGONY OF A BREAKING HEART?
YOU KNEW ME ONCE, MANY YEARS AGO!
--AS TODAY YOU KNOW MY BROTHER --THE EVER-FAITHFUL HEIMDALL!
CAN IT BE--? THOU ART SIF! THE RAVEN-TRESSED CHILD WHOM ONCE I DANGLED UPON MY KNEE!
BUT, BY MY MALLET --THOU ART CHILD NO LONGER!

AS A YOUNG GIRL--SILENTLY WATCHING YOU GALLOP INTO BATTLE, I HAVE LOVED YOU, SON OF ODIN! I HAVE LOVED YOUR SPIRIT, YOUR STRENGTH--YOUR MATCHLESS COURAGE--AS ONLY A CHILD CAN LOVE!
BUT, NOW YOU HAVE CHANGED! AN AURA OF SORROW PERVADES YOUR MANNER--!
AY! EVEN A GOD MAY KNOW THE PANGS OF DESPAIR!

SIF, TOO, HAS BEEN NO STRANGER TO HEARTBREAK! EVER SINCE CHILDHOOD HAVE I SUFFERED THE ACHE OF LOVE UNREQUITED!
--A HOPELESS LOVE--FOR ONE WHO EVER HAD EYES FOR ANOTHER--ONE TO WHOM SIF WAS NAUGHT BUT A FORGOTTEN MEMORY!
MINE EARS HEAR THY WORDS--BUT MY HEART CANNOT BELIEVE THAT ANY COULD FORGET ONE SUCH AS THEE!

THOU ART FAIR BEYOND MEASURE --VALIANT AS ONLY A GODDESS CAN BE--AND I, LOVELY SIF, HAVE BEEN BLINDEST OF ALL WHO DWELL IN THE GOLDEN REALM!
VERILY, THOU HAST RESTORED THE LUST FOR LIFE TO THE SMOLDERING SOUL OF AN ERRANT THUNDER GOD!
AND YOU, MY LORD, HAVE REKINDLED AN EMOTION I FEARED HAD BEEN LOST TO ME FOREVER!
16
THEN, AS MIGHTY THOR AND THE STUNNING SIF TURN AND WALK INTO THE GATHERING TWILIGHT...
IN THINE INFINITE WISDOM, SIRE, THOU HAST THIS DAY PERFORMED A SEEMING MIRACLE!
NAY, NOT SO! I DID BUT PROVIDE THE TIME--THE SETTING--

BUT, ONLY IN THE HEART CAN BE FOUND THE FINAL, ENCHANTED INGREDIENT--MEN CALL LOVE!
AND SO SAY WE ALL!

THOR

MARVEL COMICS GROUP™

APPROVED BY THE COMICS CODE AUTHORITY

25¢ 229 NOV 02450

THE MIGHTY

THOR

GOD OF THUNDER, NIGHT OF DOOM!

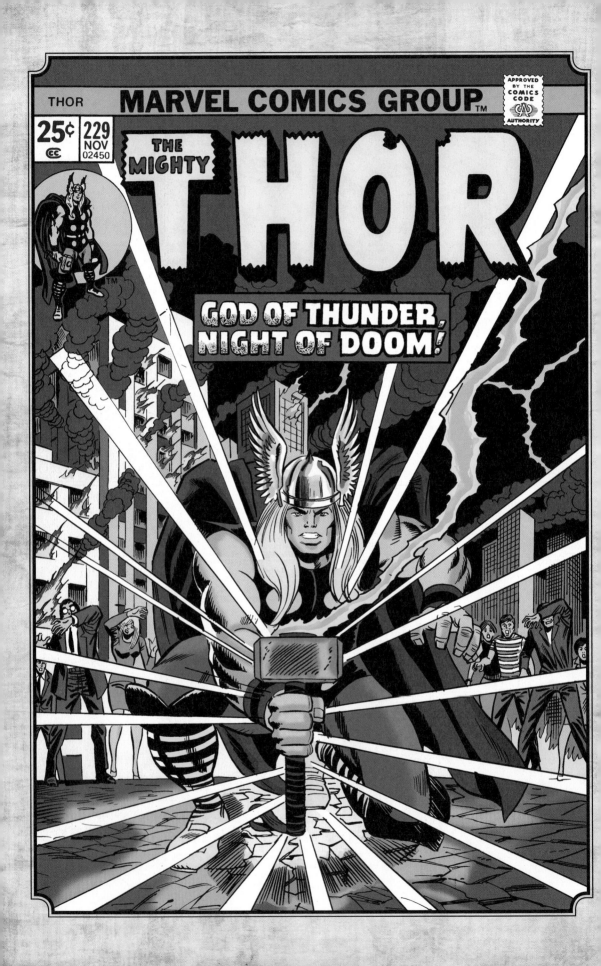

Stan Lee PRESENTS: THE MIGHTY THOR! TM
"WHERE DARKNESS DWELLS, DWELL I!"
'TIS GOOD TO FLY ONCE MORE O'ER THE WORLD OF MEN.
METHINKS I HAVE BEEN TOO LONG IN FOREIGN PARTS--
FOR, VERILY, 'TIS ON EARTH THAT MY HEART DOTH RESIDE-- NOW, AND TILL THE END OF TIME!
GERRY CONWAY AUTHOR
RICH BUCKLER ARTIST
CHIC STONE INKER
J. COSTANZA, letterer
L. LESSMANN, colorist
ROY THOMAS EDITOR

YET, EVEN AS THE THUNDER GOD, THOR, VIEWS THE WORLD BELOW HIM WITH KINDLY AMUSEMENT--

--HIS OLYMPIAN FRIEND, THE GOD CALLED HERCULES, STARES AT THE CITY STREETS--FILLED WITH AN EMOTION MUCH LIKE DESPAIR!
BY MY FATHER'S BEARD, THIS IS MADNESS!
EVERYWHERE I LOOK, THERE IS PAIN AND SORROW.
DO MORTALS ENJOY THIS LIFE? ARE THEY MAD--
GROCERY

--OR ARE THEY ACCURSED?
CHILDREN CRY FOR THEIR MOTHERS... MEN WEEP FOR DREAMS LOST OR ABANDONED ...THERE IS POVERTY, DIRE POVERTY.
POVERTY-- IN A WORLD FILLED WITH WEALTH.
EITHER I'M MAD--OR THEY ARE.
AND I THINK IT MUST BE THEY.

BUT, BEFORE HERCULES' MUSINGS CAN GO ANY FURTHER...
AAAAH
A CRY--! SOMEONE IN DANGER--!

HE'S A BRUSQUE MAN, THIS OLYMPIAN GOD--BUT HIS COARSENESS CONCEALS A WARM INTERIOR--
AAAAH

--AND A RAGING SENSE OF JUSTICE--
PLOW!
--THAT TAKES A VERY VIOLENT FORM!

THE DOOR IS LOCKED -- BUT THAT DOESN'T MATTER.
THE DOOR HASN'T BEEN BUILT WHICH CAN WITHSTAND THE SON OF ZEUS--
RRIPPPP!

--ESPECIALLY NOT WHEN HE'S ANGRY.
THE CRIES HAVE STOPPED.

IF I'M TOO LATE-- SOMEONE WILL PAY.
I SWEAR IT!

I'M TELLIN' YA, OLD MAN-- LET GO OF ME.
THE MONEY'S ALL I WANT, AN' I GOT THAT NOW-- SO I DON'T WANT TO HURT YOU, SEE--?
BUT IF YOU DON'T LET GO--

--I WILL!
DO WHAT YOU HAVE TO... I'M NOT AFRAID TO DIE... NOT WITH HIM ON MY SIDE...
HE PROMISED ME... PROMISED ME I'D LIVE IF I DIED...
SO KILL ME--I'M NOT AFRAID! I'M NOT A-

-AAAAAAAAAAAHHHH
CRAZY OLD COOT! I WARNED YA--BUT YOU WOULDN'T LISTEN!
YOU WOULDN'T LISTEN!

MORTAL, ART THOU INJURED?
THY ASSAILANT-- DID HE--?
HE PROMISED-- SAID I WOULDN'T DIE--

'TIS ONLY A SURFACE WOUND-- A MERE CUT, NO MORE.
STILL--THE FOOL COULD HAVE KILLED THEE!
NEVER DIE-- SAID-- NEVER DIE--!

BE PATIENT, MORTAL. IN TIME, THY WOUND WILL HEAL.
YET--HAD IT BEEN DEEPER--

--THY MORTAL LIFE WOULD HAVE MET A MOST UNTIMELY END!
SUCH WASTE DOTH APPALL ME!
'TIS MADNESS--

FIRE EXIT
--BLIND, UNTHINKING MADNESS-- AND, IN TRUTH--

--IT DOTH FIRE ME TO A RAGE!
SMASH!

HOLY CRUD.
THAT FIREDOOR-- YA JUST TORE IT OPEN LIKE IT WUZ CARDBOARD OR SOMETHIN'--!
I DON'T KNOW WHAT'S WITH YOU--
BUT YA BETTER STAY BACK, OR I'LL--
FIRE EXI

THOU SHALT BE GRATEFUL I CHOOSE TO SPARE THY WORTHLESS HIDE, WHELP--

--INSTEAD OF CRUSHING THEE, LIKE THE INSECT THOU TRULY ART!
BAP!
URRRRP!

THE BOY FALLS, AND AS THOUGH HE WEIGHS NO MORE THAN A SLEEPING DOG, IS SHOULDERED...
...FOR SUCH IS THE STRENGTH OF HERCULES.

YET, WHEN THE OLYMPIAN GOD RETURNS TO THE SECOND-FLOOR APARTMENT OF THE THIEF'S VICTIM...
GAS...?
THIS IS A NEW ODOR--!
WHAT--?

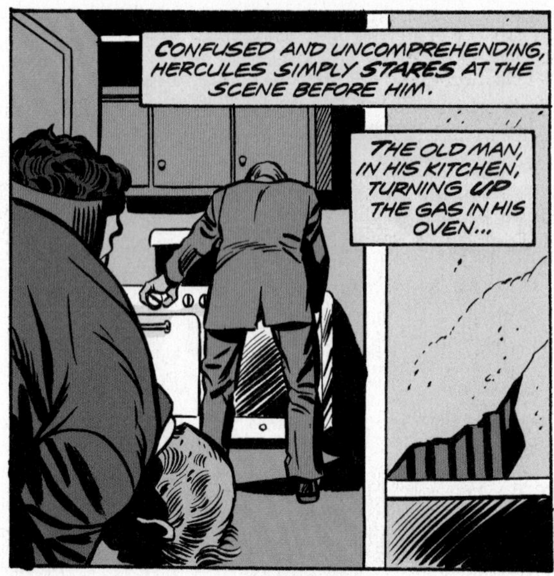
CONFUSED AND UNCOMPREHENDING, HERCULES SIMPLY STARES AT THE SCENE BEFORE HIM.
THE OLD MAN, IN HIS KITCHEN, TURNING UP THE GAS IN HIS OVEN...

...THEN, CALMLY-- SO INCREDIBLY CALMLY-- STRIKING A WOODEN MATCH--
--AND, BEFORE HERCULES CAN MOVE TO STOP HIM--

--PLACING IT AT THE MOUTH OF THE STOVE.

WHOOM

AS EXPLOSIONS GO, IT'S NOT A PARTICULARLY LOUD ONE.
BUT FOR SOME REASON IT ATTRACTS THE GOD OF THUNDER--
--AND HE SWEEPS SOUTHWARD ACROSS THE CITY--

--KNOWING THAT HE IS NEEDED!
HE-- ESPECIALLY HE.

'TWAS HERE I LEFT HERCULES, WHEN WE PARTED AFTER OUR LAST DEALING WITH GALACTUS.*
THAT WAS BUT A FEW BRIEF HOURS AGO--
--AND HERCULES, WITH NOWHERE ELSE TO TURN-- MAY WELL HAVE WANDERED THESE STREETS, AND STILL--
*LAST ISSUE, OF COURSE. --ROY.

"I WAS RIGHT! 'TIS INDEED MY OLYMPIAN FRIEND.
"AND, AS ALWAYS, HE IS MORE THAN MILDLY INVOLVED!

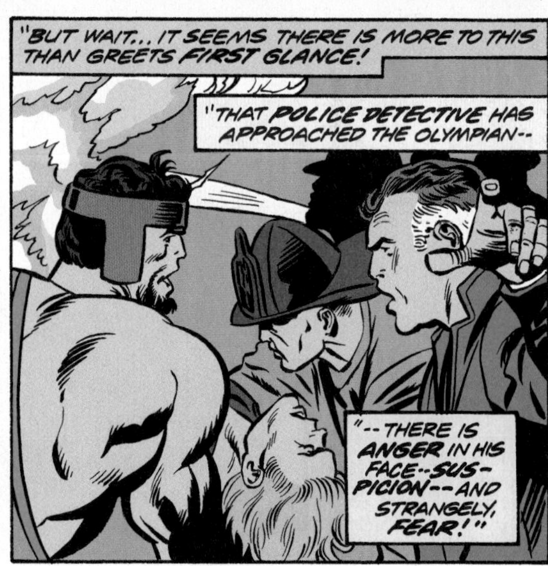
"BUT WAIT... IT SEEMS THERE IS MORE TO THIS THAN GREETS FIRST GLANCE!
"THAT POLICE DETECTIVE HAS APPROACHED THE OLYMPIAN--
"--THERE IS ANGER IN HIS FACE--SUS-PICION--AND STRANGELY, FEAR!"

YET, THESE ARE MYSTERIES WHICH MAY AWAIT THE SOLVING--
--WHILE YON FIRE CANNOT WAIT, BUT MUST BE DEALT WITH NOW!
AND WHO IS BETTER ABLE TO DEAL WITH A FIERY HOLOCAUST THAN THOR--

--WHOSE MYSTIC MALLET MAY SUMMON RAIN AND WIND--
--AND DROWN THE FIRE IN A STORM!
TWO RAPS OF THE HAMMER UPON THE GROUND--

--AND, LIKE THE WATER SUMMONED BY MOSES FROM A STONE, THE RAIN COMES FORTH--
--THE TENEMENT FIRE SMOKES--SPUTTERS--SMOULDERS--

--AND AT LAST, AS THE RAINS CEASE--

--THE FIRE GOES OUT.

PRETTY NEAT TRICK YOU'VE GOT THERE, MISTER.
I WAS JUST TELLING YOUR FRIEND--

IF WE HAD COPS LIKE YOU GUYS ON THE FORCE, CROOKS WOULDN'T STAND A CHANCE.
ON THE OTHER HAND, JOES LIKE ME WOULD BE OUT OF A JOB--
SO MAYBE IT'S A GOOD THING YOU'RE NOT WORKING FOR THE MAYOR AFTER ALL.
IN CASE I DIDN'T MENTION IT--MY NAME'S BLUMKENN.
DETECTIVE SERGEANT BLUMKENN.
LET'S US HAVE A LITTLE TALK.

SOON, IN A CAFETERIA NOT TOO FAR AWAY...
IT'S LIKE I WAS TELLING HERC OVER HERE--
THAT OLD GUY WHO SET THAT FIRE ISN'T THE FIRST TO GO CRACKERS ALL AT ONCE--
--AND I'VE GOT A FEELING HE WON'T BE THE LAST, EITHER.
MATTER OF FACT, HE'S NUMBER FOUR.

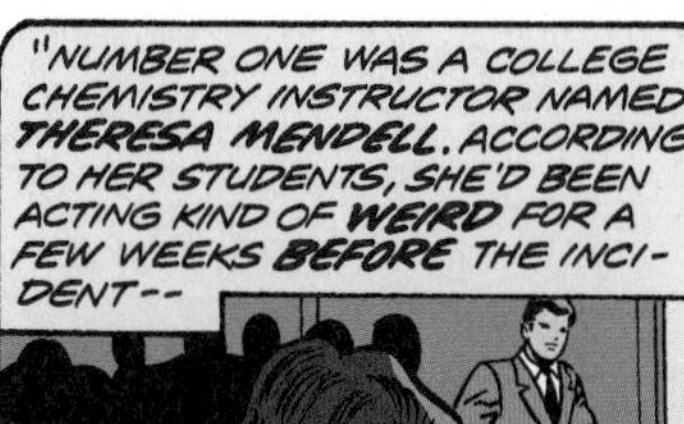

"NUMBER ONE WAS A COLLEGE CHEMISTRY INSTRUCTOR NAMED THERESA MENDELL. ACCORDING TO HER STUDENTS, SHE'D BEEN ACTING KIND OF WEIRD FOR A FEW WEEKS BEFORE THE INCIDENT--

"-- THOUGH NOT AS WEIRD AS SHE ACTED WHEN SHE MUMBLED SOME SORT OF CRAZY INCANTATION--
IN HIS HANDS, I LIVE--
IN HIS HEART, MY LIFE GOES ON FOREVER.
"--AND--WELL-- SET HERSELF ON FIRE.
"SHE DIED IN THE BLAZE-- HER BODY WAS NEVER FOUND.

"NUMBER TWO WAS A HARD-HAT CONSTRUCTION ENGINEER--MOE HARTWELL. NOBODY NOTICED ANYTHING STRANGE ABOUT HIM--TILL THAT DAY ON THE SITE--
IN DEATH I'LL GET LIFE.
HE PROMISED THAT--
TNT

--AN' I'M GONNA HOLD HIM TO IT!

"THE BLAST WIPED OUT THE SITE, A BLOCK OF ABANDONED TENEMENTS-- AND, OF COURSE, THIS GUY CALLED MOE.
BLOOM!
"THE INQUIRY CALLED IT AN ACCIDENT.
"ME, I KNOW BETTER.

"BY THIS TIME, I'D BECOME INVOLVED-- HEARD THE STORIES ABOUT WHAT THESE PEOPLE SAID BEFORE THEY DIED--AND WAS BEGINNING TO PUT TWO AND TWO TOGETHER--
"-- WHEN WE RAN ACROSS NUMBER THREE, ON A JET INTO LA GUARDIA AIRPORT.

I'LL LIVE IF I DIE-- THAT'S WHAT HE SAID--
AND I BELIEVE HIM!
POW
POW
"THE FLIGHT CONTROLLER HEARD IT ALL OVER THE RADIO.
SKREEEBOOM!
"WITH THE PILOT AND COPILOT SHOT, THE PLANE CRASHED--"

--AND THE OFFICIAL VERDICT WAS-- ACCIDENT IN THE COMMISSION OF A FELONY.
BUT WHAT EACH OF THEM SAID, JUST BEFORE THEY DESTROYED THEMSELVES-- IT'S BEEN BUGGING ME, Y'KNOW?
DOST THOU IMAGINE 'TIS A CON-SPIRACY?
HUMANS ALWAYS SEE A PLOT WHERE NONE EXISTS.

MAYBE SO--BUT ME, I'M KNOWN AS A KIND OF REALISTIC SORT OF JOE.
YA CAN'T SCARE ME WITH FANTASIES--
--AND PAL, THIS THING SCARES ME.
A LOT.

ANYWAY, I JUST THOUGHT I'D TELL YOU--IN CASE YOU HAD SOME IDEAS ON HOW TO HANDLE IT.
IF YOU WANNA LAUGH ABOUT IT, SWELL.

ME--I'VE GOT BETTER THINGS TO DO.

A LONG PAUSE, AND THEN...
HAST THOU THE THOUGHT I HAVE, THUNDER GOD?
THE POLICEMAN NEEDS OUR HELP--
AND BY ASGARD, HE'LL HAVE IT!

SOON, IN AN ALLEY NOT FAR FROM THE STILL-SMOULDERING TENEMENT...
THIS MATTER IS SO STRANGE, WE DARE NOT EXPLORE ITS MYSTERY ALONE.

RATHER, LET US LOOK TO MY FATHER FOR ADVICE--
--THAT HIS WISDOM MAY GUIDE US--
--TO THE PATH THAT IS TRUE--AND JUST!

LORD ODIN, ALL-FATHER OF ASGARD-- THY SON DOTH BESEECH THEE!
APPEAR TO US, NOW--
AND GIVE US WHAT AID THOU CANST!

THUNDER ROARS AND LIGHTNING FLARES; AND WHEN THE HEAVENS CEASE TO STIR-- ODIN APPEARS--!
MY SON, WHAT AID I GIVE THEE IS LESS THAN THOU SHALT NEED!
THERE IS ONE WHO CAN HELP THEE, HOW-EVER--

--AND SO I SEND HER TO THEE--
SPAZ!

--AND SHE WILL BE MORE HELP THAN I CAN EVER BE!
THERE IS ANOTHER CRACK OF POWER, AND THE IMAGE OF ODIN IS GONE!

YET THE IMAGE OF ODIN'S GIFT REMAINS--SIF, LADY OF ASGARD-- BELOVED LADY OF THOR!
MILORD, WE ARE REUNITED! BUT WHAT DID ODIN MEAN -- THAT I WOULD BE MORE AN AID TO THEE THAN EVEN THE ALL-FATHER HIMSELF?
MY LADY, I KNOW NOT--! I KNOW ONLY THAT MY HEART IS FULL WITH THE SIGHT OF THEE--
AND YEA, 'TIS ENOUGH!

PERHAPS 'TIS ENOUGH FOR THEE, THOR--BUT NOT FOR ME.
THERE IS A MYSTERY AFOOT IN THIS CITY--
--THOU MAY IGNORE IT, IF THOU MUST--BUT I HAVE HONOR, AND--
CANNOT.

FOR A LONG MOMENT, THOR TREMBLES ON THE VERGE OF ANGER.
AFTER ALL, HE IS A PROUD MAN-- AND NO PROUD MAN WANTS ANOTHER MAN'S REBUFF.
BUT, INSTEAD OF STRIKING OUT IN ANGER-- HE TURNS AWAY, AND GATHERING UP HIS LADY LOVE--
--FLIES.

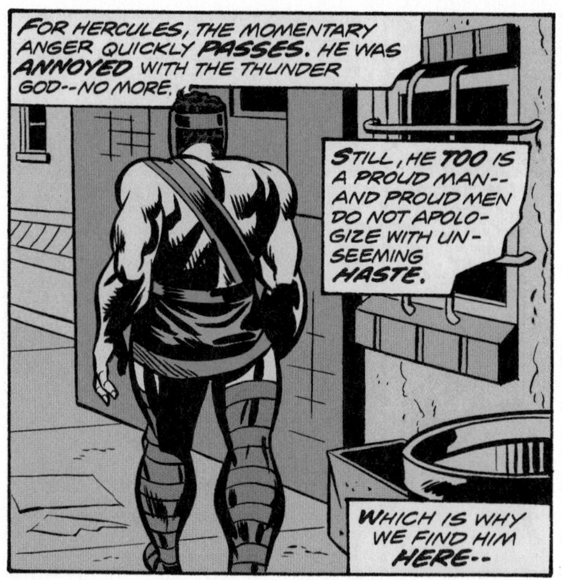
FOR HERCULES, THE MOMENTARY ANGER QUICKLY PASSES. HE WAS ANNOYED WITH THE THUNDER GOD--NO MORE.
STILL, HE TOO IS A PROUD MAN--AND PROUD MEN DO NOT APOLOGIZE WITH UNSEEMING HASTE.
WHICH IS WHY WE FIND HIM HERE--

--WANDERING BACK THROUGH THE SIDE-STREETS OF THIS RUNDOWN NEIGHBORHOOD... SEARCHING UNCONSCIOUSLY FOR A CLUE TO UNDERSTANDING THE MYSTERY WHICH SO FASCINATES HIM--
--A MYSTERY WHICH WILL SOON BE ABANDONED--

--WHEN HERCULES REALIZES THAT HE'S BEING--
--FOLLOWED?
FOR TWO BLOCKS NOW, SOMEONE HAS BEEN BEHIND ME--

--AND AS I PAUSE AT THIS CORNER, I CAN HEAR HIS FOOTSTEPS--APPROACHING.
WE SHALL SEE WHO IT IS THAT DARES PURSUE THE SON OF ZEUS--AND WE SHALL SEE IT--

NOW!
WHAT IN THE NAME OF MERCURY?

AN EMPTY SUIT OF CLOTHES?
'TIS IMPOSSIBLE--AN UTTER MADNESS!
I SENSE SORCERY HERE--A VILE, BLACK SORCERY! 'TIS ALMOST AS IF--

SPOW!

NOT MANY BLOWS ARE STRONG ENOUGH TO DROP THIS GOD OF OLYMPUS.
THIS BLOW WAS... AND AS HE LOOKS UP... ONLY SLIGHTLY DAZED, HERCULES DOES NOT KNOW WHETHER TO BE MORE SURPRISED BY THE STRENGTH OF THE BLOW--

--OR BY ITS WIELDER!
THY SKIN--'TIS ALL BUT COMPLETELY OPAQUE! THOU ART ALMOST A SHADOW-- A FIGURE FORMED OF DARKNESS ITSELF!
IS THAT HOW THOU DIDST APPEAR SO SUDDENLY--AS THOUGH FROM NOWHERE--
--BY MELTING INTO THE SHADOWS? WELL? WILT THOU ANSWER?
NO? THEN-- WILT THOU FIGHT?

SPAKO!
AYE--IT SEEMS THOU WILT!

SPAAM!
UNNNNH! THOU ART STRONG INDEED, MY SILENT FRIEND-- BUT PERHAPS-- NOT STRONG ENOUGH!

BUNT!
I KNOW NOT WHY THOU DIDST ATTACK ME--
--BUT 'TWAS AN ERROR MOST GRAVE!
FOR, IF THOU ART STRONG--
HERCULES IS STRONGER A THOUSANDFOLD!
SO SPEAK AT LAST, MUTE ONE.
WHY DIDST THOU ASSAULT ME? AND MORE-- WHO ART THOU? NEVER HAVE I SEEN SUCH A BODY AS THINE, SAVE IN MY MOST DARK DREAMS--

--MY MOST CONFOUNDING--
SCRAPE

--NIGHTMARES?
FATHER ABOVE! DEMONS!
HE HAS NO TIME TO WONDER ABOUT THIS NEW MENACE--EVENTS MOVE TOO SWIFTLY FOR THOUGHT--
--AND BY THE TIME EVEN HIS REFLEXES BEGIN TO REACT--
--HE IS CAUGHT--

--AND IS DRAWN BY A HUNDRED CLAWING HANDS--
NOOOOOOOOOOOOOOOO
--FROM THE NIGHT--
--INTO THE PITS OF DARKNESS.

NOW, AS MEN AND WOMEN THROW OPEN WINDOWS, CURIOUS ABOUT THAT BLOOD-CHILLING SCREAM--
--THE SILENT ATTACKER LAUGHS--
--SILENTLY.

MORE THAN AN HOUR LATER, IN A HOSPITAL SUITE NOT FAR FROM THE MIDTOWN LOCATION OF THE AVENGERS MANSION...
MILORD, CHEER THYSELF. WHEN HERCULES RETURNS, THOU WILT MAKE AMENDS, THE HARSH WORDS WILL BE FORGOTTEN--
AND THOU WILT BE FRIENDS, AS ALWAYS.
YEA, I KNOW THIS-- AND YET--
AND YET, THOU ART SORRY FOR THY ANGER--AS HERCULES, NO DOUBT IS SORRY FOR HIS ANGER.
PLEASE, MILORD --ABANDON THESE THOUGHTS. COME, LOOK AT HOW WELL KRISTA IS--

--WALKING ONCE MORE, THANKS TO THEE.
THANKS TO THY HUMAN HALF, DOCTOR DONALD BLAKE, WE SHOULD SAY.
'TWAS HE WHO OPERATED UPON ME, AFTER MY ADVENTURE WITH PLUTO.*
AND APPARENTLY HE OPERATED WELL--
*WAY BACK IN THOR #224.--ROY.

--FOR THOU DOST SEEM AS STRONG AND LOVELY AS EVER.
CAREFUL, MILORD, SPEAK MORE KINDLY OF HER--AND THOU WILT MAKE ME JEALOUS.
SIF, THOU DOST FLATTER ME.
ASGARD KNOWS 'TIS ONLY THEE THOR LOVES.
BUT--MY LORD, WHAT OF HERCULES? WHERE IS HE WHO ALSO SAVED ME?

FOR A LONG, PAINFUL MOMENT, THOR HESITATES, RECALLING THE BROODING GUILT OF A SHORT TIME BEFORE.
THEN, JUST AS HE BEGINS TO ANSWER THE YOUNG ASGARDIAN'S QUESTION--
THRUMP!

--FATE ANSWERS IT FOR HIM!
HERCULES!

HEIMDALL'S EYES... HE CAN BARELY STAND!
HIS SKIN IS COLD AND CLAMMY --HIS BODY SHAKES, AS THOUGH STRICKEN WITH DISEASE!
BY ALL THE GODS WHO LIVE--WHAT HAPPENED TO THEE?

FIVE WORDS ARE WHISPERED, IN A VOICE BARELY AUDIBLE TO THE THUNDER GOD'S EARS.
NO MORE THAN THIS--FIVE GRIM WORDS--

--AND THEN--NOTHING.
SLUMP!

MILORD, IS HE ALL RIGHT? WHAT DID HE SAY TO THEE?--HE SPOKE SO SOFTLY, I COULD NOT--
HE SAID-- "WHERE DARKNESS DWELLS, DWELL I!"
I KNOW NOT NOW WHAT IT DOTH MEAN--
--BUT BY ALL THE LEGIONS OF ASGARD, I SWEAR ON MY HONOR I WILL LEARN ITS SECRET--
AND HERCULES WILL BE AVENGED!
NEXT ISSUE
THE SKY ABOVE, THE PIT BELOW!

THOR

MARVEL COMICS GROUP™

25¢ CC

230 DEC 02450

THE MIGHTY

THOR

THE SKY ABOVE-- THE PIT BELOW!

HERCULES! STAND THEE AT MY SIDE AGAINST THESE HELLSPAWN--

--OR ALL THE EARTH IS DOOMED!

BUCKLER + SINNOTT

SPECIAL NOTE: YOU'LL NEVER GUESS THE SHOCKING SURPRISE-STAR WHOSE COMING IS HERALDED IN THIS ISSUE!!

Stan Lee PRESENTS: THE MIGHTY THOR! TM
THE SCENE: A QUIET RESIDENTIAL STREET IN MANHATTAN'S EAST EIGHTIES, LOCATION OF THE AVENGER'S MANSION. THE PLAYERS: AN ASGARDIAN NAMED THOR, AND AN OLYMPIAN NAMED HERCULES. THE SITUATION: IN A WORD... DESPERATE!
THE SKY ABOVE...
COME WITH US ON A TREK INTO THE MYSTIC BEYOND... A JOURNEY THAT WILL TAKE US TO--
...THE PITS BELOW!
GERRY CONWAY, AUTHOR
RICH BUCKLER, ARTIST
JOE SINNOTT, EMBELLISHER
COSTANZA & JETTER, letterers
STAN GOLDBERG, colorist
ROY THOMAS, EDITOR

BOOTED FEET LAND ON CONCRETE PAVEMENT.
AN IRON GATE SWINGS WIDE.
BEARING A STRANGELY LIFE-LESS HERCULES, THE GOD OF THUNDER ENTERS THE MANSION'S GROUNDS

HE LOOKS NEITHER TO THE RIGHT NOR THE LEFT. HE SEEMS UNAWARE OF THE WORLD AROUND HIM.
HE IS--INTENT.

I HEAR HIM COMING NOW, LADIES.
THANKS FOR WARNING ME. I'D BETTER SEE IF I CAN HELP.

IRON MAN!

IF FRIEND THOU ART, THEN THOU MUST AID ME.

READY YON MEMORY INDUCER--FOR WE MUST PROBE THE MIND OF HERCULES, AS ONCE WE PROBED BEFORE*--!

PRAY THAT THIS TIME, WE MEET WITH MORE SUCCESS THAN LAST.

*CHECK IT IN AVENGERS #99, FEARLESS FACT-FOLLOWER!--ROY.

--AND WITH IT, LEARN WHAT HAPPENED IN THAT MISSING HOUR!

IT WON'T BE EASY, THOR. AS WE FOUND OUT LAST TIME, HERCULES IS RESISTANT TO THIS KIND OF PROBE.

STILL--WE HAVE MADE SOME IMPROVEMENTS ON THE MEMORY INDUCER--

--AND WITH MYSTIC MJOLNIR TO POWER THE MACHINE--WE MAY YET PREVAIL!

TURN THE SWITCH, IRON MAN--

THE MOMENT TO ACT--IS NOW!

SOFTLY AT FIRST, THEN WITH INCREASING LOUDNESS, A RHYTHMIC HUM BEGINS TO THROB WITHIN THE LOW-CEILINGED CHAMBER...! WITH EACH PASSING SECOND, IT GROWS EVER LOUDER... UNTIL IT BECOMES AN EAR-SPLITTING WHINE...
MMMMMM
...AND SEEMS TO WAKE THE UNCONSCIOUS HERCULES!

BY MY FATHER'S BEARD-- NO!
RIPP

I WILL NOT REMEMBER!
LET PLUTO TEAR ME FROM THIS WORLD --LET ZEUS EXILE ME FROM FAIR OLYMPUS--
WHAM
PLOW!

--I--

--WILL NOT--

REMEMBER?

DEMONS! DEVILS!
THOU HAST RETURNED TO HAUNT ME ANEW!
APPROACH, AND I'LL DESTROY THEE!
I SWEAR IT BY MY UNDYING SOUL!

SIR, THE TWO YOUNG LADIES YOU TOLD ME ABOUT HAVE ARRIVED.
SHALL I SEND THEM IN, OR WOULD YOU PREFER--
OH MY LORD!

WHAK!
BEGONE, DEMON!
I COMMAND THEE, GET THEE BEHIND ME!

WHOA, BIG FELLA--IF YOU KEEP THIS UP, WE'LL LOSE OUR INSURANCE ON THIS PLACE!
GIVE ME A HAND HERE, THOR--HE'S--

SPAROOM!

WE HAVE TO DO SOMETHING--HE'S DESTROYING EVERYTHING!
PERHAPS IF I--
NOT THEE, MORTAL.

I OWE MY LIFE TO THIS GODLING, AS MUCH AS I OWE IT TO THOR.
IF A RISK MUST BE TAKEN--
I MUST TAKE IT!

HEIMDAL'S EYES! KRISTA, 'TIS NOT THE HERCULES THOU DOST KNOW--
TAKE CARE LEST HE--
--BUT A GOD GONE MAD!

"HE WILL DO NOTHING, THOR," THE YOUNG GODDESS SAYS SOFTLY. "HE IS FRIGHTENED-- AFRAID-- AND YES, DELUDED.

"BUT HE WILL NOT HARM ME. HIS NOBILITY IS FAR TOO GREAT, TOO MUCH A PART OF HIM.

"HE WILL SEE ME-- AND HE WILL KNOW ME--

"--AND FOR THE MOMENT--

"--HIS NIGHTMARE--
"--WILL BE GONE."

THE MOMENT STRETCHES TO A MINUTE, THE MINUTE TO AN HOUR, AND WHEN HERCULES STIRS ONCE MORE... HIS EYES ARE LIT WITH THE GLOW OF REASON...
THE WOMAN SAVED ME, THOR. MY MIND WAS ASWIRL WITH A THOUSAND PHANTOMS--
--TILL SHE BROKE THROUGH THE MIST AND RE-TURNED MY SANITY.
CANST THOU NOW REM-EMBER THE HOURS THAT WERE COST TO THEE?

AYE... AND THE MEMORY IS ALMOST AS TERRIBLE AS THE EVENT ITSELF.
HAVE NO FEAR, ASGARDIAN-- I'M NOT ABOUT TO LOSE CONTROL AGAIN.
STILL, I MUST HAVE TIME-- TIME TO AB-SORB WHAT I NOW RECALL. THEN WE'LL TALK, THEE AND I--
AND WHEN WE HAVE FINISHED TALKING, WE'LL MAKE OUR PLANS-- TO FIGHT!

PERHAPS THE GENTLEMEN AND LADIES WOULD LIKE SOME TEA.
IF YOU WISH, I CAN ALSO PREPARE A SMALL SNACK --SOMETHING TO TIDE YOU OVER UNTIL DINNER--?
THANK YOU, JARVIS--BUT I DON'T THINK THAT'LL BE NECES-SARY.
FEELING ANY BETTER, HERCULES?

AS WELL AS I CAN FEEL, WITH THESE VISIONS HAUNTING MY BRAIN.
DID I TRULY SEE WHAT I REMEMBER SEEING--OR WAS IT ONLY ANOTHER DELUSION--
--THE IMAGININGS OF A MIND INSANE?
THOU MUST NOT TORMENT THYSELF, HERCULES.

TORMENT? WHAT CANST THOU KNOW OF TORMENT?
BY MY SOUL, I'VE ALWAYS COUNTED MYSELF A BRAVE MAN--
BUT CAN EVEN BRAVERY MATTER, 'GAINST THE FOUL-NESS I HAVE SEEN?

"IT BEGAN SEVERAL HOURS AGO, IN EARLY EVENING, AS I LEFT THOR* AND WANDERED THROUGH THE DARK-ENED SIDESTREETS OF THIS CITY'S SLUM.
*LAST ISSUE.--ROY.

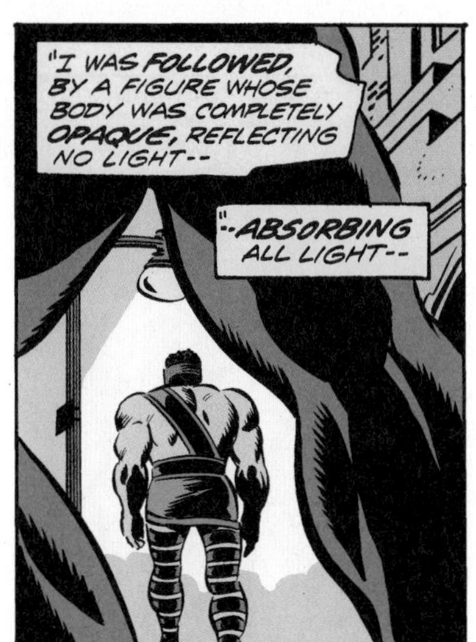
"I WAS FOLLOWED, BY A FIGURE WHOSE BODY WAS COMPLETELY OPAQUE, REFLECTING NO LIGHT--
"--ABSORBING ALL LIGHT--
"--A MAN OF UTTER BLACKNESS, LIKE NOTHING IN THIS OR ANY OTHER WORLD!

"HE ATTACKED ME.
"WE FOUGHT.
"AND IN THE MIDST OF THE BATTLE, SOMETHING CLUTCHED ME FROM OUT OF THE DARKNESS--
"--AND I WAS DRAGGED INTO THE DEPTHS OF THE EARTH--
"--TO A PLACE WHERE NO LIGHT REACHED AT ALL!"

AND THEN, HERCULES? PRAY, TELL US--
--WHAT HAPPENED THEN?
WOMAN, I SWEAR TO THEE-- 'TIS GONE FROM MY MEMORY!
YET WHEN I THINK UPON THAT TIME--
--I FEEL A DREAD --SUCH AS I HAVE NEVER KNOWN!

THINKEST THOU WE CAN FIND THIS STREET, OLYMPIAN?
'TIS SEARED IN MY BRAIN, THUNDER GOD.
THEN LET US BE OFF.
GIVE US ONE HOUR, IRON MAN. IF WE DO NOT RETURN IN THAT TIME--FOLLOW US, IF THOU CANST!
I PRAY THEE--FOLLOW THEN, AND NOT BEFORE!

MANY ARE THE DRAMAS WHICH UNFOLD IN TIME AND SPACE; BEFORE WE LEARN WHAT TERROR AWAITS THOR AND HERCULES BENEATH THE PLANET EARTH--
--LET'S LOOK FOR A MOMENT AT ANOTHER DRAMA, UNFOLDING IN ETERNAL ASGARD--
--A PLAY WHICH INVOLVES A WOMAN CALLED HILDEGARDE, SISTER TO THE FAIR-HAIRED KRISTA. LO, THE DRAMA BEGINS:
AWAY WITH THEE, WOMAN. ODIN HATH COM-MANDED--HE IS NOT TO BE DISTURBED.

'TIS MOST PASSING STRANGE! FOR NIGH ON SEVEN DAYS, ODIN HATH BEEN HIDDEN FROM ALL PRYING EYES.
AND EVEN WHEN HIS SON DID ASK HIM FOR AID*--
*LAST ISSUE. --ROY.

--ODIN REFUSED IT, AND SENT THE LADY SIF TO THOR INSTEAD!
'TIS ODD--IT WORRIES ME!
PERHAPS IF I TRY ANOTHER ENTRANCE--

BUT NO--! THESE GUARDS SEEM AS STERN AS THE OTHER PAIR.
IT LEAVES ME LITTLE CHOICE.
I MUST SEE THE ALL-FATHER...

AND NONE MAY SAY ME NAY!
THRAMM!

ALL-FATHER ODIN, I BEG THEE--FORGIVE THIS TRESPASS AGAINST THEE.
I SWEAR, 'TWAS ONLY MY CONCERN WHICH--

BY BIFROST'S GOLDEN SPAN!

THE THRONE ROOM IS EMPTY--
THE LORD OF ASGARD IS GONE!

WHAT I FEAR CANNOT BE TRUE!
I MUST SEARCH EVERY ROOM--EVERY CHAMBER--TILL THE FEAR CAN NO LONGER BE DENIED!

FOR--IF MY FEARS ARE TRULY FOUNDED ON FACT--
--METHINKS ASGARD'S GRAVEST HOUR IS NIGH!

AND SEARCH, SHE DOES... UNTIL, ALMOST AN HOUR LATER, HER WEARY FEET CARRY HER TO THE DARKEST OF THE ODIN-KEEP'S TOWER ROOMS, WHERE...
ODIN'S SEER AND CONFIDANT--THE VIZIER!
IF ANY DOTH KNOW THE ALL-FATHER'S HIDING PLACE..!TWOULD BE HE!

BUT, INSTEAD OF ALLAYING THE GODDESS HILDEGARDE'S FEARS... THE AGE-WEARY VIZIER CONFIRMS THEM...
YES, HILDEGARDE-- ODIN HAS VANISHED!
EVEN I, HIS MOST TRUSTED SERVANT, KNOW NOT WHERE HE MAY BE.
FOR IF I DID, I WOULD WARN HIM OF THE DANGER FACED BY THOR--

"--WHO EVEN AS WE SPEAK--

"--DESCENDS TO THE PITS OF DARKNESS!"
ART THOU CERTAIN THIS IS THE PLACE OF THY ABDUCTION, HERCULES?
AYE. MY HEART POUNDS --MY BLOOD CONGEALS--!
THIS IS INDEED THE PLACE, ASGARDIAN...
...FOR THE VERY THOUGHT OF ENTERING THIS BLACKNESS AGAIN... DOTH MAKE MY SKIN CRAWL!
STEEL THYSELF, HERCULES.
NO DREAM OR MEMORY ALONE IS ENOUGH TO BREAK A MAN--!
SO SAYEST THOU.
THOU WHO HATH NEVER TASTED FEAR AS A TANGIBLE-- WAIT!
"A SNATCH OF MEMORY-- I SEEM TO RECALL BEING HERE, SOMETHING I COULD NOT RECALL BEFORE!
"AND THE SHADOWS--I REMEMBER THE SHADOWS, ASGARDIAN-- SO DEEP, SO FULL OF HIDDEN IMPLICATIONS--! BY MY SOUL, MY MIND REELS!"

FEAR NOT, OLYMPIAN. 'TIS ONLY A MEMORY.
A TRICK OF THE IMAGIN-ATION, TAKING THE UNREAL-- MAKING IT REAL UNTIL--
HEIMDAL'S EYES! 'TIS A DEMON IN THE DARK-NESS BEFORE US!
BACK, YE MINIONS OF HELL!
WHAM!
GET THEE BACK, OR FEEL THE POWER OF MINE MYSTIC MALLET--
THE POWER OF MY HAMMER, MJOLNIR--
EH?
THE DEMONS-- DIS-APPEARED--?
YET, HOW COULD THEY FADE SO QUICKLY--
UNLESS--THEY WERE NEVER THERE?
PERHAPS NOW, THOU DOST BEGIN TO UNDER-STAND.
WHATEVER POWER IS BEHIND THIS MYSTERY--'TIS A POWER WE CANNOT TOUCH.
'TIS A POWER WHICH DOTH AFFECT--
--THE MIND!
MORE THAN THE MIND, THOR-- IT SEEMS TO HAVE ITS WILL OVER OUR VERY SOULS!
IN THAT CASE, WE MUST INDEED LOCATE THIS POWER--
--AND HAVING LOCATED IT--
--WE MUST DESTROY IT!

THE GRIM OLYMPIAN ONLY NODS IN ANSWER, AS HE CONTINUES TO LEAD THE WAY DOWNWARD THROUGH THE DARK ABYSS... DEEP INTO THE BEDROCK UNDERLYING THE CITY OF MANHATTAN... THROUGH A MAZE OF TUNNELS AND BURROWINGS WHICH IMPLY A HORROR GREATER THAN THOR EVER IMAGINED...
THEN, WHEN THE AIR--ALREADY STIFLING--HAS BECOME SO DENSE IT ALMOST SUFFOCATES...
HERCULES.. ....IN THE BECKONING GLOOM AHEAD...

DOST THOU SEE?
A SHAPE--A SHADOW--A FORM WITHOUT DIMENSION OR DEPTH--?
BY BIFROST'S RAINBOW SPAN--

--TIS AS THOUGH THE DARKNESS WERE ALIVE!
BUT HOLD! THE FORM DOTH VANISH--

--AND DOTH BECOME BUT A SHADOW ONCE MORE--

--AS THOUGH IT WERE BUT A TRICK OF MINE EYES--

--ONLY THIS, AND NOTHING MORE!
WE MUST BE WARY OF OUR SUSPICIONS, HERCULES. THEY'LL BETRAY US YET.
HERCULES...?

ODIN'S BLOOD! MATERIALIZING FROM ALL SIDES--
DEMONS--OF EVERY SIZE AND SHAPE!
THEN--TWAS NO ILLUSION--
AAARRR
--THE DARKNESS IS ALIVE--
--AND IT STRUGGLES AGAINST US--
--SEEKING OUR VERY LIVES!
KAPLOW!!
WHAM!
NAY, THOR--THESE WERE NOT THE MONSTERS WHICH ATTACKED ME!
THEY ARE A LESSER BREED -- QUICKLY ROUTED--
--EASILY DESTROYED!

THE DEVILS I FOUGHT WERE STRONGER, MORE QUICK-WITTED THAN THESE DEMON DRONES!
I FEAR THEY ARE BUT MEANT TO WEARY US!
--TO READY US FOR AN ATTACK BY THEIR MASTER--
"HE WHO DWELLS IN DARKNESS!"
HE IS THE THREAT!
HE IS THE POWER--THAT IS UNKNOWN!

BUT THOR DOESN'T HEAR THE SHOUTING HERCULES --RATHER, HIS ATTENTION IS ALL BUT CONSUMED BY THE ATTACKERS SWARMING OVER HIM--
--AND THE OLYMPIAN'S WARNING GOES UNHEARD--AND UNHEEDED!

BELATEDLY, HERCULES UNDERSTANDS THAT THIS MAY BE THE TRUE THREAT--

--AND WITHOUT A WORD TO HIS COMRADE IN ARMS, HE WHIRLS ABOUT--AND RUNS!

HE KNOWS HE CANNOT DESTROY US --IN A PHYSICAL ATTACK--
--THEREFORE, HIS ATTACK CANNOT BE PHYSICAL--DESPITE THESE SWARMING MONSTERS!

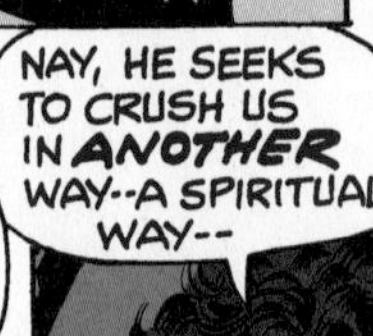

NAY, HE SEEKS TO CRUSH US IN ANOTHER WAY--A SPIRITUAL WAY--
--BY OVERWHELMING US WITH INCREDIBLE ODDS--AND FOR JUST A MOMENT--

--MAKING US DESPAIR!
IN DESPAIR, HE WILL CONQUER US --IN DESPAIR HE WILL CAPTURE OUR VERY SOULS!

MAY THE HALLOWED HIGH-LORDS OF OLYMPUS PROTECT ME--
THIS MUST NOT BE!
REACHING A NARROW POINT IN THE MUSTY TUNNEL, WHERE THE CEILING ALMOST MEETS THE RUBBLE-STREWN FLOOR--THE SON OF ZEUS THROWS HIS ARMS ABOVE HIS HEAD--
--PLANTS HIS FEET LIKE ROCK UPON THE ROCK--
--AND STRAINS UPWARD, WITH ALL THE MIGHT OF A GODLING BORN!

AT ONCE, THE EARTH **HEAVES** A THOUSAND FEET ABOVE--AS A VAST GRANITE **PLUG** SLOWLY RISES FROM THE GROUND--
RUMMMN
--A PLUG PUSHED FROM **BENEATH** BY THE GOD WHOM MEN CALL **HERCULES**--WHOSE MUSCLES BAND AND **RIPPLE**--WHOSE BODY GLISTENS WITH **SWEAT**--
--TILL THE COLUMNS OF EARTH **BLAST FREE!**
KAAHOOOM!
HERCULES, WHERE ART THOU?
FOR EACH DEMON I DISPATCH, **TEN MORE** APPEAR! THEIR NUMBERS SEEM **ENDLESS!**
ALMOST IT MAKES ME--

BEFORE THE THUNDER GOD CAN **COMPLETE** HIS SENTENCE, A BRILLIANT SHAFT OF DAWN **SUNLIGHT** WASHES OVER HIM--
--SHATTERING THE **GLOOM**---
--AND SENDING THE DEMONS **SCURRY-ING**--FOR **DARKNESS!**

PRAISE, ZEUS, THOU DIDST NOT SPEAK THE WORD, ASGARDIAN!
IF THOU DIDST **DESPAIR**--'TWOULD HAVE BEEN THE **END** OF THEE--
--FOR **HE** DOTH FEED UPON DESPAIR--'TIS HOW HE SPENDS **ETERNITY!**
"HE"?

I REMEMBER HIM NOW, ASGARDIAN. HE DWELLS IN DARKNESS--BECAUSE HE CANNOT ABIDE THE LIGHT!
WHO IS THIS "HE" THOU DOST SPEAK OF?
SOME MONSTER--SOME DEVIL WHO LIVES BENEATH THE EARTH?
THOU DOST WISH TO SEE HIM, THOR?
THEN--LOOK THERE!

'TIS HIS SHADOW! THE CREATURE I CAUGHT BUT A GLIMPSE OF BEFORE--
--HE DOTH HIDE IN YONDER TUNNEL!

THINK SO, THUNDER GOD?
ATTACK HIM--AND TELL ME WHAT THOU DOST THINK THEN!

AYE! I'LL ATTACK HIM--! WITH THE AID OF MINE MYSTIC MJOLNIR, I SHALL--
EH?

NOTHING!
NAUGHT BUT HIS SHADOW EXISTS--ALL ELSE IS ILLUSION!
BUT--IF HE HAS NO FORM --THEN WHO--?

PERHAPS THE GREATEST DEMON OF ALL, ASGARDIAN-- WHO DWELLS NOT ONLY IN DARKNESS, BENEATH THE EARTH--
--BUT IN US ALL, ONLY WAITING TO ESCAPE-- AND DESTROY US.
WE TRIUMPHED OVER HIM THIS TIME, THOR--
--BUT NEXT TIME?
NEXT TIME-- THE TRIUMPH MAY WELL GO TO THAT MOST INTANGIBLE DEVIL-- FEAR!
NEXT ISSUE: WHEN ODIN DISAPPEARS!

DEAD OF NIGHT
MARVEL COMICS GROUP™
APPROVED BY THE COMICS CODE AUTHORITY
25¢
11
AUG
02909
DEAD OF NIGHT™
featuring
THE SCARECROW
™
ALL-NEW! MARVELDOM'S #1 SHOCK-STAR!
A FEARSOME NIGHT-PROWLER VS. A CENTURIES-OLD CULT OF BLOOD!
FIRES OF REBIRTH.. FIRES OF DEATH!

Stan Lee PRESENTS: THE SINISTER SCARECROW!™
THE DEAD OF NIGHT:
ON A NIGHT SUCH AS THIS, MOST CITY-DWELLERS HIDE IN THE SHELTER OF THEIR HOMES, AFRAID TO RESPOND TO THE SLIGHTEST OUTSIDE SOUND, AFRAID TO GET INVOLVED--
--AFRAID OF THEMSELVES.
YET THERE ARE THOSE WHO DO NOT FLEE FROM EVIL--BUT RUSH TOWARDS IT, LIKE MOTHS TO A CANDLE FLAME.
THE SCARECROW WAITS... FOR THEM!

SKREEEEEE...

SKREEEEB...

COME ON...

THE SILENCE OF A TOMB IS BROKEN HERE... THE SAME SORT OF DEATHLY SILENCE WHICH NOW HOLDS THE OWNER OF THIS GALLERY SO TIGHTLY IN ITS GRIP.
THE PAINTING'S IN HERE, SOMEWHERE. ALL WE HAVE TO DO IS FIND IT. SO START LOOKING!
HE WAS A QUEER DUCK, SOME WOULD SAY... HE MADE CERTAIN PROVISIONS WHICH MANY HAD TOLD HIM WERE QUITE--

-- INADEQUATE!
HOLD IT RIGHT THERE! I'LL PLUG THE FIRST ONE THAT MOVES!

IS THAT RIGHT, GRANDPA?

YOU KNOW-- YOU'RE TOO OLD TO BE MAKIN' THREATS YOU CAN'T BACK UP!
A SHAME YOU AIN'T GONNA BE GETTIN' ANY OLDER!
CH-POW
CH-POW
CH-POW

SO THE FAITHFUL GUARD NOW JOINS HIS EMPLOYER... IN DEATH.
OKAY-- LET'S GET DOWN TO WORK!

YEAH. AS SOON AS THAT SCARECROW PAINTING IS IN OUR HANDS...

...THE CULT OF KALUMAI WILL RULE THE WORLD ONCE MORE!

Y'KNOW, I AIN'T NEVER SEEN SO MANY PAINTINGS IN MY WHOLE--
SHADDUP, WILLYA! JUST KEEP LOOKIN'!
BENEATH A VENEER OF SOPHISTICATED CALLOUSNESS OR INFANTILE HUMOR, THERE OFTEN LURKS A FEARFUL CHILD.

SHEESH! A MAN CAN'T EVEN WHISTLE WHILE HE WORKS ANYMORE! 'USTA BE THAT YOU COULD...
CAPSULE STUDY: THE CRIMINAL WITH DELUSIONS OF GRANDEUR, SPENDING THE LAST FEW MOMENTS OF A SOMEWHAT WASTED LIFE COMPLAINING...
...THUS PROVING THAT HE IS NOT TRULY SO DIFFERENT FROM THE REST OF US.

EXCEPT THAT HIS TIME HAS COME-- NOW!

HE SPINS IN HIS LAST FEW MOMENTS, THIS MOUSE OF A MAN. HE SPINS TO SEE HIS PERSONAL INCARNATION OF DEATH -- THAT WHICH PREVIOUSLY TOUCHED HIS TATTERED EXISTENCE ONLY AS SOME NEBULOUS ABSTRACTION--
--BUT NOW HAS COME FORTH TO TOUCH HIM PHYSICALLY...

...AND ITS TOUCH IS DEATHLY COLD!
... THE SCARECROW...

IF THE DEAD MAN HAD LIVED, PERHAPS HE WOULD HAVE WARNED HIS PARTNER...
WHA?
...BUT KNOWING THE NATURE OF THAT DEAD MAN...
...IT'S DOUBTFUL!
SO IT'S HALLOWE'EN TIME, EH, JOKER. GUESS I'LL JUST HAVE TO REMOVE YOUR MASK... THE HARD WAY!

STEEL-JACKETED PROJECTILES PIERCE CLOTH... AND IF THERE IS ANY EARTHLY FLESH HIDDEN BENEATH...
...NOTHING SHOWS TO PROVE IT. NO BLOOD SPRAYS FORTH FROM GAPING WOUNDS. ONLY PUFFS OF DUST AND A FEW STRAY WISPS OF STRAW STAND WITNESS TO THE FACT THAT BULLETS HAVE VISITED THE SCARECROW'S FORM.

THEN, WITH A SPEED BELYING THE GRACE OF A RUDOLPH NUREYEV, IF NOT QUITE THE BEAUTY...
WAIT! GET BACK!
...A COMPLETELY UNHARMED SCARECROW RUSHES FORWARD...

...A NIGHTMARE STEALING FORTH UPON THE LAND OF THE LIVING...

...TO CARRY HOME A VICTIM TO THE LAND OF THE DEAD!
CRACK!

ENTER: THE SCARECROW
THE SCARECROW REARS BACK HIS MISSHAPEN HEAD AND LAUGHS THE LAUGH OF A MADMAN... HIS HUGE GAPING WOUND OF A MOUTH PAYING TESTAMENT TO THE INHUMAN NATURE OF THE CREATURE.
THE MERCILESS MANIACAL ROAR OF THIS BEING WHO WOULD OTHERWISE BE ONLY A SYMBOL OF TRICK-OR-TREATING, HAYRIDES, AND PUMPKIN PIES... WOULD TERRIFY THE TWO DEAD MEN AT HIS FEET... IF THEY COULD HEAR IT.
HE SEEMS TO ENJOY THESE DEATHS...TO REVEL IN THEM...TO BATHE IN THE WAVES OF PAIN WHICH THE DYING MEN SEND FORTH FROM THE DEPTHS OF THEIR SOULS.
HEEE HEEE HEEE HEEE HEEEE
ANY SANE MAN WOULD LOOK SILENTLY ON THIS SCENE, UNABLE TO LAUGH... AND WONDER, PERHAPS... "WHAT'S THE JOKE?"
WRITTEN BY SCOTT EDELMAN
DRAWN BY RICO RIVAL
COLORED BY GLYNIS WEIN
LETTERED BY MARCUS
EDITED BY LEN WEIN

CUT!
ARE THERE ANY MORE BIDS? DO I HEAR ANOTHER BID?
FACE IT, JESS...

...IT'S YOURS. YOU'VE SCARED AWAY EVERYONE ELSE HERE!
CAN THE CONGRATULATIONS, DAVE! THE MINUTE YOU GET TOO OPTIMISTIC IS WHEN EVERYTHING BEGINS TO FALL AP--
FIVE THOUSAND, ONE HUNDRED.

SORRY, MY FRIEND, IF I GOT YOUR HOPES UP TOO HIGH...
...BUT THIS IS MORE TO ME THAN JUST A CHILDREN'S GAME.
YOU KNOW HIS TYPE, JESS DUNCAN...

YOU'VE SEEN HIS KIND AT EVERY AUCTION. THE MAN WITH THE DIVIDE-AND-CONQUER MENTALITY. HE'LL SIT BACK AND LET OTHERS DO ALL THE WORK.
RIGHT AGAIN, JESS. CAN'T YOU EVER BE WRONG?

FIVE THOUSAND, FIVE HUNDRED!

I THOUGHT THAT I WAS THE ONLY ONE AFFLICTED WITH A DESIRE FOR THIS PAINTING. SUCH A PITY THAT YOU'RE GOING TO LOSE.
SIX THOUSAND.

YOU'VE ALWAYS BEEN PROUD, HAVEN'T YOU, JESS. MAYBE TOO PROUD?
BUT WHEN YOU CANNOT EVEN TURN TO YOUR BROTHER FOR HELP...

... WHAT DO YOU DO WHEN YOU NEED SOMEONE?
WHERE ARE YOU GOING, DAVE?
DAVE DOES NOT ANSWER.

SIX THOUSAND, ONE HUNDRED.
OH! PARDON ME!
--OOF!

DO I HEAR ANY MORE BIDS?
SILENCE.

GOING ONCE!
I'M TERRIBLY SORRY, SIR.

HERE. LET ME HELP YOU UP.
GOING TWICE!

GONE!
SOLD--FOR SIX THOUSAND, ONE HUNDRED DOLLARS!

OH, JESS! AT LAST!

I DON'T UNDERSTAND, DAVE. WHY DID THAT MAN GIVE UP? HE SEEMED SO DETERMINED.
WE'VE BOTH SEEN OTHERS LIKE HIM, JESS. HE'S THE GUY WHO BLUFFS AT POKER WITH AN EMPTY WALLET.

I REMEMBER THAT TIME JUST BEFORE I LEFT HOME, WHEN YOU--
WAIT!

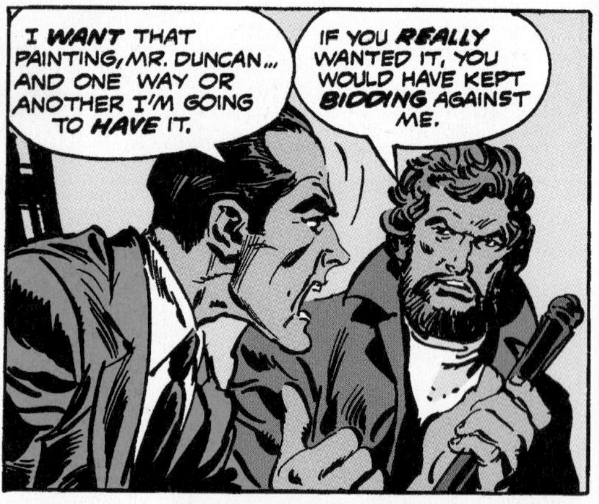
I WANT THAT PAINTING, MR. DUNCAN... AND ONE WAY OR ANOTHER I'M GOING TO HAVE IT.
IF YOU REALLY WANTED IT, YOU WOULD HAVE KEPT BIDDING AGAINST ME.

JESS HAS WANTED THIS PAINTING ALL HIS LIFE, AND HE'S NOT ABOUT TO GIVE IT UP NOW. SURELY YOU MUST UNDERSTAND THAT FEELING OF FULFILLMENT?
I CAN'T BE SWAYED BY HOMILIES, MISS. WE SHALL MEET AGAIN.

I PROMISE YOU... WE SHALL MEET AGAIN.

AND IF ANY OF THE TRIO HAS ABSORBED THE THREAT INHERENT IN THE WORDS OF GREGOR ROVIK...

...THEY LEAVE IT BEHIND IN THE PARKING LOT. THERE IS NO PLACE FOR MALICE IN THE SOHO LOFT OF JESS DUNCAN.
I'VE WANTED THIS FOR A LONG TIME, DAVE. YOU NEVER KNEW BACK THEN, 'CAUSE YOU'D ALREADY LEFT HOME. YOU WERE ON YOUR OWN UNICORN HUNT, I GUESS. SEEMS I'VE FOUND MY UNICORN FIRST.
WE CAN'T ALL BE WINNERS, JESS. AT LEAST NOT WHEN YOU'RE AROUND.

Y'KNOW--ER-- IT'S FUNNY. I'VE BEEN GETTING WEIRD VIBES FROM THIS CANVAS ALL AFTERNOON. THINK IT HAS ANYTHING TO DO WITH ITS SUPPOSED MYSTICAL PROPERTIES?
WHAT PROPERTIES, JESS? YOU'VE BEEN EVADING MY QUESTIONS FOR MONTHS... EVER SINCE YOU FIRST TOLD ME ABOUT THE PAINTING'S EXISTENCE.

YOU KNOW MORE THAN YOU LET ON, DAVE. I'VE GOT THE GUT FEELING YOU'RE WORKING ON A FEATURE ARTICLE FOR THAT MAGAZINE OF YOURS!
IT SHOWS, HUH? YEAH -- SO FAR I'VE FOUND THAT THE FIRST RECORDED OWNER OF THE PAINTING WAS A RELIGIOUS HERETIC! HE'D EVEN FALLEN OUT WITH THE MORE ORTHODOX HERESIES -- SUCH AS THE CULT OF KALUMAI.
WHATEVER HAPPENED TO THE CULT, DAVE?
WELL--
THAT MUCH I KNOW! IT DIED OUT MANY YEARS AGO HARMONY. AS FAR AS I CAN TELL, THIS PAINTING IS ALL THAT REMAINS.

THEY WERE BELIEVED TO HAVE HAD SOMETHING TO DO WITH THE PAINTING CENTURIES EARLIER, BUT EXACTLY WHAT HAS BEEN LOST TO HISTORY.

JESS DUNCAN WOULD HAVE MADE AN EXCELLENT PLAYRIGHT...

HE HAS A MARVELOUS SENSE OF IRONY... AND TIMING!
THE EFFECT IS ASTOUNDING... AS A CULT THOUGHT DEAD FOR CENTURIES, EVEN BY MOST OF ITS ADHERENTS, COMES CRASHING THROUGH THE THICK OAKEN DOORS OF JESS DUNCAN'S STUDIO LOFT-- THE KALUMAI LIVE!
JESS?
HER WORDS SEEM TO ASK, "IS THIS ANOTHER OF YOUR CHILDISH JOKES?"

SADLY, IT IS NOT.
SOON OUR LORD SHALL WALK THE EARTH ONCE MORE! TAKE THE PAINTING!

NO! YOU CAN'T DO THIS!

SOK
JESS!

DO NOT FORGET THE GIRL! IT IS ONLY FITTING THAT THE SACRIFICE WHICH WILL BRING OUR GOD BACK TO LIFE BE THAT OF SHE WHO HELPED STEAL HIM FROM OUR GRASP.
HARMONY!
TAKE HER!
NO, HARMONY MAXWELL. THIS IS NO JOKE--

--NOT EVEN A VERY GOOD ONE-LINER.
HARMONY! WATCH OUT!

DON'T WORRY, DAVE. I CAN TAKE CARE OF MYSELF!

WHICH IS MORE THAN CAN BE SAID FOR YOU, FRIEND!
DUCK!

Y'KNOW, HARMONY--

--ALL MY LIFE I'VE WANTED TO PROVE JESS WRONG. JUST ONCE.

WOULDN'T YA KNOW I'D HAVE SUCH CRUMMY TIM-- NGGG!

CLUNKK!
FOR A MOMENT, THERE IS SILENCE...

...AND THEN THE TENSION, SO THICK IT CAN ALMOST BE BREATHED, IS SHATTERED BY A FINAL COMMAND!
TAKE HER!

ER-- CAN I GET ANY OF YOU GUYS SOMETHING TO EAT?
I DIDN'T THINK SO.
THIS TIME, HARMONY MAXWELL CANNOT BUY HER WAY OUT WITH HUMOR.

AGAINST SUCH OVERWHELMING ODDS, HARMONY QUICKLY FALLS..
..AND AS SHE IS DRAGGED STRUGGLING FROM JESS' APARTMENT, SHE GLANCES AT THE TWO STILL FORMS THAT LIE SPRAWLED IN THE EVER DEEPENING DUSK...
AND SINCE ONE IS THE FORM OF THE MAN SHE LOVES, THE SCENE IS DOUBLY DARK.

THE SUN ALWAYS SEEMS TO SET MORE QUICKLY WHEN YOU NEED THE LIGHT..
... AND IN THE DIM MOONGLOW, TWO UNIDENTIFIABLE FORMS LIE UNMOVING...

... UNTIL ONE WRENCHES ITSELF PAINFULLY TO ITS FEET...

...SHAMBLES AWKWARDLY ACROSS THE ROOM...

... AND EXITS.

FRIENDS, THE DAY OF DAWNING IS AT LAST AT HAND!

IN BUT A FEW SHORT MOMENTS, OUR LORD SHALL WALK THE EARTH AGAIN, ONCE MORE ALIVE...

...AND NOT MERELY A PAINTING COVERED OVER BY A HERETIC'S NIGHTMARE--BY THIS BLASPHEMOUS SCARECROW!
IN MOMENTS, THE CANVAS WILL STAND RESTORED TO ITS ORIGINAL STATE--
--AND THE VISAGE OF KALUMAI SHALL SHINE UPON US ONCE MORE!

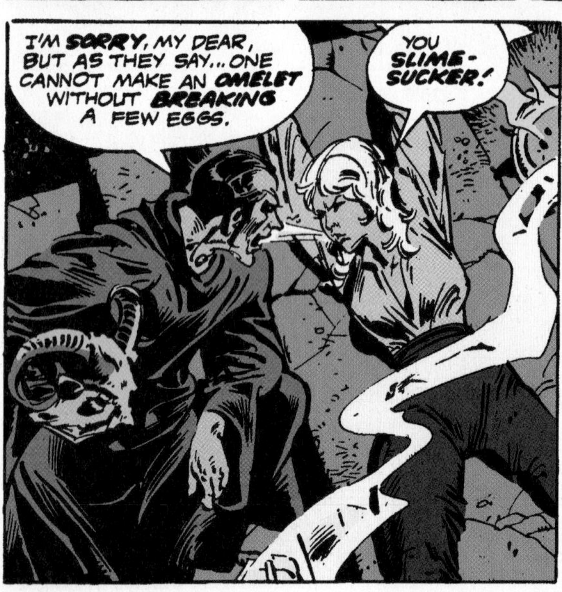
I'M SORRY, MY DEAR, BUT AS THEY SAY...ONE CANNOT MAKE AN OMELET WITHOUT BREAKING A FEW EGGS.
YOU SLIME-SUCKER!

TSK, TSK... YOURS WAS GOING TO BE A PAINLESS DEATH, BUT NOW I THINK THAT I SHALL RATHER ENJOY THE DEED.

A QUARTER-HOUR PASSES, AND THE SMELL OF INCENSE ENGULFS THE ROOM. CANDLE WAX DRIPS HEAVILY UPON THE FLOOR, AND SONOROUS INCANTATIONS BEGIN TO RISE AND FALL IN INTENSITY...
IF NOT FOR THE DANGER ABOUNDING IN HER PRESENT SITUATION, HARMONY COULD ALMOST DRIFT OFF TO SLEEP.
EN--? THAT SHARD OF GLASS--?! WHO--?

IF DANTE HAD KNOWN OF THE SCARECROW, HE WOULD SURELY HAVE INCLUDED HIM AS THE TASKMASTER OF HIS FAMOUS INFERNO!
THE HAND OF FEAR TIGHTENS AROUND THE HEARTS OF THE MINIONS OF KALUMAI... FOR TO SEE A CACKLING LIVING INCARNATION OF THE PAINTING THEY SO DESPISE IS AKIN TO BEING ALONE IN A WAX MUSEUM... AND TO HEAR BREATHING NOT YOUR OWN. IT CAN'T HAPPEN! IT CAN'T BE TRUE!
HE HE HE HE HE
HE HE HE HE
BUT THE LAUGHTER SHRIEKING OUT OF THE SCARECROW'S GAPING MAW CRIES THAT IT IS TRUTH!
THE SCARECROW LIVES!

AND HE COMES WITH A THOUSAND SAVAGE SERVANTS BESIDE HIM!

TALONS RIP OPEN FLESH... BEAKS SCRATCH STREAMERS OF BLOOD ACROSS THE ROOM... AS THE HELL-SPAWNED BIRDS CLAIM THROBBING BITS OF FLESH FOR THEIR OWN.

... AND THROUGH IT ALL, ANY WHO DARE TO LOOK STRAIGHT INTO THE SCARECROW'S EYES...

... ARE INSTANTLY FROZEN IN FEAR! THEY CANNOT TEAR THEIR GAZE FROM THE DEATHLY VISAGE...
... EVEN AS ITS OWNER QUICKLY ENDS THEIR MISSPENT LIVES!

THEY FALL QUICKLY... ALMOST TOO QUICKLY...
... FOR THE SCARECROW SEEMS TO BE ENJOYING THIS.

GREGOR ROVIK KNOWS WHEN HE IS BEATEN. HIS UNHOLY GOD WILL NOT HELP HIM WITHOUT THE PRESCRIBED DROP OF SACRIFICIAL BLOOD.
HE FLEES... AND HE IS SHORN OF ALL RATIONALIZATIONS.

HE IS NOT "ADVANCING IN ANOTHER DIRECTION." HE IS RUNNING AWAY.
OR MORE PRECISELY, BEING PUSHED FORWARD BY THE LAUGHTER AT HIS BACK...
...BEING BUOYED FORWARD--

--BY STARK, UNRELENTING FEAR!
STAY BACK!
STAY BACK OR I SWEAR...THE WOMAN DIES!
YES, GREGOR ROVIK KNOWS WHEN HE IS BEATEN. AND IF HE WERE A BRAVER MAN, HE MIGHT CONFRONT THAT KNOWLEDGE.

LET ME BY OR I'LL SLAY HER!
AND HER BLOOD WILL BE ON YOUR HANDS!
UNFORTUNATELY SOME THINGS YOU DO NOT NEED COURAGE TO CONFRONT...

... BECAUSE NO MATTER WHICH WAY YOU TURN...
HUH?

...THEY'LL CONFRONT YOU!
NOOOOOO!

THE--THE TREES--! THEY'RE ALIVE!

SCARECROW! HELP MEEEEEEE

THREE DAYS FROM NOW, THE POLICE WILL FIND THE BODY OF GREGOR ROVIK. EVERY BONE WILL BE BROKEN. NOT ONE MUSCLE WILL BE UNTORN; NOT ONE ORGAN UNRUPTURED.

THE POLICE WILL, OF COURSE, BE BAFFLED. THEY WILL CLASSIFY THE DEATH AS UNEXPLAINED.

A SHAME THEY WILL NOT KNOW ENOUGH TO CLASSIFY IT UNDER ITS PROPER HEADING.
RETRIBUTION!

EPILOGUE: SUNRISE, AND HARMONY MAXWELL AWAKENS TO FIND HERSELF SPRAWLED ONCE MORE ON THE SACRIFICIAL ALTAR. GONE IS THE LEERING SARDONIC SCARECROW, PROTECTING HER FROM THE MINIONS OF KALUMAI. NOW THERE IS ONLY JESS DUNCAN AND DAVE MONROE KNEELING BESIDE HER, SHIELDING HER FROM THE COOL MORNING BREEZE.

HARMONY! WAKE UP, HARMONY!
CAN YOU HEAR ME, HARMONY? ANSWER ME!

HEY--HER EYES ARE OPENING, JESS. SHE'S OKAY!
WHAT HAPPENED? WHERE ARE ALL THOSE RAM'S-HEADED DUDES?

THEY'RE... GONE.
BUT LET'S NOT TALK ABOUT THAT, ONLY...
JESS, I FEEL SO SORRY FOR YOU. YOUR POOR PAINTING... THEY'VE DESTROYED YOUR PAINTING.

MY PAINTING? YOU MUST'VE BEEN DREAMING, HARMONY. NO ONE'S DAMAGED THE PAINTING. THERE'S NOTHING WRONG WITH IT AT ALL.
NOTHING? I WOULDN'T BE TOO SURE OF THAT, JESS...

...I DON'T THINK HE WAS SMILING BEFORE!
JESS DUNCAN'S ONLY RESPONSE IS SILENCE.
A TERRIBLY, TERRIBLY LONG SILENCE.
END

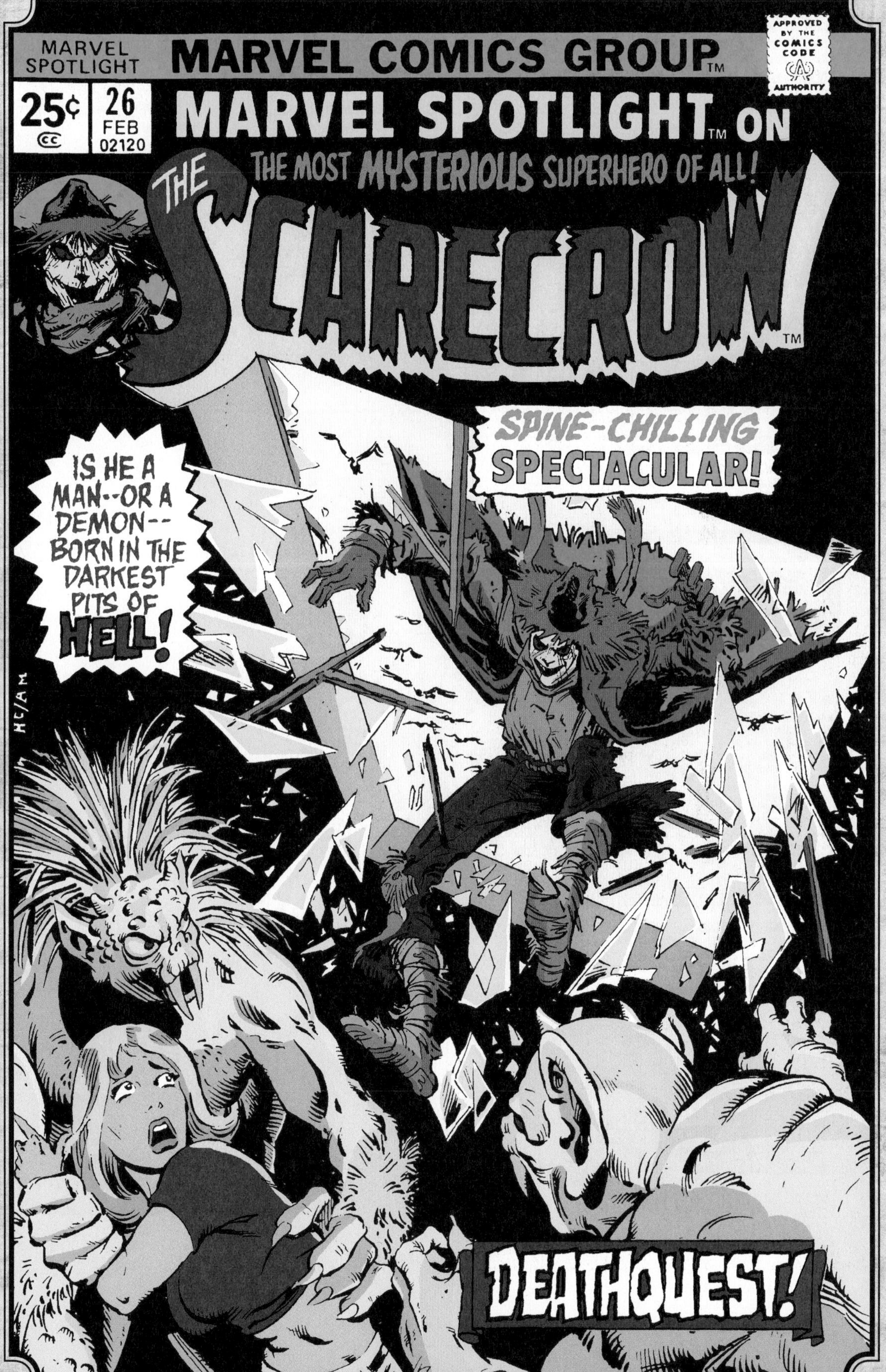
MARVEL SPOTLIGHT
MARVEL COMICS GROUP
APPROVED BY THE COMICS CODE AUTHORITY
25¢
26 FEB 02120
MARVEL SPOTLIGHT ON
THE MOST MYSTERIOUS SUPERHERO OF ALL!
THE SCARECROW
SPINE-CHILLING SPECTACULAR!
IS HE A MAN--OR A DEMON--BORN IN THE DARKEST PITS OF HELL!
DEATHQUEST!

Stan Lee PRESENTS: THE SINISTER SCARECROW!™

SCOTT EDELMAN AUTHOR * RUBEN YANDOC ILLUSTRATOR * PETRA GOLDBERG COLORIST * SAN JOSÉ LETTERER * MARV WOLFMAN EDITOR

FINGERTIPS... HAND...WRIST...
...EACH IN TURN APPEARS...
...UNTIL FULL-BLOWN GROTESQUERIES OF EVIL STAND IN THE SOHO LOFT OF JESS DUNCAN.
THREE NIGHT DEMONS PLAY CHESS WITH WORLDS... WORLDS NOT THEIR OWN...
FOR THOUGH THE CULT OF KALUMAI IS DEAD-- ITS LORD, KALUMAI, LIVES ON!
DEATH WATERS OF THE RIVER STYX

THESE SUB-HUMAN CREATURES SHAMBLE SLOWLY ABOUT A ROOM IN A WORLD THEY HAVE NEVER BEFORE SEEN...
...A WORLD ALMOST BOUGHT WITH THE BLOOD OF HARMONY MAXWELL!

AND ALTHOUGH THAT PRICE WAS TOO DEAR FOR THE LIKES OF JESS DUNCAN...
POLICE
...THE CULT OF KALUMAI THOUGHT IT A BARGAIN TO PAY FOR THEIR GOD.

A GOD WHO HAS WATCHED HIS MINIONS FAIL TO FREE HIM...*
* SEE DEAD OF NIGHT #11--MARV.

...A GOD WHO HAS DECIDED TO TAKE ACTION...FOR HIMSELF!
WHAT THE--! HEY, RILEY! GET YOUR ASPIRATIONS OVER HERE--

--BEFORE THESE HALLOWE'EN REFUGEES DECIDE TO END MINE!
BRAM
POW

BUT RILEY DOES NOT ANSWER.

HE TURNS AND RUNS AS MOST MEN WOULD AT THE SIGHT OF A FEARFUL DEATH...
BRA-GAM
HEY! C'MON, GUYS, IT'S TIME FOR THE CAVALRY!

...SO RILEY LIVES OUT THIS DAY...
RILE--AUKKKK!
WOOSH
BUT ANOTHER DOES NOT.

THESE FIENDS SEEK THE HORN OF KALUMAI.
CRASH
A HORN WHICH WILL, WHEN USED IN BLOOD SACRIFICE, OPEN A DIMENSIONAL DOORWAY TO MORE THAN JUST A GOD'S UNDERLINGS...

BUT TO THE GOD HIMSELF!
A HORN WHICH CAN FREE A TERROR WHOM ONE HAS SWORN TO KEEP ENTRAPPED...
...THE ONE CALLED--
-- THE SCARECROW!
PROTECTOR OF A HELLISH DIMENSION-- AND, FOR CENTURIES...
HEEEHEEEHEHEEHEHEEEEHHEEEH
...GUARDIAN TO A PAINTING WHICH SAINTS AND SAGES HAVE TRIED FRUITLESSLY TO DESTROY...
...FOR, IT IS THE SOLE LINK BETWEEN OUR DIMENSION AND THAT OF KALUMAI.
AND SHOULD THE SCARECROW FALTER IN HIS ASSIGNED MISSION, THE EARTH WILL CRUMBLE!
TWO RUN FORWARD AT THE PLAYING OF UNEARTHLY PIPES...
HEE HE HEE
HEE
...WHICH WOULD SEND CHILLS DOWN THE SPINE OF ANY MAN...
...IF THERE WAS ONE PRESENT!
CRACK
HHEEHEE

ONE STAYS BEHIND AT THE BIDDING OF THE MUSICAL LURE...
HEEHE HEEHHEE
...ONE TO WHOM THE LOSS OF COMRADES MEANS NOTHING...

...ONE TO WHOM ONLY ONE THING HAS VALUE--

--DEATH!
CRASHHH

AND WHEN DEATH DOES NOT OCCUR...
...PANIC SETS IN.
PANIC WHICH MAY ONLY BE DISPELLED BY THE NOTES OF AN OTHERWORLDLY INSTRUMENT...

...AND WHICH MAY LEAD TO OTHER--
TUNK
--OVERSIGHTS!

THE SUBHUMAN CREATURE GROWS ANGRY... BUT DOES NOTHING...
...UNTIL THAT ANGER IS CHANNELED BY AN UNEARTHLY TUNE...

...AND DIRECTED AT THE SCARECROW!
TSAK
HEE-HE-HEE

BUT THE SCARECROW IS UNAFFECTED...
ZIP
...THOUGH ONE MIGHT GUESS DIFFERENTLY--

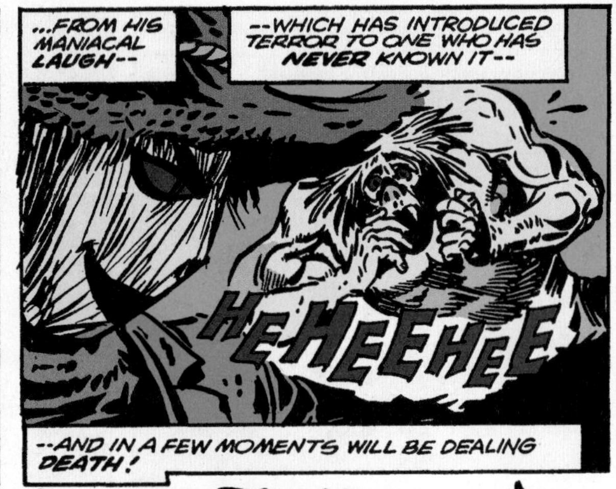
...FROM HIS MANIACAL LAUGH--
--WHICH HAS INTRODUCED TERROR TO ONE WHO HAS NEVER KNOWN IT--
HEHEHEEHEE
--AND IN A FEW MOMENTS WILL BE DEALING DEATH!

KA-ROCK
HEE HEE EEEE
SILENCE.

THE MUSIC IS MUTED LIKE THE PULLING OF A CORD OF AN ETHERAL JUKE BOX.
IT DIES!
AND WITH THAT DYING, FOR A FEW MORE MOMENTS...
...THE WORLD LIVES!

THE PRIZE HAS BEEN WON... TO THE VICTOR FALLS THE SPOILS--
--THE SACRIFICIAL HORN OF KALUMAI, WREST FROM HIS OWN HEAD BY THE SCARECROW'S HANDS CENTURIES AGO IN A DEATH-BATTLE WHICH RESULTED IN THE ENTRAPMENT OF A GOD.
SOMEWHERE, TONIGHT, THAT GOD IS WATCHING.
AND HE DOES NOT LIKE WHAT HE SEES.

IT IS STILL THE DEAD OF NIGHT WHEN THE SCARECROW RETURNS TO JESS DUNCAN'S SOHO LOFT. RETURNS...
...HOME.
WHEN ONE LIVES ONLY FOR BATTLE, EACH MOMENT IS PRECIOUS...
...AND A MOMENT SPENT IN CONTEMPLATION MUST SEEM LIKE A MOMENT LOST!

FOR THE SCARECROW HAS BUT SECONDS UNTIL HE MUST RETURN TO HIS RESTING PLACE... HOME WITH HIS--

--PRIZE?
CLINK

THE HORN OF KALUMAI, TAKEN FROM THE POLICE WHO HAD FOUND IT BESIDE THE MUTILATED BODY OF GREGOR ROVIK...
...UPON WHOM VENGEANCE WAS TAKEN BY THE SCARECROW...*
TOK
TUNK
*DEAD OF NIGHT #11--MARV.

...IS ONE STEP CLOSER HOME.
--DON'T CARE WHAT YOU SAY, HARMONY... THAT KAUFMAN IS A FUNNY GUY!

WHEN WILL YOU LEARN, JESS? MUST YOU BE PERPETUALLY FOOLED BY FLASHINESS AND OVER-ENTHUSIASM?
AND YOU'RE NOT, eh?
I'D LIKE TO THINK I'M NOT!

WELL... OKAY, MAYBE YOU'RE NOT! AND THAT'S WHY YOU'VE ALWAYS HATED MY PAINTINGS!
JESS! I--
YOU KNOW I'M RIGHT, HARMONY! EVER SINCE I MET YOU, I'VE HAD TO STOP SAYING, "LOVE ME, LOVE MY WORK!"

THAT'S NOT TRUE, JESS! I'VE NEVER HATED YOUR PAINTINGS! I'VE JUST...
...NEVER LIKED THEM.
BUT WHAT DO YOU EXPECT FROM AN ART CRITIC--?

...LIES AND VENEER? GET THEM FROM A MOVIE REVIEWER! I DON'T--
JESS?
LOOK HERE...

I THINK WE'VE BEEN PAID A VISIT...
MAY I... COME IN?

DAVE! WHAT BRINGS MY OLDER BROTHER AROUND IN THE MIDDLE OF THE NIGHT?
I DON'T...

...KNOW...
DAVE!

WHAT'S WRONG WITH, HIM, JESS?
CAN'T TELL, BUT I COULD GUESS THAT IT PROBABLY HAS TO DO WITH ONE OF THOSE NUTTY STORIES OF HIS!

I'VE BEEN WANTING TO TALK TO YOU ABOUT THOSE STORIES!
HE KEEPS DRAGGING YOU OFF ON HIS NEW JOURNALISTIC CRUSADE...
...LEAVING ME TO ATTEND PLAYS WITH AN EMPTY SEAT BESIDE ME AS MY ESCORT!

ISN'T IT ABOUT TIME YOU BOTH STOPPED HUNTING SHADOWS?
AHHRR

IF EITHER OF YOU WOULD BE KIND ENOUGH TO TELL ME EXACTLY HOW I GOT HERE, I'D GREATLY APPRECIATE IT!
YOU JUST WALKED IN AND COLLAPSED, DAVE...

...RIGHT AFTER HARMONY FOUND... THIS!
DOES THIS HORN LOOK FAMILIAR, HARMONY?

IT'S THE ONE THEY TRIED TO KILL ME WITH, JESS! THE VERY SAME!
MY GOD! I DIDN'T REALIZE IT WAS THIS LATE! WE'D BETTER GET GOING!

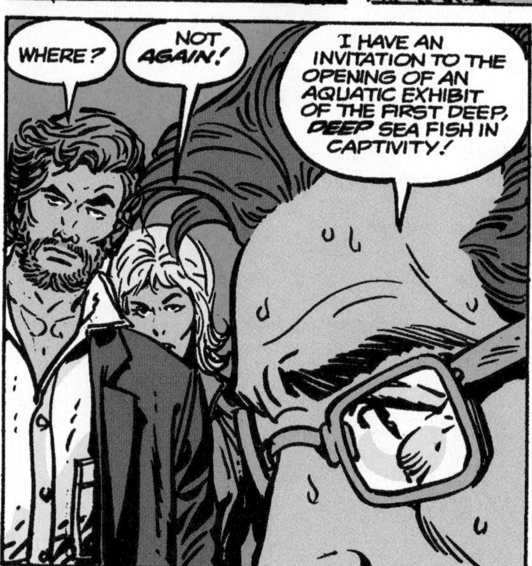
WHERE?
NOT AGAIN!
I HAVE AN INVITATION TO THE OPENING OF AN AQUATIC EXHIBIT OF THE FIRST DEEP, DEEP SEA FISH IN CAPTIVITY!

YOU SURE YOU'RE FEELING ALL RIGHT, DAVE?
JESS, ASIDE FROM NOT REMEMBERING WHAT I WAS DOING AN HOUR AGO I'M AS FIT AS EUELL GIBBONS!
BUT, IF THE HORN COULD SPEAK...

WITHIN THE HOUR, HARMONY, JESS AND DAVE ARRIVE AT THE AQUARIUM...
AQUARIUM
...AND EACH STARES IN AWE AT WHAT, IF SEEN IN LESS CIVILIZED TIMES, WOULD BE CONSIDERED A GOD.
THEY HALF EXPECT SACRIFICES TO BE LAID AT ITS FEET...

... SUCH AS THEY ARE.

THE CREATURE RADIATES LIGHT, HIS EERIE PHOSPHORESCENCE GAINED FROM THE DARKNESS OF THE DEPTH AND UNTOLD YEARS OF LORD-KNOWS-HOW-MANY TONS OF AQUATIC PRESSURE PER SQUARE INCH.

IT DOES NOT LIKE BEING ON DISPLAY.

I DON'T UNDERSTAND WHAT HAPPENED...

WE SENT INVITATIONS TO ALL THE MAJOR MAGAZINES, NEWSPAPERS, RADIO STATIONS--EVERYONE INVOLVED IN PUBLICITY --BUT YOU'RE THE ONLY ONES WHO SHOWED!

THAT'S DAVE, I GUESS!

AND ALL THE FOOD WE CATERED IN FOR THE PRESS... WHAT AM I GOING TO DO WITH TEN POUNDS OF CHOPPED LIVER?
HOW ABOUT FEEDING IT TO THE FISH, MR. GROSMAN?

SORRY, MR. MONROE-- HE'LL ONLY EAT MY MOTHER'S COOKING!
WAS THAT MEANT TO BE FUNNY?
YES!
THERE THEY GO... OFF TO SWAP BAD JOKES FOR AN HOUR OR TWO!
OH!
BUT WHAT ELSE SHOULD I EXPECT FROM A WRITER?
SSSSSHH...

STARTED A POEM ALREADY, HUH?
WELL, I MIGHT AS WELL GET MY SKETCH BOOK OUT OF THE CAR!
I NEVER EXPECTED A FISH LIKE THIS!

whew! WHEN I DIE THEY'LL LIST "IAMBIC PENTAMETER" AS CAUSE!
WHO--?

OH, NO--

HAVE I BECOME A "WEIRDO" MAGNET OR IS IT MY PERFUME?
NO ANSWER?
THIS IS ONE OF THE TIMES I'M THANKFUL FOR THOSE STREET FIGHTS I USTA GET IN...

BUT TO TELL YOU THE TRUTH--
HEE
HEE
HEE
HEH
--I'M GETTING SICK OF ALL YOU THINGS ATTACKING ME!

THEN...
THE SCARECROW!

HARMONY'S EYES TRACE THE AIR LOOKING FOR JESS HURRYING BACK WITH HIS SKETCHBOOK...

...FOR THIS IS A SIGHT THAT AN ARTIST SHOULD NOT MISS.
WRACK

SCIENTISTS: COOL, CACULATED OBSERVERS.
LET ME OUT OF HERE!
OUTTA MY WAY!
SCIENTISTS-- PSHAW!

BUT EVEN THEY MIGHT BE EXCUSED FEAR AT THE SIGHT OF THE SCARECROW!
I DON'T KNOW HOW MUCH LONGER I CAN KEEP THIS UP--

--BUT...
...I'VE GOT TO, OR IT'S GOODBYE HARMONY!
WOOSH
POW

WHAT HAPPENS WHEN EVERYONE IS FOLLOWING THE PIPER, AND THE PIPER'S CONFUSED? IT'S THEN WE MUST TURN TO THE BANDLEADER.
O GREAT KALUMAI! HEAR ME AND HARKEN TO MY CALL! YOUR FAITHFUL SERVANT, BARTOLOME, REQUIRES YOUR AID!
BY THE GLOW FROM THE SEA CREATURE, ANOTHER RADIANCE IS SEEN "GROWING"-- FORMING INTO--

--KALUMAI!

O MOST WISE AND BENIFICENT LEADER! WHAT SHALL I DO NOW?
WHATEVER YOUR WISHES BE, I SHALL HEED THEM! WE HAVE LOST THE HORN... BUT WHAT OF THE GIRL?

FOOL! FORGET THE GIRL! DESTROY THE SCARECROW!
KILL HIM!

WITH THE PRONOUNCEMENT OF DEATH, BARTOLOME CLOSES HIS EYES...
...AND A DIFFERENT MUSIC SHATTERS THE AIR...
...AS EVERY SUB-HUMAN SLAVE FREEZES...

WHAT'S HAPPENING?
BUT THE SCARECROW DOES NOT ANSWER...HE RUSHES FORWARD TO CONTINUE HIS ATTACK...

...AS THE MONSTERS BURST INTO FLAME!

NO! SCARECROW-- STAY BACK!

YOU'LL BURN TO A CINDER!

NOW IT IS THE SCARECROW'S TURN TO STAND STOCK STILL--FOR THOUGH THERE IS NOTHING HE FEARS--

--THERE IS BUT ONE THING BY WHICH HE CAN BE DESTROYED.

WOULDN'T YA KNOW I BURRIED THE PAD BENEATH THAT ROLL OF CANVAS!
DAVE AND HARMONY ARE PROBABLY READY TO LEAVE ALREADY!
HUH? DOOR'S LOCKED!

WHAT! THE SCARECROW AND--
--HARMONY!

LEMME IN THERE! OPEN UP! HARMONY! HARMONY!
YOU'RE GONNA GET YOURSELF KILLED!
HARMONY!
TOK
POK
TOK

BUT JESS DUNCAN HAS LITTLE TO FEAR, FOR HARMONY IS IN BETTER HANDS NOW THAN SHE HAS BEEN IN MOST OF HER LIFE--
--REGARDLESS OF WHETHER THOSE HANDS ARE OF FLESH AND BLOOD OR RAGS AND STRAW!
THE MAN-BEASTS LEAP AT THE SCARECROW, AND HE BUT LAUGHS AND WAVES HIS HANDS...

...TO CALL HIS ALLIES!
TUNK
POK
PRAK
THE FISH BANGS OVER INTO THE GLASS SIDES OF THE TANK, WHICH, DESPITE ITS INCREDIBLE THICKNESS, MUST EVENTUALLY--

--BREAK!

"APRÈS MOI LE DÉLUGE," SAID KING LOUIS THE FIFTEENTH.

CRAACKK

CRASH

WHOOSH

"WHILE I'M **HERE**, THE FLOOD!" DEMANDS **THE SCARECROW**.

AS THE TSUNAMI-STRENGTH **SAVAGERY** STARTS TO SUBSIDE, THE SCARECROW ADDS A MADNESS OF HIS **OWN**.
AND ALL THE WHILE, A SINGLE SET OF EYES WATCHES **FEVERISHLY**.

EYES BELONGING TO-- **JESS DUNCAN**...

EYES WHICH CAN **SEE** AND WHICH COME WITH HANDS THAT CAN **DRAW**...
HANDS WHICH MOVE ALMOST WITH A **SENTIENCE** OF THEIR OWN... AS JESS STARES, HYPNOTIZED BY THE SCENE--

THE WATERS SLOWLY RISE AND FALL AS THE SCARECROW WILDLY GESTICULATES... UNTIL THERE EXISTS A HELL ON EARTH!

ALL IS TRAPPED WITHIN THE FORCE OF THE WHIRLPOOL-- BARTOLOME, THE SUB-MEN, AND THE FISH...

...WHO IS NOW AT LEAST FREE...

ONE BY ONE THESE CREATURES ARE DRAGGED TO THE CENTER...AND ONE BY ONE THESE CREATURES DISAPPEAR!

WHEN THE WATER IS PURIFIED OF ITS FILTH, THE SCARECROW LOWERS HIS ARMS AND GAZES UPON HIS WORK...
...AND SEES THE WATERS HAVE ALSO LOWERED...
...AND HE IS PLEASED.

THE WATERS EBB UNTIL THEY DISAPPEAR ENTIRELY...LEAVING TRACE OF NEITHER SUB-MEN...
...NOR PIPER...
...NOR FISH.

AND, AS THE SCARECROW PLACES HARMONY ON DRY GROUND, SHE GAZES IN AWE UPON HIM...
...AND SEARCHES HER MIND FOR A CLUE AS TO WHY THIS HAS HAPPENED TWICE TO HER.
WAIT! WHERE ARE YOU--?
SHE FINDS NO ANSWER.

THE WORK IS DONE.
THE SPELL IS BROKEN.

AND IT IS TIME FOR THE SCARECROW TO...

...LEAVE?
WHA? WHERE'S HE GO?

BUT JESS' CONCERN SOON TURNS ELSEWHERE...
HARMONY!

JESS RUNS TO HARMONY, REALIZING PERHAPS FOR THE FIRST TIME, THAT HE TRULY CARES...NO, LOVES THIS WOMAN...
...LEAVING BEHIND HIS OWN DRAWING... WHICH HE WILL LATER FIND...

...AND NOT EVEN REMEMBER HAVING DONE!
HARMONY, WHAT'S BEEN GOING... HOW ...WHO WAS THAT...
HER STARE STOPS HIM. IT'S AS IF SHE'S SAYING, "ASK ME NO QUESTIONS. I KNOW NO MORE THAN YOU."

BUT THERE IS ONE QUESTION HE MUST ASK.
WHERE'S DAVE?

I...I DON'T KNOW...
THEY LOOK AT EACH OTHER... AND IN THEIR GAZE THERE IS UNSPOKEN AGREEMENT...
...AGREEMENT IN THEIR OWN DOUBT.

HARMONY... SOMETHING VERY... WRONG IS GOING ON HERE...
WRONG?

MY FREEDOM HAS BEEN STOLEN AGAIN, THAT'S WHAT'S WRONG!
BUT THIS IS THE LAST TIME THE SCARECROW WILL SQUELCH MY PLANS. FOR WHEN NEXT WE MEET...
...THE SCARECROW DIES!
TO BE CONTINUED... SOMEDAY!

25¢
CC
18 AUG
MARVEL COMICS GROUP
APPROVED BY THE COMICS CODE AUTHORITY
02906
MARVEL TWO-IN-ONE
PRESENTS
THE THING
AND THE
SCARECROW
WITH YOU DEAD, MONSTER-- THE DEMON CULT WILL RULE SUPREME!
WANNA BET, BOZO?
JUST TAKE A PEEK AT WHO'S COMIN' UP BEHIND YA!

Stan Lee PRESENTS: THE THING AND THE SCARECROW -- TOGETHER!
JV317
PLOT--BILL MANTLO & SCOTT EDELMAN / STORY-BILL MANTLO | ART RON WILSON | INKS MOONEY-ADKINS | LETTERS RAY H. | COLORS H. PALEY | EDITOR M. WOLFMAN
DARK, DARK DEMON-NIGHT!
LATE-NIGHT GALLERY OPENINGS ARE THE RULE RATHER THAN THE EXCEPTION IN THE SOHO AREA OF NEW YORK CITY.
STILL, SOME SHOWS ARE MORE EXCEPTIONAL THAN OTHERS-- SUCH AS THIS ONE, SPONSORED BY PAINTER JESS DUNCAN AND HOUSED IN HIS GREENE STREET LOFT. ITS THEME: THE OCCULT.
AND THAT SUBJECT MATTER WILL DRAW QUITE A CROWD BEFORE THIS NIGHT IS DONE!
BEN, I'D LIKE YOU TO MEET HARMONY MAXWELL, THE ART CRITIC, AND OUR HOST, JESS DUNCAN!
THEY'RE THE ONES WHO ASKED ME TO BRING YOU TO THE OPENING!
PLEASED TO MEET YOU, MR. GRIMM.
ALICIA'S TOLD US SO MUCH MORE ABOUT YOU THAN THE NEWSPAPER STORIES HAVE, BEN!
YEAH? SHE TELL YA HOW MUCH I JUST LOVE DRESSIN' UP FER PARTIES?

YOU'LL HAVE TO EXCUSE BEN, HARMONY! HE'S SO USED TO DISPLAYING HIS GRUFF MANNERISMS FOR SUPER-VILLAINS-- THAT HE SOMETIMES FORGETS HOW TO TALK TO REAL PEOPLE!
OWWW! I WAS ONLY JOKIN', BABY! YA DIDN'T HAVE TO GO AN' KICK ME!
I UNDERSTAND HOW YOU MUST FEEL, MR. GRIMM.
YEAH? WHEN WAS THE LAST TIME YOU TRIED TO SQUEEZE FIVE HUNNERT POUNDS INTO A TUXEDO? OWWW!

SOMETHING WRONG, DARLING?
OH, NO, BABY! NUTHIN' I CAN THINK OF!
SERIOUSLY, MR. GRIMM! WE WOULDN'T HAVE ASKED ALICIA TO DRAG YOU DOWN HERE--
--UNLESS WHAT WE HAD TO TELL YOU WAS OF THE UTMOST IMPORTANCE!

LADY-- I'M MISSIN' SPACE:1999 FOR THIS HERE SHINDIG-- AN' TO ME--THAT IS OF TH' UTMOST IMPORTANCE!
SO WHAT YOU GOTTA SAY BETTER BE AWFUL BLASTED GOOD!
THEN MAYBE I'D BETTER START AT THE BEGINNING...
GO AHEAD, HARMONY. BEN WON'T BE BORED--
--I PROMISE YOU!
ALL RIGHT, THEN--

"--IT BEGAN A FEW MONTHS AGO, WHEN JESS BOUGHT A PAINTING AT AN AUCTION, A PAINTING HE'D WANTED NEARLY ALL HIS LIFE."
"A PAINTING OF-- THE SCARECROW!"*
OH! JESS! AT LAST!
CONGRATULATIONS, BIG BROTHER!
THANKS, DAVE!
*DEAD OF NIGHT #11--MARV.

BUT IT WASN'T THAT SIMPLE, BEN. THERE'D BEEN ANOTHER BIDDER AT THE AUCTION! HE BID ME PRETTY HIGH--
--AND THEN HE SUDDENLY STOPPED BIDDING!
I DIDN'T REALIZE TILL LATER THAT THE REASON WAS MY BROTHER DAVE--
--WHO'D MANAGED TO PLANT A FAST ELBOW IN THE FELLOW'S STOMACH!
"THE JOKER'S NAME WAS ROVIK--
I WANT THAT PAINTING, MY FRIEND!
AND I'M GOING TO HAVE IT!
"--AND HE WAS PRETTY MAD!"
"I WROTE HIM OFF AS A NUT, MR. GRIMM.
"I WAS WRONG!
"NEARLY DEAD WRONG!
"'CAUSE ROVIK WAS MORE THAN JUST NUTS... HE WAS INSANE!"
THERE IS NO NEED TO HURRY, MY FRIENDS--
--FOR ONCE THE PAINTING IS OURS, WE WILL HAVE PLENTY OF TIME!
ALL THE TIME IN THE WORLD!!
HEY! WHAT DO YOU THINK YOU'RE--
--DOING... UNFF!!
DAVE!
WRAK!
JESS!!
BRING THE GIRL!
A SACRIFICE WILL BE NEEDED!
"I DON'T KNOW IF YOU BELIEVE ANY OF THIS, BEN--
"--BUT THEY STRETCHED ME OUT ON A SLAB AND CAME VERY CLOSE TO KILLING ME--IN THE NAME OF SOME GOD THEY CALLED KALUMAI--

"--WHEN SUDDENLY THERE WAS THE SOUND OF GLASS BREAKING AS THE SKYLIGHT SHATTERED INWARDS--
"--THE SOUND OF EERIE, STRANGLED LAUGHTER--
HEE HEE HEE HEE HEE
"--AND THE FIGURE IN JESS' PAINTINGS CAME ALIVE!
"THE SCARECROW LIVED!!

"HE NEVER SAID A WORD! NO SOUND BUT THAT AWFUL SOUL-RENDING LAUGH--
HEE HEE HEE

"--AND I FAINTED...
"...WAKING HOURS LATER, WONDERING IF IT HAD ALL BEEN A DREAM!"

BUT IT WASN'T A DREAM, BEN! I SAW THE SCARE-CROW AGAIN*--AND THIS TIME JESS SAW HIM, TOO!
MEBBE YA BOTH ATE AT THE SAME BLIMPIE BASE THE NIGHT BEFORE!
YOU DON'T... BELIEVE ME, DO YOU, MR. GRIMM?
OH, SURE I DO! LOOK, LADY-- I LIKE FAIRY TALES AS MUCH AS THE NEXT GUY--
--MEBBE MORE, SEEIN' AS HOW I COULD PASS FOR ONE!
*MARVEL SPOTLIGHT #26--MARV.

BUT YERS JUST DON'T WASH! NOW IF YA EXCUSE ME-- I CAN STILL CATCH THE LAST HALF HOUR OF "SPACE" AN' SAVE THE NIGHT FROM BEIN' A TOTAL LOSS!
BENJAMIN J. GRIMM!

I'M SORRY, HARMONY-- JESS. BEN'S NEVER DONE ANYTHING LIKE THAT BEFORE!
FORGET ABOUT IT, ALICIA.
A FEW MONTHS AGO, I WOULD'VE WALKED AWAY IN DISGUST MYSELF IF SOMEONE HAD TRIED TO SELL ME THE SAME STORY!

AH, BUT HERE'S MY BROTHER DAVE! LATE--
--AS USUAL!
QUITE A CROWD YOU'VE ASSEMBLED HERE, JESS. AND SOME OF THE EXHIBITS ARE--

--ABSOLUTELY BEAUTIFUL!
MS. MASTERS, I PRESUME!
OH! WELL--I... YES!
YOU PRESUME TOO MUCH, DAVID--AS ALWAYS!
ONLY IF ALICIA-- MAY I CALL YOU ALICIA--?

--SAYS SO!
WHY--ARE YOU WITH SOMEONE, ALICIA? I THOUGHT I HEARD A GRUNT!
MMMFFFF!

NAH! SHE AIN'T WITH NOBODY, WISE GUY!
I'M A POTTED PALM SHE BROUGHT ALONG TO KEEP OFF THE RAIN!
I BEG YOUR PAHDON!
HUH?
YOU BIG OAF! IF YOU THINK YOU'RE GOING TO GET AWAY WITH SPILLING MY CHAMPAGNE--

--BY PRETENDING NOT TO HAVE SEEN ME...
LADY, I'M HAVIN' A HARD TIME TRYIN' TA FIGGER OUT HOW I COULDA MISSED YA!

WHY! IN ALL MY LIFE I'VE NEVER--
ME NEITHER! C'MON, GRIMM--
--WHAT'S BUGGIN' YA?

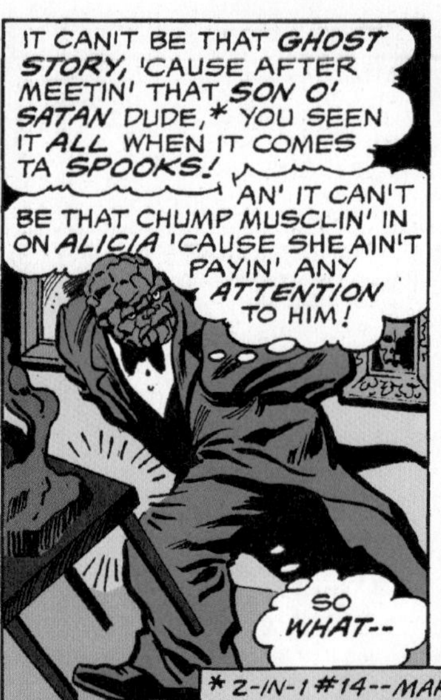
IT CAN'T BE THAT GHOST STORY, 'CAUSE AFTER MEETIN' THAT SON O' SATAN DUDE,* YOU SEEN IT ALL WHEN IT COMES TA SPOOKS!
AN' IT CAN'T BE THAT CHUMP MUSCLIN' IN ON ALICIA 'CAUSE SHE AIN'T PAYIN' ANY ATTENTION TO HIM!
SO WHAT--
* 2-IN-1 #14--MARV.

SKRASH!

UNH-UNH! I AIN'T EVEN GONNA LOOK! ALICIA TOLD ME THAT SOME OF THESE HERE SCULPTURES WAS WORTH MILLIONS!

AHEM. PARDON ME, SIR.
OKAY! YA GOT ME! I CONFESS!
I BROKE IT! BUT IT WAS AN ACCIDENT, PAL, AN'--

SIR? I WAS JUST WONDERING WHY YOU WERE SO UPSET OVER HAVING BROKEN THAT ASH TRAY!
IS THERE ANYTHING WRONG, MR. GRIMM?
WRONG?

'COURSE THERE AIN'T NUTHIN' WRONG!
WHY'D YA ASK?

YOU APPEARED... WELL, RATHER STRAINED, SIR! IF YOU DON'T MIND MY SAYING--
WHAT'S TA MIND?
NOW WHAT SAY I GIVE YA A HAND CLEANIN' UP THIS MESS?
WHY... THAT'S AWFULLY KIND OF YOU, SIR!
'TAIN'T NUTHIN', CHUM! BELIEVE ME!

I HOPE I HAVEN'T PRESUMED TOO MUCH ON OUR FRIENDSHIP TONIGHT, ALICIA.
YOU KNOW YOU HAVEN'T, JESS! IT'S JUST THAT BEN CAN BE SO--
--SO DIFFICULT SOMETIMES!
BUT MAYBE IF I TRY TO TALK TO HIM--

BEN?
AW, ALICIA! DON'T SAY IT!
YOU HEARD THAT COCK-AN'-BULL STORY!
GIMME ONE GOOD REASON WHY I SHOULD BELIEVE IT!
BECAUSE I'M ASKING YOU TO, BEN DARLING.

YOU WIN! C'MON-- LET'S GO FIND YOUR PAINTER FRIEND AN' TELL HIM I THOUGHT THINGS OVER--
--AN' THEY COME UP JUST AS SCREWY!
COMIN', MASHER?
I'LL BE ALONG, MR. GRIMM--

--LATER!
VOICES BECOME ECHOES AS THE GUESTS RECEDE TO THE RECEPTION AREA...
...LEAVING DAVE MONROE QUITE...
...ALONE.

FIRST CHANCE I'VE HAD TO LOOK AT YOU IN DAYS, SCARECROW! YOU DON'T CHANGE MUCH, THOUGH!
AS A PAINTING, YOU'RE STILL AS UGLY AS SIN!

BUT PEOPLE HAVE DIED FOR YOU-- AND MY BROTHER THINKS YOU'RE ALIVE!
WHICH JUST GOES TO SHOW YOU--

--THAT IT TAKES ALL KINDS TO MAKE A WORLD!
YES, FOOL! ALL KINDS!
AS YOU SHALL SHORTLY SEE!

WELL, I'M HERE TO DO A STORY--
SO I GUESS I'D BETTER GET STARTED!
THE FIGURE MOVES STEALTHILY, ENFOLDED IN DARKNESS.

THERE IS A GLINT OF MADNESS IN HIS EYES.
A MADNESS THAT WAS NOT THERE AN HOUR AGO...

...WHEN HE WAS BUT ONE OF THE MANY SEEKING KNOW-LEDGE THROUGH THE WORK OF OTHERS...
SKRAK!
UNNHH!
...UNTIL SOMETHING EVIL TOUCHED HIS MIND...

...AND HE FOUND LEARNING OF QUITE A DIFFERENT KIND!
I... HEED YOUR CALL!

WHISPERS. URGING HIM ON.
PULLING AT HIM. CALLING HIM.

UNTIL HE CAN STAND IT NO LONGER...

...AND HE IS TAKEN--
HEE HEEHEEHEE HEE HEE
--LEAVING A ROOM FILLED WITH EERILY ECHOING LAUGHTER.

I TELL YOU I SAW THE SCARECROW, MR. GRIMM! I SKETCHED IT AS IT FOUGHT THOSE DEMONS TO PROTECT HARMONY!
I'M FROM MISSOURI, PAL!
AN' YOU KNOW WHAT THAT MEANS!

IT'S NO USE, ALICIA!
I JUST CAN'T BUY IT!
OH, BEN!

WELL, AT LEAST YOU TRIED TO UNDERSTAND, BEN. THANK YOU FOR THAT MUCH!
ANY TIME, SISTER! MAYBE SOMETIME I CAN HELP YA WITH A REAL PROBLEM.
LIKE GETTIN' YER CAT OUT OF A TREE OR SOMETHIN'!

WE'LL BE SURE TO CALL YOU, MR. GRIMM-- IN THAT CASE!
YOU DO THAT, DUNCAN! HEY!
WHERE'S YER GIRLFRIEND?

SHE WENT TO ASK THE BUTLER FOR ALICIA'S COAT, I BELIEVE, AND--
--GOOD LORD!!
EEEEEEEEE

WHERE'D IT COME FROM, DUNCAN?
I THINK-- YES!
IT HAD TO COME FROM--
--THE GALLERY!
JESS! JESS! IT-- IT CAME OUT OF THE SCARECROW PAINTING!
--STARED AT ME! MADE ME FEEL LIKE I WAS DEAD!
IN HEAVEN'S NAME, JESS-- WHAT IS IT!??

IT'S INDIGESTION, KID! IT'S GOTTA BE!
THINGS JUST DON'T UP AN' WALK OUT O' PAINTINGS!

NO? HAVE YOU SO SOON, THEN, FORGOTTEN THE SPIRIT OF RAVENSTORM* ENCOUNTERED IN THE ARIZONA DESERT?
*2-IN-1 #14--MARV.
OR IS IT THAT YOU WISH YOU COULD FORGET?

FOR IT'S HARD TO ADMIT, ISN'T IT, BEN GRIMM, THAT A MAN SUCH AS YOURSELF...
...CAN SO EASILY FIND HIMSELF FRIGHTENED BY THE SUPERNATURAL?

HARD... BUT TRUE.
FLAMES! FROM HIS HANDS!
BURNIN' THE TUX RIGHT OFF ME!

BUT THAT AIN'T SUPPOSED TA HAPPEN!!
STRETCH MADE THESE DUDS SPECIAL! OUTTA THEM SAME UNSTABLE MOLECULES WHAT THE TORCH WEARS!
THEY AIN'T SUPPOSED TA BURN!!
BUT THEY DO!

AND THEN A SHADOW FALLS ACROSS THE MOON.
HEEHEEHEEHEEHEEHEEHEEHEEHEE
WHAT IN BOLTIN' BLAZES--??

IT'S THE PITCHER! THE ONE THEY WAS TELLIN' ME ABOUT!!
THE SCARECROW!!
AN' HE'S ALIVE!!

AND AS BEN WATCHES, UNABLE TO MOVE...
...HE SEES THAT SUPERNATURAL, WHICH HE SO FEARED, COME TO VERY REAL LIFE ABOUT HIM!
HEEHEEHEEHEE
GUARDIAN! I HAVE BEEN SENT FOR YOU!
THE LORD KALUMAI DESIRES YOUR DEATH!
THE SCARECROW VOICES NO ANSWER.
YET ALL WHO HEAR HIS MOCKING LAUGHTER--
--ARE STRUCK TO THE HEART--
--WITH DREAD!
I HAVE COME FOREARMED AGAINST YOUR POWER, GUARDIAN!
I WILL NOT BE STOPPED--
--UNTIL THE GOD MAY LIVE!!

--AND STILL YOU STAND AND WATCH, THING.
GOD? GUARDIAN? WHAT'S HE TALKIN' ABOUT, DUNCAN?

WE--WE THINK THE SCARECROW PAINTING IS SOME KIND OF INTER-DIMENSIONAL DOOR, BEN!
AND SOMETHING ON THE OTHER SIDE-- A LORD OF DEMONS CALLED KALUMAI-- HAS BEEN TRYING FOR CENTURIES TO GET OUT!
BUT, SOMEHOW THE SCARE-CROW WAS SET OVER THAT DOORWAY AS A GUARDIAN, GRIMM!
AND IF THE GUARDIAN FAILS--

DON'T TELL ME! LET ME GUESS!
THE WHOLE FATE OF THE WORLD IS AT STAKE, RIGHT?
WELL I'M GONNA PROVE TO YA BOTH THAT SOME JOKER'S PULLIN' YER LEGS--

--AN' I'M GONNA PROVE IT RIGHT NOW!

SORRY, FIREBALL--
--BUT THE PARTY'S OVER!

HEEHEEHEEHEE
AS OF RIGHT NOW!!

GOWAN AN' LAUGH, BUTTER-CUP--
--'CAUSE AS SOON AS I FINISH WITH THIS TWO-BIT HUMAN TORCH--

HEEHEEHEE
--IT'S GONNA BE YOUR TURN!

AWRIGHT, LAUGHIN' BOY!
START SPILLIN' WITH THE EXPLANA-TIONS!
GRIMM! BEHIND YOU!
HUH?

AARRGGHH!
THIS BODY HAS KNOWN PAIN BEFORE... BUT ALWAYS IT HAD BEEN A PAIN OF THE FLESH.

THIS PAIN-- GNAWING, CHILLING, BURNING, DEVOURING...
...THIS PAIN IS OF THE SOUL.
AND THUS THE BODY FALLS!

NOW, GUARDIAN, IT IS JUST WE TWO!

HEEHEEHEEHEEHEEHEE
THE LAUGHTER STOPS THE DEMON--

--AND AS IF IN THAT INSTANT MIND HAD MET MIND AND ONE READ THE INTENT OF THE OTHER...
...THE BEING CREATED BY KALUMAI STARES AT THE STARS-- OBLITERATED STARS.
HIDDEN BY CLOUDS BEARING--

--RAIN!
--SUMMONED BY THE SCARECROW!!
SSSSSSSS

THE FIRES OF EVIL ARE DAMPED.
SSSSSSSSSSS

THE CHILL OF A SOUL IS DISPELLED!
WHOLE PLACE IS FULLA STEAM!
WHAT'S GOIN' ON?

DUNCAN! YOU AN' THE GIRL BEAT IT! AN' TAKE ALICIA WITH YOU!
GOOD LUCK, GRIMM!
ME--I'M GONNA GET ME SOME ANSWERS!

YEAH! I MAY NEED IT!
AWRIGHT, BLUE-EYES! SO THE SCARECROW'S FER REAL--AN' HE'S DOIN' A DARN SIGHT BETTER'N YOU DID AGAINST OL' SCALE-SKIN!

BUT ARE YOU GONNA LET SOME REFUGEE FROM OZ MAKE YOU LOOK LIKE A MONKEY?
YOU BET YER NOT!!
GANGWAY, STRAW MAN! IT'S CLOBBERIN' TIME!
HEE HEE HEE

GEEZ! HE HIT THE WALL AN' THEN JUST DISAPPEARED!
AN' NOW THE WHOLE BLASTED PLACE IS ON FIRE!

BUT NUTHIN'S BURNING!!
FLAMES ARE JUST WHIRLIN' AROUND--
--AN' NOW THEY'RE RE-FORMIN' INTO SOME KINDA SHAPE!

IT'S HIM! HE'S BACK!!
BUT BEFORE ANYTHING AT ALL CAN BE DONE ABOUT IT--

--THE INSANE LAUGHTER OF THE SCARECROW CALLS DOWN THE NIGHT!
HEEHEEHEHEEH

LIVING SHAPES FIGHT THEIR WAY THROUGH THE DARK.
THIS WILL NOT KEEP ME FROM YOU GUARDIAN!

I'M BEGINNIN' TA WISH I COULD TAP MY FEET TOGETHER THREE TIMES--
--AN' SEND MYSELF TO KANSAS!

HEE HEE
GUARDIAN?

YOU APPEAR!
THE SCARECROW MUST KNOW THAT HIS PUNCH CANNOT BEGIN TO SLOW THE DEMON...
...BUT PERHAPS HE MEANT IT AS NO MORE THAN A DISTRACTION.

GIVING ANOTHER A CHANCE TO...
STRAM!
NICE GOIN', HAY-STACK--

--LIFTIN' THE DARK SO'S WE CAN SEE HIM--

--BUT HE CAN'T SEE US!
FOR A MOMENT BEN AND THE STRANGE BEING EACH ACKNOWLEDGE THE OTHERS REALITY...

...AND THEN THE BATTLE IS RESUMED!
STILL YOU GUARD THE DOORWAY, SCARECROWS?

IT IS MY TASK TO SEE THAT YOU BE REMOVED!
THAT KALUMAI MAY WALK THE EARTH AGAIN!!
THE PORTRAIT-DOORWAY ERUPTS IN SUPERNATURAL FLAMES.

YA CRUMB! YA WENT AN' KILLED HIM!!
SHA-KOOM!
EVEN YOU, BEN GRIMM, MUST STOP AND WONDER AT THAT STATEMENT.

--BEGINS TO CHANGE.
LAYERS OF PAINT BUBBLE AWAY TO REVEAL A FORMER IMAGE ON THE BURNING CANVAS-- A FAR MORE MENACING VISAGE--
--THAT SEEMS TO SEETHE WITH FRUSTRATED WRATH, AS IN TURN IT IS DEVOURED.

THE GATEWAY, IMPERVIOUS TO REAL FIRE, AS WELL AS ALL OTHER AGENTS OF DESTRUCTION KNOWN TO MORTAL MEN--
--IS IRREVOCABLY CONSUMED BY THE MYSTIC FLAMES OF THE NETHERGOD. AND THEN...

EVEN AFTER THE PROCEEDING EVENTS THIS BIZARRE IMMOLATION SHOCKS YOU.
BUT AFTER ALL... WHAT NEED IS THERE OF A GUARDIAN... NOW?

GONE! THE SCARECROW! THE PAINTING! THE DEMON!
THE WHOLE BLASTED LOT OF 'EM! GONE!!
AN' I BET YOU CAN'T REMEMBER A THING!
WHAT AM I DOING HERE?--

THAT'S WHAT I THOUGHT!
YOU CAN COME IN NOW, FOLKS! SHOW'S OVER!
THE PAINTING--?

BURNT UP! WITH THE SCARECROW INSIDE IT! LOOKS LIKE YER DOORWAY IS CLOSED--
--FOR GOOD!
BUT--YOU DON'T UNDERSTAND, BEN!

JESS' BROTHER DAVE IS--IS MISSING!
--AND WE'D BEGUN TO SUSPECT THAT HE WAS THE SCARECROW!
IF--IF THE SCARECROW IS... DEAD--
--THEN WHAT ABOUT DAVE??

IS THIS THE END OF THE MOST MYSTERIOUS SUPERHERO OF THEM ALL...?
THE SCARECROW
MEANWHILE, BE WITH US NEXT ISSUE WHEN BEN GRIMM MEETS
TIGRA
The WERE-WOMAN!

MARVEL TEAM-UP TM

MARVEL® COMICS GROUP

APPROVED BY THE COMICS CODE AUTHORITY

35¢ CC 68 02147

MARVEL TEAM-UP TM

FEATURING

SPIDER-MAN®

AND THE

MAN-THING TM

DARK SWAMP, DEEP FEAR!

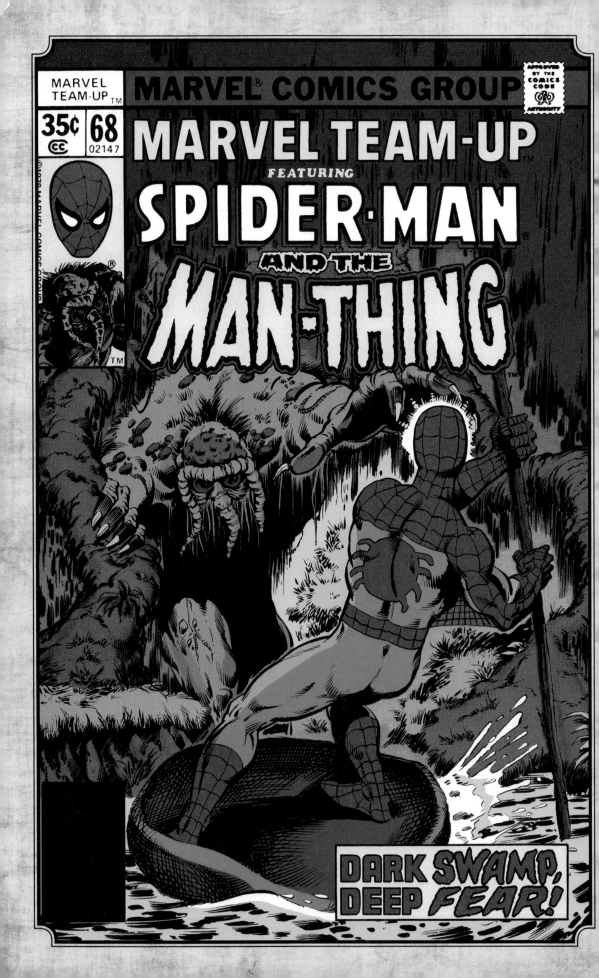

Stan Lee PRESENTS: SPIDER-MAN AND MAN-THING!
CHRIS CLAREMONT AUTHOR * JOHN BYRNE ARTIST * BOB WIACEK INKER * BRUCE -LETTERER PHIL R.-COLORIST * ARCHIE GOODWIN EDITOR
THE MEASURE OF A MAN!
BEGINNINGS: IT SEEMS THAT IT'S THE DEAD OF NIGHT, AN UNREAL, STYGIAN BLACKNESS ONLY SLIGHTLY BROKEN BY SILVER BANDS OF MOONLIGHT GLANCING OFF THE ANCIENT, GNARLED, MOSS-COVERED TREE LIMBS THAT SHROUD THE SWAMP...
...AND THE CREATURE THAT LURKS WITHIN.
LORD IN HEAVEN!
THE MAN-THING-- HE'S LUNGING RIGHT AT ME!!
PERHAPS-- BUT APPEARANCES CAN BE DECEIVING.

WHAT APPEARS TO BE THE SWAMP THAT IS THE MUCK BEAST'S HOME, TURNS OUT TO BE A SOPHISTICATED HABITAT...
...AND AS FOR MAN-THING'S "LUNGE"!...
SPLUTCH!
MY MISTAKE. HE'S COLLAPSING!

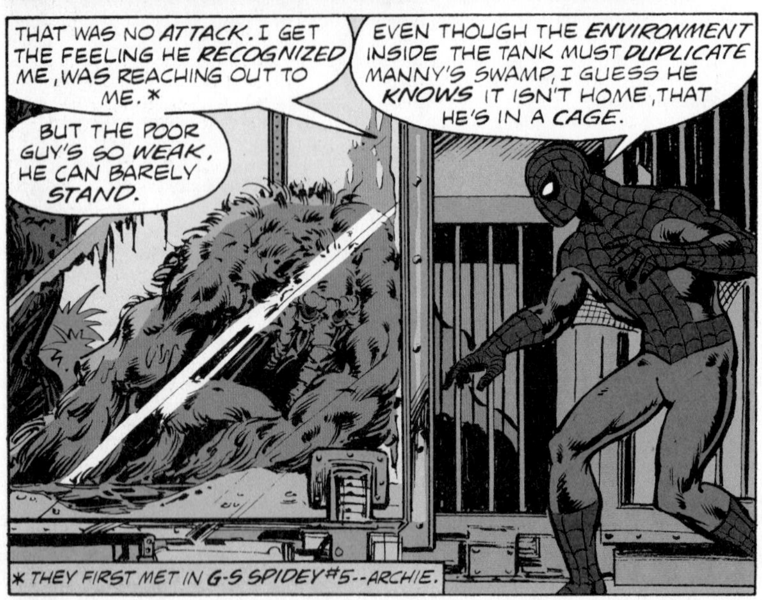
THAT WAS NO ATTACK. I GET THE FEELING HE RECOGNIZED ME, WAS REACHING OUT TO ME. *
BUT THE POOR GUY'S SO WEAK, HE CAN BARELY STAND.
EVEN THOUGH THE ENVIRONMENT INSIDE THE TANK MUST DUPLICATE MANNY'S SWAMP, I GUESS HE KNOWS IT ISN'T HOME, THAT HE'S IN A CAGE.
* THEY FIRST MET IN G-S SPIDEY #5--ARCHIE.

AND LIKE ANY TRULY WILD ANIMAL, TRAPPED IN A CAGE HE CAN'T ESCAPE FROM--
--HE'S LOST THE WILL TO LIVE.

BEGINNINGS: WHERE SPIDEY'S CONCERNED, THEY WERE INNOCENT ENOUGH. AS PETER PARKER, HE AND MARY JANE WATSON HAD GONE TO THE CIRCUS.
IT WAS MEANT TO BE A NO-HASSLE DAY, A DAY FREE OF ANY THOUGHTS OF DOOM AND GLOOM, OF SCHOOL AND WORK. A DAY OFF.
IT DIDN'T WORK OUT THAT WAY.
PETEY--WHAT IS THAT THING?! IS IT... ALIVE?!?
YEAH, MJ, I'M AFRAID IT IS.
MAN-THING?!? THE WIRE-SERVICES REPORTED MANNY ON A RAMPAGE IN ATLANTA--BUT THAT WAS MONTHS AGO.*
WHAT'S HE DOING HERE?!
*MAN-THING #'S 19-22 --A.G.

PETEY, WHAT ARE YOU DOING? WE'RE SUPPOSED TO BE ON A DATE!
I KNOW, MARY JANE. BUT THAT GUY IS AMOS JARDINE, THE CIRCUS OWNER.
MR. JARDINE!

I'D LIKE TO ASK YOU SOME QUESTIONS ABOUT THE MAN-THING! I, UH, DO SOME WORK FOR THE DAILY BUGLE, AND--
YOU CLOWNS NEVER GIVE UP, DO YOU? WELL, BUG OFF, KID. I'M TIRED OF TALKING. I GOT NO COMMENT.
WHAT GIVES YOU THE RIGHT TO EXHIBIT HIM?

RIGHT? I FOUND HIM, BUCKO. AND CAPTURED HIM. AND I'LL DO WITH THAT WALKING MOUND OF MUCK AS I SEE FIT.
UH-OH. PETER.
NOT NOW, MJ.

I'D LISTEN TO YOUR LADY FRIEND, KID. SAVE US ALL A LOT OF UNNECESSARY GRIEF.
I HOPE YOU FOLKS ENJOYED MY SHOW, BECAUSE YOU'VE JUST SEEN ALL OF IT YOU'RE GOING TO SEE. ESCORT THEM TO THE DOOR, BRUNO.
AND TELL SECURITY I DON'T WANT TO SEE THEM AROUND HERE AGAIN --EVER.

"NICE TALKING WITH YOU, MR. PARKER OF THE DAILY BUGLE."
FIRST ROUND TO YOU, JARDINE, BUT I'LL BE BACK.

SORRY IT TOOK SO LONG, PAL, BUT IT COST ME A STEAK DINNER AND A MOVIE TO CALM MJ DOWN.
AND THEN, AT MY PLACE, ONE THING LED TO ANOTHER AND ...WELL, YOU KNOW.

NO, HE DOESN'T. HE'S A THING, NOT A--
--CRIPES!
SECURITY!
HOLD IT, BUSTER!

"THERE WASN'T MUCH LEFT O' HIM WHEN THE FLAMES DIED DOWN, BUT JARDINE DIDN'T CARE. DEAD OR ALIVE, HE FIGURED MAN-THING'D MAKE ONE HECK OF AN ATTRACTION.

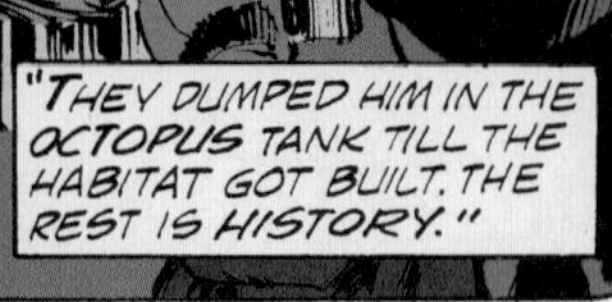

FRIEND, WHEN YOU'VE GOT THE PROPORTIONATE STRENGTH OF A SPIDER, THERE ISN'T MUCH YOU CAN'T DO.
HEY!!
SHEESH!

THAT CAGE IS PRIVATE PROPERTY! PUT IT DOWN!!
BOSS, THAT'S SPIDER-MAN!
I DON'T CARE IF IT'S THE MORMON TABERNACLE CHOIR. HE'S STEALING MY MAN-THING! STOP HIM!

FIRST OF ALL, BLUBBER-GUT, HE ISN'T YOUR MAN-THING. NOT NOW, NOT EVER!
AND AS FOR STOPPING ME...
THWIP!

I'M TAKING HIM HOME, JARDINE, BACK TO HIS SWAMP. AND IF YOU KNOW WHAT'S GOOD FOR YOU, YOU'LL LEAVE HIM THERE.
DON'T JUST STAND THERE, YOU HIPPIE TWERP! YOU'VE GOT A GUN! SHOOT HIM!

RRRGLEMUMMPH!
SORRY, MR. JARDINE, I CAN'T DO THAT. I JUST QUIT.

MEANWHILE, UP ON THE ROOF...
NOW WHAT? I SAID I'D GET YOU HOME, MANNY. QUESTION IS, HOW?
HOO-BOY THIS HABITAT IS HEAVY.
IT'S A CINCH I'M NOT GONNA CARRY IT DOWN TO FLORIDA ON MY BACK. NEITHER OF US WOULD LIVE TO SEE NEWARK.
WE NEED HELP-- AND I THINK I KNOW JUST THE GUY TO ASK.

AND SO, THE VERY NEXT AFTERNOON...
HOW WE DOIN', NINA? ANY IDEA WHEN WE'LL REACH THE SWAMP?
WE'VE BEEN OVER IT FOR THE PAST FIFTEEN MINUTES.
OH. IT'S...UH, BIG.
THAT IT IS. FIVE THOUSAND SQUARE MILES, SOME OF IT STILL UNEXPLORED, EVEN TODAY.

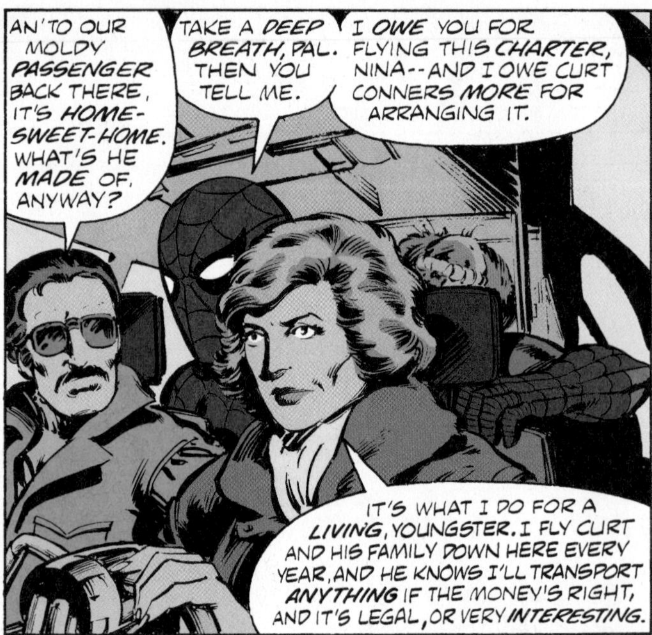
AN' TO OUR MOLDY PASSENGER BACK THERE, IT'S HOME-SWEET-HOME. WHAT'S HE MADE OF, ANYWAY?
TAKE A DEEP BREATH, PAL. THEN YOU TELL ME.
I OWE YOU FOR FLYING THIS CHARTER, NINA--AND I OWE CURT CONNERS MORE FOR ARRANGING IT.
IT'S WHAT I DO FOR A LIVING, YOUNGSTER. I FLY CURT AND HIS FAMILY DOWN HERE EVERY YEAR, AND HE KNOWS I'LL TRANSPORT ANYTHING IF THE MONEY'S RIGHT, AND IT'S LEGAL, OR VERY INTERESTING.

AN' THANKS TO DANE GAVIN AN' THE NEW YORK ECOLOGICAL HISTORY MUSEUM,* CONNERS AIN'T EVEN FOOTIN' THE BILL.
BETTER FLASH CITRUSVILLE OMNI. LET 'EM KNOW--
--HOLEE--!
SHZAK!
* SEE G-S MAN-THING #2- A.G.

NINA, WHAT-- HIT US?!
I--I DON'T KNOW...BUT ONE ENGINE'S GONE, AND A GOOD CHUNK OF WING WITH IT!
HANG ON! WE'RE GOING DOWN!

IT'S A NIGHTMARE DESCENT, NINA TRYING DESPERATELY TO LEVEL THE MORTALLY WOUNDED AIRCRAFT BEFORE IT HITS.
SHE DOES HER BEST, BUT THE PLANE HAD BEEN TOO LOW, GOING TOO FAST. THERE SIMPLY ISN'T ENOUGH AIRSPACE. OR TIME.
BUT THEN, AS THE BEECH BARON RIPS THROUGH A GROVE OF CYPRUS TREES AND DISINTEGRATES IN THE BLINK OF AN EYE...
FA-CHOOM!

THE UNGAINLY BALL DOESN'T BOUNCE FAR BEFORE COMING TO ITS FINAL RESTING PLACE.
PHLOPT!

AND THEN...
MAIN FLOOR, EVERYBODY OUT!
I D-DON'T BELIEVE IT. WE'RE... ALIVE!
THANKS TO YOUR FLYING AND MY WEB-BALL, LADY, WE SURE ARE.

YOU KEPT THE PLANE LEVEL JUST LONG ENOUGH FOR ME TO SPIN THIS COCOON AROUND US, AND, LIKE I FIGURED, THE IMPACT CATAPULTED US OUT OF THE WRECK.
HOW'S YOUR PARTNER?
I'LL LIVE, THANKS. JUS' CAUGHT SOME SHRAPNEL FROM THE ENGINE IN MY ARM.

WE WERE LUCKY. MAN-THING WASN'T. THE FIRE MUST'VE BURNED HIM TO A CRISP.
POOR GUY. WE'D ALMOST GOTTEN HIM HOME, TOO!
SPIDER-MAN-- LOOK!

WHAT THE--?!
MAN-THING?!?
BUT THAT'S IMPOSSIBLE-- UNLESS...

I KNOW THIS SOUNDS CRAZY, BUT IT'S THE ONLY ANSWER THAT MAKES SENSE. SOMEHOW, THE SWAMP'S REVITALIZED MANNY, RESTORED HIM TO HEALTH!
AND YET, I STILL GET THE FEELING THAT HE'S IN PAIN, THAT WHATEVER HURT HIM BEFORE HASN'T GONE AWAY...

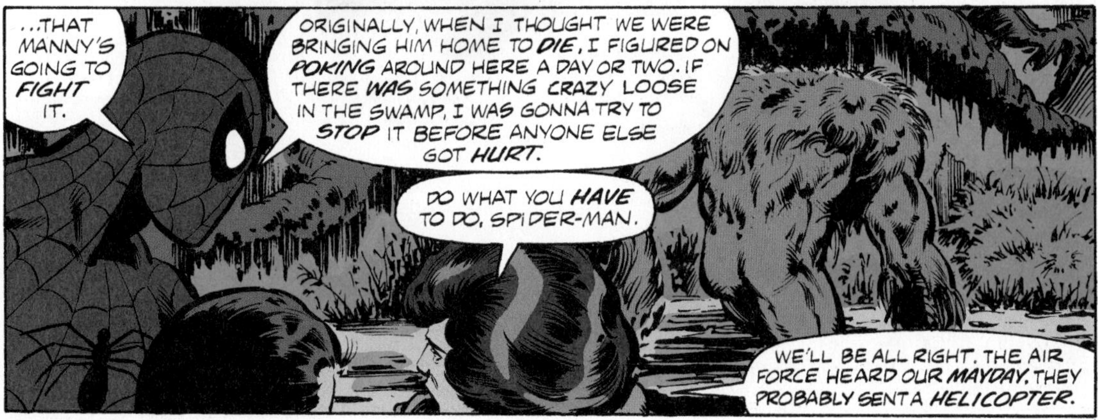
...THAT MANNY'S GOING TO FIGHT IT.
ORIGINALLY, WHEN I THOUGHT WE WERE BRINGING HIM HOME TO DIE, I FIGURED ON POKING AROUND HERE A DAY OR TWO. IF THERE WAS SOMETHING CRAZY LOOSE IN THE SWAMP, I WAS GONNA TRY TO STOP IT BEFORE ANYONE ELSE GOT HURT.
DO WHAT YOU HAVE TO DO, SPIDER-MAN.
WE'LL BE ALL RIGHT. THE AIR FORCE HEARD OUR MAYDAY. THEY PROBABLY SENT A HELICOPTER.

"WE'LL BE OUT OF HERE BEFORE YOU KNOW IT."
THAT IS ONE HECKUVA LADY.
AND I'M BEGINNING TO FEEL LIKE ONE HECKUVA JERK.
I OUGHTTA HAVE MY HEAD EXAMINED. I'VE BEEN PADDLING THROUGH THIS QUAGMIRE FOR THREE HOURS! I'M TIRED, I'M LOST, IT'S GETTING DARK, AND--
--HMM! WHAT'S THIS?
"A SHACK, IN THE MIDDLE OF NOWHERE, COMPLETE WITH AN OLD MAN AND A GIRL TIED UP ON THE FRONT PORCH!"
DAKIMH, LOOK! MAN-THING'S RETURNED, AS YOU SAID HE WOULD!
AND HE'S BROUGHT HELP!
HELP, JENNIFER KALE? HE'S BROUGHT ONE MAN, AND A MORTAL, TO BOOT, WHO CAN NO MORE STAND AGAINST MY POWER...
...THAN YOUR PET QUAG-BEAST COULD WHEN HE FIRST TRIED TO RESCUE YOU.
HEAR ME, LITTLE MAN. I AM D'SPAYRE!
IF YOU VALUE YOUR LIFE AND YOUR IMMORTAL SOUL, RUN FROM HERE! IF YOU STAY BOTH ARE FORFEIT!
MISTER, I'VE NEVER RUN FROM A FIGHT IN MY LIFE, AND I DON'T INTEND TO START TONIGHT.
HUH?! MANNY'S STOPPING ME! BUT WHY?!
HE CAN'T ANSWER, AND EVEN IF HE COULD, SPIDER-MAN WOULDN'T UNDERSTAND.
SPIDEY IS HUMAN, MAN-THING IS NOT. HE'S THE SOUL OF BIOLOGIST TED SALLIS, MERGED WITH THE RAW SUBSTANCE OF A PART OF THE EVERGLADES THAT HAPPENS TO BE THE NEXUS OF A NUMBER OF MYSTIC DIMENSIONS.

AND BECAUSE MAN-THING IS A FREAKISH **SYNTHESIS** OF SCIENCE GONE MAD AND AGE-OLD MYSTIC POWER, HIS PERCEPTION OF **REALITY** IS SOMEWHAT... **DIFFERENT** THAN OURS.

WHERE **SPIDEY SEES A WEATHER-BEATEN SHACK**, MAN-THING SEES AN **OBSIDIAN TOWER**, REARING A **MILE HIGH** ABOVE THE SWAMP...

...A TOWER WHOSE ESSENCE IS SO **MALIGN** THAT THE MAN-THING FINDS HIMSELF **DROWNING** IN A MIASMA OF PURE **EVIL**.

AND AS FOR THE TWO HELPLESS BACK-WOODS TYPES, THEY ARE HARDLY THAT. THE OLD MAN IS THE TECHNICALLY **DEAD GRAND SORCERER OF LEGEND-- DAKIMH THE ENCHANTER**.

THE GIRL IS HIS DISCIPLE, **JENNIFER KALE**.

THEY'VE FOUGHT **HARD** THESE PAST WEEKS, BUT TO NO AVAIL, AS D'SPAYRE'S TOWER **LEECHED** FROM THEM LIFE AND **HOPE**.

AND NOW, **BOTH** KNOW THAT IF THEY ARE NOT FREED **TONIGHT**, THEY WILL NOT LIVE TO SEE TO-MORROW'S **SUNRISE**.

BUT SPIDEY KNOWS NONE OF THIS. TO HIM, IT'S A MATTER OF TWO PEOPLE BEING **THREATENED** BY YET ANOTHER BRAND-NEW SUPER-VILLAIN ABOUT TO LEARN THE **ERROR** OF HIS WAYS.

AND SPIDEY RESPONDS ACCORDINGLY.

I **APPRECIATE** THE CONCERN, MANNY, BUT THAT BOZO'S LOOKING FOR **TROUBLE**--

--AND AS FAR AS **I'M** CONCERNED, HE JUST **FOUND IT**!

YOU ARE EITHER BRAVE OR A FOOL, LITTLE MAN.
WHICHEVER, YOU WILL SOON BE DEAD.
BETTER MEN THAN YOU HAVE SAID THAT, SPOOKY, BUT I'M STILL HERE.

I'LL GO FOR BROKE WITH MY FIRST SHOT-- TAKE THE OPENING HE'S GIVEN ME.
NO TELLING WHAT KIND OF POWERS OR WEAPONS HE'S PACKING--
KRAK!
--AND I'D RATHER NOT FIND OUT THE HARD WAY.
MY HAND!!

YOU DARE CHALLENGE ME, MORTAL?
HIS JAW-- LIKE BELTING GRANITE, OR... BEN GRIMM. NEVER SEEN ANYONE... REACT SO... FAST.
HAND... LIKE IRON CLAMP AROUND... NECK.
CHURL! YOU ARE BEATEN BEFORE YOU BEGIN.

THE SCREAM COMES OUT OF NOWHERE, TORN FROM THE VERY CORE OF SPIDER-MAN'S BEING.
YAARRRGH!!
AND IF HE HAD A MOUTH, MAN-THING WOULD ECHO THAT SCREAM AS HIS EMPATHIC SENSES ARE SUDDENLY RAVAGED BY THE ONE EMOTION HE ABHORS ABOVE ALL OTHERS -- FEAR.
FEEL MY POWER, HUMAN! FEEL THE AWESOME, UNSTOPPABLE POWER OF-- D'SPAYRE!!
AS IT IS, HE CAN ONLY STAGGER UNDER THE ONSLAUGHT AND WATCH, AS SPIDER-MAN'S VERY SOUL IS TORN APART BEFORE HIS EYES.

FINALLY, THE SWAMP-DWELLER CAN STAND NO MORE. TRUE, SPIDER-MAN IS HIS FRIEND. BUT HIS FEAR PAINS MAN-THING AS IF IT WERE SALT LAID ACROSS AN OPEN WOUND.
NO MATTER WHAT THE COST, THIS AGONY MUST END.

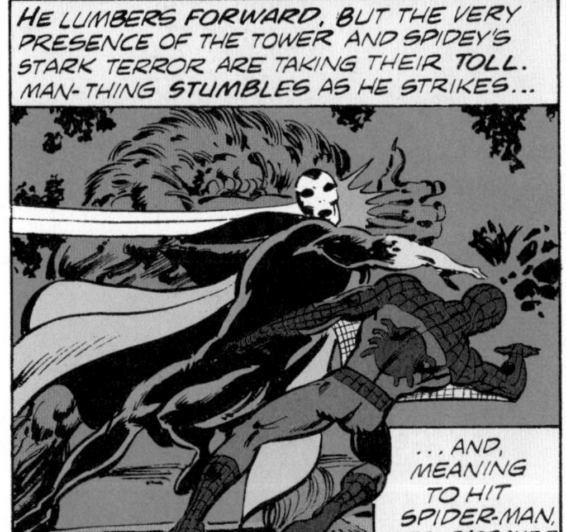
HE LUMBERS FORWARD, BUT THE VERY PRESENCE OF THE TOWER AND SPIDEY'S STARK TERROR ARE TAKING THEIR TOLL. MAN-THING STUMBLES AS HE STRIKES...
...AND, MEANING TO HIT SPIDER-MAN, HITS D'SPAYRE INSTEAD.

BOG-BEAST, WILL YOU NEVER LEARN?
I MUST TEACH YOU A LESSON EVEN YOUR MINDLESS FORM WILL NEVER FORGET!

THERE'S A FLASH OF LIGHT...
AND, IN THAT INSTANT, FEAR SEIZES MAN-THING--AWESOME, PRIMAL, CANCEROUS ABSOLUTE FEAR--NOT EMPATHICALLY "FELT" FROM OUTSIDE...
...BUT FROM WITHIN. THIS TIME, MAN-THING HIMSELF IS AFRAID.
AND WHATEVER KNOWS FEAR BURNS AT THE MAN-THING'S TOUCH!

HE GLOWS LIKE A MINIATURE STAR, FLAMES EATING HIM UP FROM WITHOUT AND WITHIN...
...AS HE INSTINCTIVELY STAGGERS TOWARDS THE SWAMP AND, HOPEFULLY, SALVATION. A SENTIENT BEING WOULD GO MAD WITH THE UNIMAGINABLE PAIN.

BUT MAN-THING, HAVING NO MIND AND, THEREFORE, NO SUCH ESCAPE...
...CAN ONLY ENDURE AND, PERHAPS, SURVIVE.

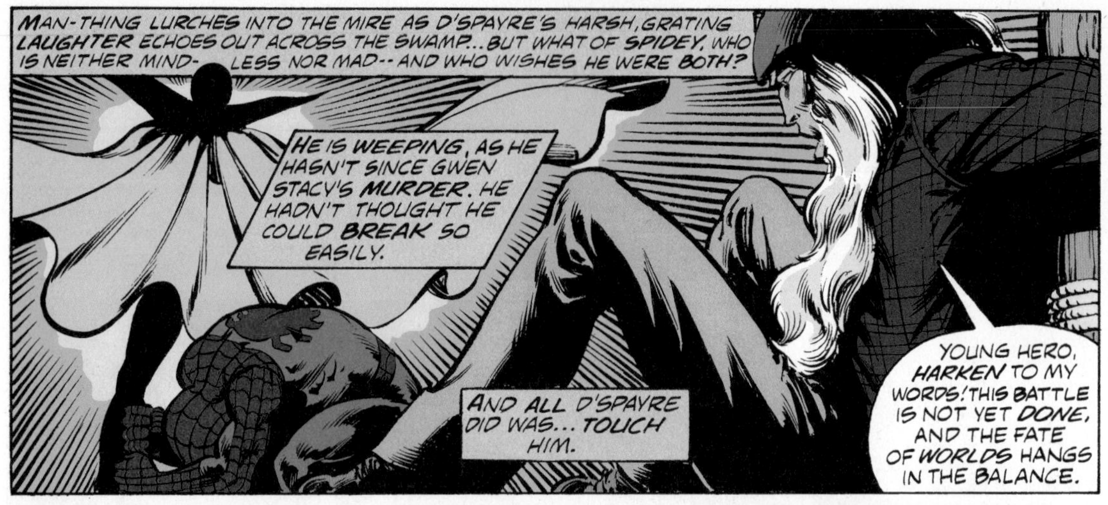
MAN-THING LURCHES INTO THE MIRE AS D'SPAYRE'S HARSH, GRATING LAUGHTER ECHOES OUT ACROSS THE SWAMP... BUT WHAT OF SPIDEY, WHO IS NEITHER MIND- LESS NOR MAD-- AND WHO WISHES HE WERE BOTH?
HE IS WEEPING, AS HE HASN'T SINCE GWEN STACY'S MURDER. HE HADN'T THOUGHT HE COULD BREAK SO EASILY.
AND ALL D'SPAYRE DID WAS... TOUCH HIM.
YOUNG HERO, HARKEN TO MY WORDS! THIS BATTLE IS NOT YET DONE, AND THE FATE OF WORLDS HANGS IN THE BALANCE.

SPIDEY DOESN'T ANSWER, AND FOR ALL THE OLD MAN KNOWS, HE'S BEYOND HEARING, HIS SPIRIT CRUSHED AND THROWN INTO THE ABYSS. BUT DAKIMH HAS TO TRY...
I AM DAKIMH, CALLED THE ENCHANTER. AND ON THESE PLANES OF EXISTENCE, I AM COUNTED A FORCE FOR GOOD.

"D'SPAYRE IS MY OPPOSITE, THE EMBODIMENT OF ULTIMATE EVIL. I KNEW OF HIM, BUT HAD NOT REALIZED THE EXTENT OF HIS POWER UNTIL IT WAS TOO LATE.
"HE CAPTURED JENNIFER AND ME AND BOUND US TO THIS TOWER. HE IS USING ITS POWER TO TWIST OUR SOULS TO HIS SHAPING, SO THAT WHEN IT HAS DONE ITS DAEMONIC WORK...
"...WE WILL BE REBORN IN HIS IMAGE, SERVANTS OF EVIL, OUR UNIVERSE-SPANNING POWERS PLEDGED FOR ALL TIME TO THE SERVICE OF D'SPAYRE."

I-IF I WEREN'T S-SO S-SCARED I'D... LAUGH, M-MISTER. WH-WHAT T-TOWER, HUH? ALL... I SEE IS A SHACK.
IN TERMS YOU CAN UNDERSTAND THEN, SPIDER-MAN-- IF D'SPAYRE IS NOT STOPPED, HE WILL KILL US ALL.

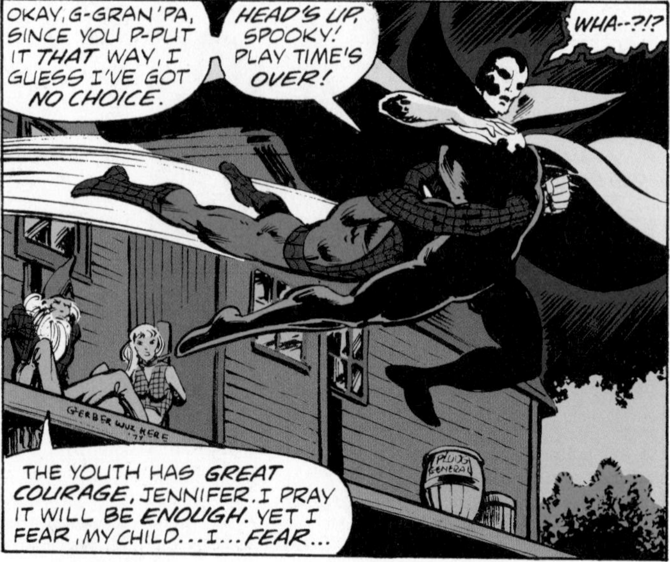
OKAY, G-GRAN'PA, SINCE YOU P-PUT IT THAT WAY, I GUESS I'VE GOT NO CHOICE.
HEAD'S UP, SPOOKY! PLAY TIME'S OVER!
WHA--?!?
GERBER WUZ HERE
THE YOUTH HAS GREAT COURAGE, JENNIFER. I PRAY IT WILL BE ENOUGH. YET I FEAR, MY CHILD... I... FEAR...

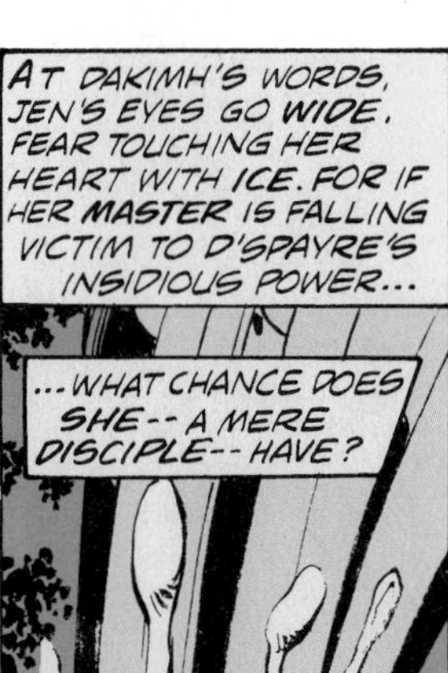

AT DAKIMH'S WORDS, JEN'S EYES GO WIDE. FEAR TOUCHING HER HEART WITH ICE. FOR IF HER MASTER IS FALLING VICTIM TO D'SPAYRE'S INSIDIOUS POWER...
...WHAT CHANCE DOES SHE-- A MERE DISCIPLE-- HAVE?
SPLORT!

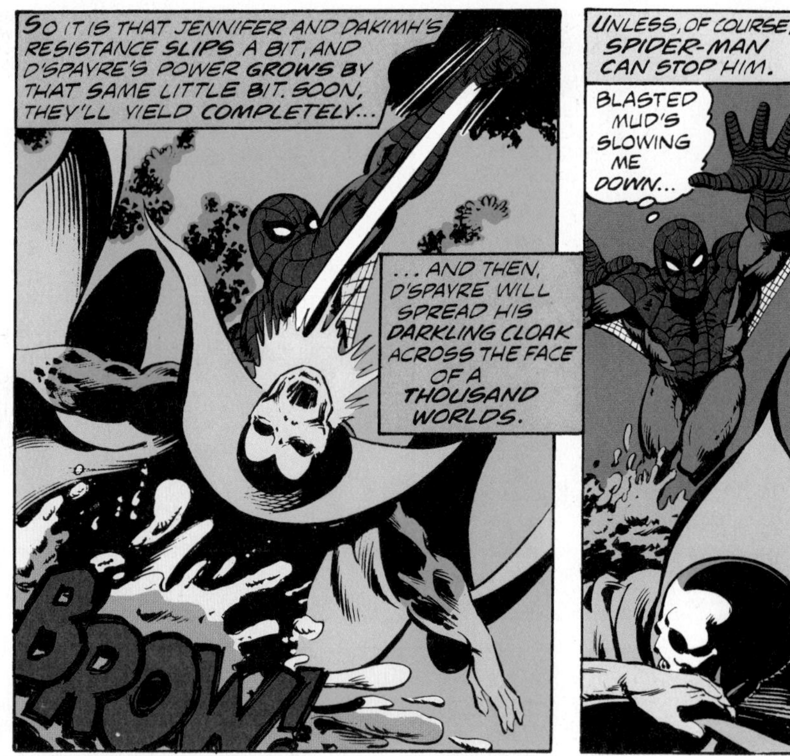

SO IT IS THAT JENNIFER AND DAKIMH'S RESISTANCE SLIPS A BIT, AND D'SPAYRE'S POWER GROWS BY THAT SAME LITTLE BIT. SOON, THEY'LL YIELD COMPLETELY...
...AND THEN, D'SPAYRE WILL SPREAD HIS DARKLING CLOAK ACROSS THE FACE OF A THOUSAND WORLDS.
BROW!
UNLESS, OF COURSE, SPIDER-MAN CAN STOP HIM.
BLASTED MUD'S SLOWING ME DOWN...

...GIVING SPOOKY TIME TO--
OH...NO!!
HE SCREAMS-- TURNED IN AN INSTANT FROM A HUMAN BEING...
...INTO A WHIMPERING, CRINGING... THING THAT HAPPENS TO WEAR A HUMAN FORM.

NO BRAVADO NOW, MORTAL?
PLEASE ...NO MORE...

YOU WERE SO PROUD A MOMENT AGO, LITTLE MAN-- SO DEFIANT, SO SURE OF YOURSELF AND YOUR POWER. AND D'SPAYRE HAS TAKEN ALL THAT AWAY.
I CAN DO ANYTHING I WISH--TO YOU OR WITH YOU--AND YOU WILL NOT LIFT A FINGER TO STOP ME.
SHAKAM

BEG ME FOR YOUR LIFE, SPIDER-MAN. OR MUST YOU FEEL MY TOUCH OF FEAR AGAIN?

ON YOUR KNEES-- EH? MAN-THING!
REBORN ONCE MORE, BUT THIS TIME, INEXPLICABLY, GOING NOT FOR SPIDER-MAN, THE ONE WHO FEARS--
--BUT FOR THE TRUE SOURCE OF THAT FEAR.

I GROW WEARY OF THIS FARCE, BEAST.

HE BURNS.
AND THE SWAMP, AS MINDLESS, AS ELEMENTAL AS MAN-THING HIMSELF...
...MAKES HIM WHOLE.

SO, HE BURNS AGAIN--
--D'SPAYRE'S POWER TOUCHING THAT MINUTE PART OF MAN-THING THAT WAS ONCE TED SALLIS...

...MAKING IT FEAR AND TURNING THE MAN-THING'S FURY AGAINST HIMSELF.

THOUGH EACH BLAST SHRIVELS HIM, STILL THE QUAG-BEAST DOES NOT STOP.
HE IS DRIVEN, PERHAPS, BY THAT SAME PART OF TED SALLIS WITHIN HIM WHICH D'SPAYRE IS USING TO DESTROY HIM.
AND SO, THE GAME GOES ON, AND ON...

...D'SPAYRE LOVING EVERY MINUTE OF IT.
MANNY'S GIVING HIS LIFE FOR ME... AN' HIS... FRIENDS, AN' ALL... I'M DOING IS... WATCHING!
GOTTA... HELP HIM! BUT IF I DO, D'SPAYRE'LL BLAST ME AGAIN!
HE STARTS SHAKING, TEARS STAINING HIS MASK...
...THE MEMORY OF WHAT HAPPENED ENOUGH TO SEND HIM INTO A PANIC. FOR A LONG MOMENT, HE DOES NOTHING...

...AND THEN...
MAN, IT'D BE SO EASY TO GIVE UP. THAT'S ALL SPOOKY WANTS. THEN, THERE'D BE NO MORE PAIN...
I MEAN, WHO SAID I HAD TO WIN 'EM ALL?

BUT...IF I LOSE TO SCUM LIKE YOU, D'SPAYRE--
--IT'S NOT BECAUSE I'VE GIVEN UP. IT'S BECAUSE I'M DEAD!
KRAKOW!

HIS ATTACK IS SO SUDDEN, HIS MOVES SO BLINDINGLY FAST, IT'S HARD TO TELL WHAT'S HAPPENING. HIS FISTS SMASH INTO D'SPAYRE LIKE SLEDGEHAMMERS--
--HIS MIND SHORT-CIRCUITING FROM THE PUNISHMENT IT'S TAKEN, SLIPPING EVER-SO-SLIGHTLY ACROSS THE THRESHOLD OF INSANITY.
BOK!

HE FEELS NO PAIN, NO EMOTION AT ALL BEYOND A BLIND BERSERKER FURY THAT SWEEPS ALL BEFORE IT.
DAKIMH, WHAT'S HAPPENING?
D'SPAYRE HAS SOWN THE WIND, MY CHILD, AND NOW, I THINK, REAPS THE WHIRLWIND.
CHOOM!

YOU SHOWED ME A PART OF MYSELF NO ONE SHOULD SEE, BUSTER, AND THEN YOU LAUGHED!
FWAK!

I DON'T HEAR ANY LAUGHTER NOW, SPOOKY!
HOW DOES IT FEEL TO BE ON THE RECEIVING END FOR A CHANGE, HUH? ANSWER ME, D'SPAYRE!
ANSWER ME!!
KROW!

ENOUGH, MY YOUNG FRIEND.
OR WILL YOU NOT BE SATISFIED UNTIL YOU'VE TAKEN THIS DEMON-SPAWN'S LIFE?
H-HUH...?
I--I--OH, MY LORD, WHAT HAVE I DONE?

SAVED US, HERO, FROM DEATH AND WORSE THAN DEATH.
S-SURE. ANYTIME.
HEY! YOUR CLOTHES... AND D'SPAYRE'S FACE! I THOUGHT HE WAS WEARING A MASK BUT...
YOU SAW US BEFORE AS D'SPAYRE'S SPELL MADE YOU SEE US, SPIDER-MAN. YOU SEE US NOW AS WE ARE.

I UNDERSTAND, DAKIMH. ONCE THE TOWER'S DESTROYED, D'SPAYRE'S POWER IS BROKEN.
QUICKLY, JENNIFER. LINK YOUR POWER WITH MINE. THERE IS ONE TASK WE MUST YET PERFORM.

"ALAS, IF THAT WERE ONLY SO," DAKIMH SAYS, AS THEIR TWIN SPELLS WEAVE A GOLD AND SILVER WEB AROUND THE TOWER, "BUT SO LONG AS THERE IS HOPE, IT MUST BE BALANCED... BY DESPAIR.
"WE CAN REDUCE HIM FOR A TIME. BUT WHILE THERE IS LIFE ITSELF, HE WILL EXIST."
AND THEN, WITH A SOUND LIKE SOFT, SILVER BELLS-- PEACEFUL, YET MORE AWESOME THAN THE LOUDEST THUNDER-CLAP-- THE TOWER SHATTERS...

...AND FALLS, IN A BILLION-BILLION IRIDESCENT CRYSTAL SHARDS THAT GLITTER IN THE MOONLIGHT LIKE NEWBORN STARS.
OH!
TRULY, SPIDER-MAN, YOU ARE A MAN OF INFINITE RESOURCES.
DON'T WORRY JENNIFER. MY WEB-UMBRELLA WILL PROTECT US FROM THE BUSTED GLASS.
TELL THAT TO MY PROFESSORS, HUH, DAKIMH? THEY ALL THINK I'M A FUMBLE FINGERED KLUTZ.

OKAY, THE SHOWER'S OVER. AND IF THE TWO OF YOU DON'T MIND I'D LIKE SOME EXPLAN-ATIONS.
LIKE, WHAT THE HECK'S BEEN HAPPENING HERE ?!?
CALL IT A DREAM, IF YOU LIKE. MORE THAN THAT I'M AFRAID I CANNOT SAY.
THE PATHS OF FATE ARE WONDROUS TO BEHOLD, MY FRIEND. MAYHAP WE THREE SHALL MEET AGAIN SOMEDAY.

UNTIL THAT TIME, KNOW THAT YOU HAVE THE ETERNAL THANKS OF...
SILENCE.

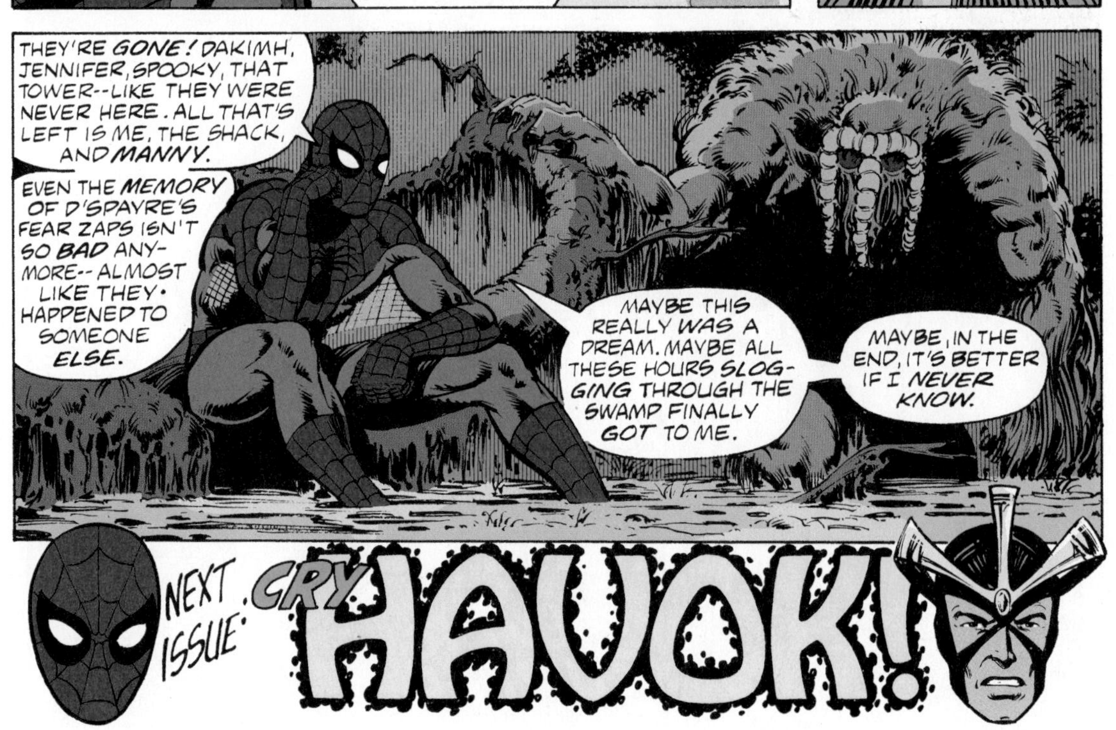

THEY'RE GONE! DAKIMH, JENNIFER, SPOOKY, THAT TOWER--LIKE THEY WERE NEVER HERE. ALL THAT'S LEFT IS ME, THE SHACK, AND MANNY.
EVEN THE MEMORY OF D'SPAYRE'S FEAR ZAPS ISN'T SO BAD ANY-MORE-- ALMOST LIKE THEY HAPPENED TO SOMEONE ELSE.
MAYBE THIS REALLY WAS A DREAM. MAYBE ALL THESE HOURS SLOG-GING THROUGH THE SWAMP FINALLY GOT TO ME.
MAYBE, IN THE END, IT'S BETTER IF I NEVER KNOW.

NEXT ISSUE: CRY HAVOK!

Writer & Artist: Al Milgrom • Colorist: Gregory Wright • Letterer: Jim Novak
Assistant Editor: Mike Rockwitz • Editors: Terry Kavanagh & Michael Higgins

THE GREAT BEAST CHEWS SLOWLY ON THE METALLIC ALLOYS OF THE ASTEROID, SAVORING THE TANGY ELEMENTS WHICH GIVE IT SUSTENANCE.
IT DOES NOT HURRY, FOR BEING ONE OF THE VERY FEW CREATURES THAT CAN LIVE UNASSISTED IN THE VACUUM OF SPACE, IT HAS KNOWN NO PREDATORS--KNOWN NO FEAR...

UNTIL NOW!

FLAILING IN A BLIND PANIC THE BEHEMOTH REARS BACK...
AND LOSING CONTROL OF ITS BODILY FUNCTIONS IT EXPELS THE CARBON-METHANE GASES WHICH IT HAD STORED DEEP IN ITS AUXILIARY LUNG COMPARTMENTS.

AND SO... IT DIES. NEVER AGAIN TO KNOW THE HARD, PIQUANT TASTE OF THE ROCKY DIET IT LOVED SO WELL.
AND NEVER TO KNOW THE PREDATOR WHO HAS BROUGHT IT LOW...

THE FEAR EATER!
BAH! SUCH MEAGER FARE! FEAR OF DEATH! IT SUSTAINS ME! IT DOES NOT INTEREST ME!

IF I COULD FIND SOME UNIQUE LIFE FORM. SOME UNIQUE FORM OF FEAR...
THAT WOULD BE A FEAST I COULD RELISH!
FOOLISH! IT WILL BE UNTOLD PARSECS BEFORE I EVEN FIND ANOTHER LIFE FORM TO NOURISH ME!
BUT WAIT--THAT FLASH OF LIGHT! IT IS LIKE NOTHING I HAVE EVER OBSERVED BEFORE. WHAT COULD IT BE?
THE SILVER SURFER
...FEAR ITSELF!

EH?! WHAT'S THIS? AN ASTEROID EATER FROM DENAK IV.
NORMALLY THEY RETURN TO THEIR HOME GALAXY WHEN THEY SENSE IT IS THEIR TIME TO DIE...

BUT NO--THIS ONE DID NOT DIE OF NATURAL CAUSES! SOMETHING HAS FELLED THE GENTLE BRUTE!
BUT WHAT COULD POSSESS THE POWER...?
WHILE THE SURFER'S COSMICALLY ATTUNED SENSES ARE FOCUSED ON THE PUZZLE BEFORE HIM--

--THE FEAR EATER STRIKES!
UNNOTICED IT PHASES EXTRA-DIMENSIONALLY INTO THE SHINING BEING DOING NO PHYSICAL DAMAGE--
--BUT FORMING A MENTAL/EMOTIONAL LINK WITH ITS INTENDED VICTIM!

ONCE SAFELY ENSCONCED, IT "READS" ITS PREY!
BY THE GREAT TIMELESS ONES! THIS CREATURE, ONCE A MORTAL BEING KNOWN AS NORRIN RADD, IS A FORMER HERALD OF MIGHTY GALACTUS!
MANY ARE THE FEASTS I HAVE ENJOYED ON THE FEAR-FILLED VICTIMS OF THAT WORLD-DEVOURING POWER!
THIS...SILVER SURFER IS AN ENTITY POSSESSED OF AWESOME COSMIC POWER AND SEEMS TO KNOW OTHER EQUALLY UNUSUAL MORTALS. FROM A PLANET CALLED EARTH.

THIS IS JUST THE SORT OF FARE I HAVE BEEN CRAVING!
BUT CAN SUCH A BEING KNOW FEAR?

YES! I SENSE IT! A DEEP ABIDING TERROR OF BEING IMPRISONED!
GOOD THEN! I CAN USE MY POWER TO TRANSPORT THIS SILVER SURFER TO THE SITE OF HIS MOST RECENT INCARCERATION...
EARTH!
NO! IT CANNOT BE!
WHAT DEVLISH POWER HAS BROUGHT ME HERE, BACK TO THE WORLD WHERE MY VENGEFUL FORMER MASTER HAD CONDEMNED ME?!
I WILL NOT BE DENIED THE GLORIES OF THE UNIVERSE A SECOND TIME!
WHOOMP
THE RESTRAINING BARRIER IS STILL IN PLACE!
BUT I WILL NOT BE A PRISONER!
NOT NOW!
NOT EVER AGAIN!

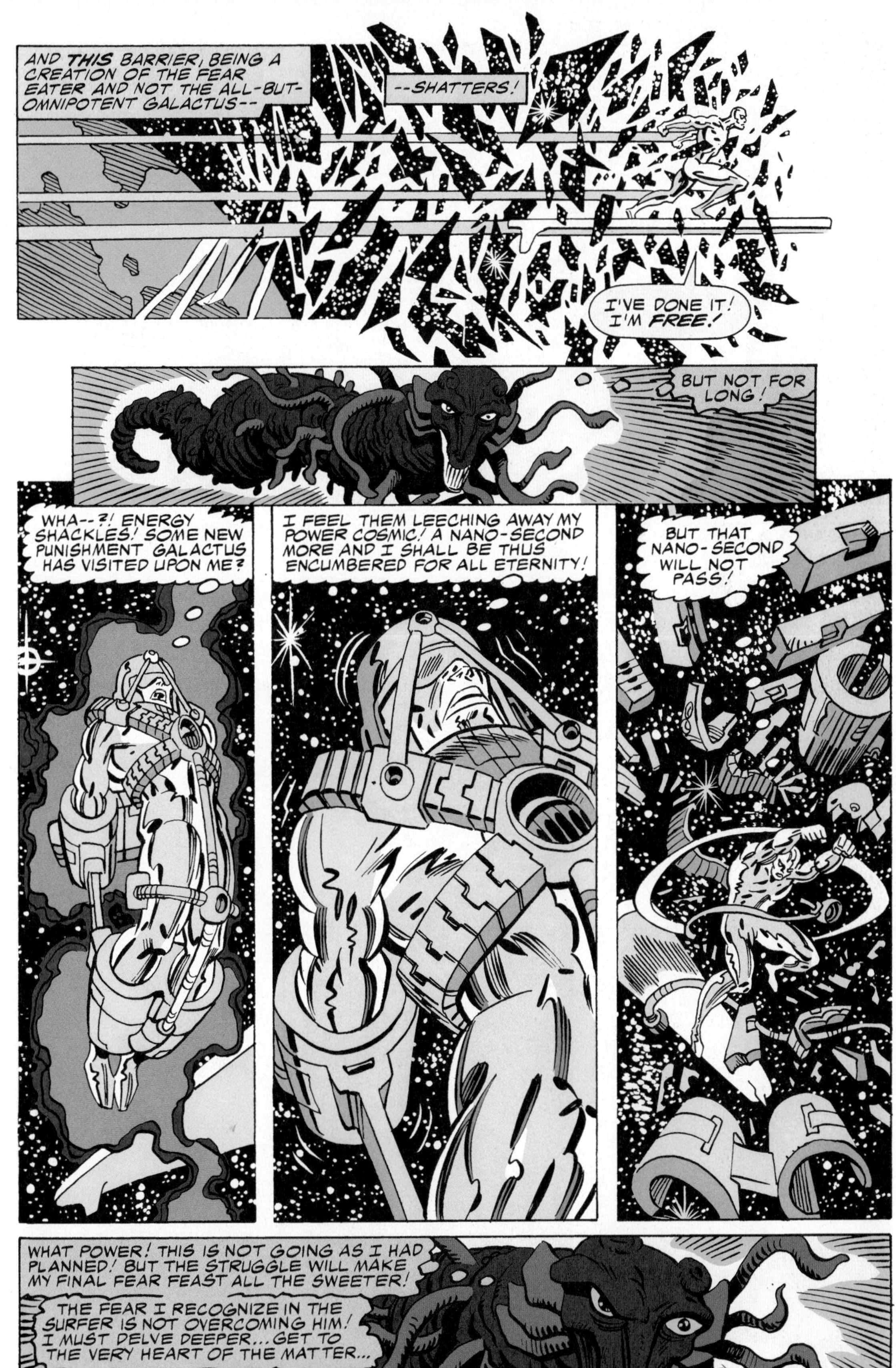
AND THIS BARRIER, BEING A CREATION OF THE FEAR EATER AND NOT THE ALL-BUT-OMNIPOTENT GALACTUS--
--SHATTERS!
I'VE DONE IT! I'M FREE!
BUT NOT FOR LONG!
WHA--?! ENERGY SHACKLES! SOME NEW PUNISHMENT GALACTUS HAS VISITED UPON ME?
I FEEL THEM LEECHING AWAY MY POWER COSMIC! A NANO-SECOND MORE AND I SHALL BE THUS ENCUMBERED FOR ALL ETERNITY!
BUT THAT NANO-SECOND WILL NOT PASS!
WHAT POWER! THIS IS NOT GOING AS I HAD PLANNED! BUT THE STRUGGLE WILL MAKE MY FINAL FEAR FEAST ALL THE SWEETER!
THE FEAR I RECOGNIZE IN THE SURFER IS NOT OVERCOMING HIM! I MUST DELVE DEEPER...GET TO THE VERY HEART OF THE MATTER...

AH, YESSSS... THERE'S THE ANSWER... I'LL PLACE HIM IN THE ULTIMATE PRISON...

...THE FLESHLY CONFINES OF HIS OWN MORTAL PERSONA!
UNNH! WHAT NEW DEVILMENT ASSAILS ME? I CANNOT STAY BALANCED ON MY BOARD!
I'LL PROTECT HIM FROM THE RIGORS OF SPACE--SO I CAN FEED!

HOW CAN THIS BE?! I'VE BECOME NORRIN RADD ONCE AGAIN!

THE VASTNESS OF SPACE--ONCE A WELCOME HAVEN--NOW SPINS ABOUT HIM SENDING TENDRILS OF FEAR SNAKING DOWN DEEP WITHIN.

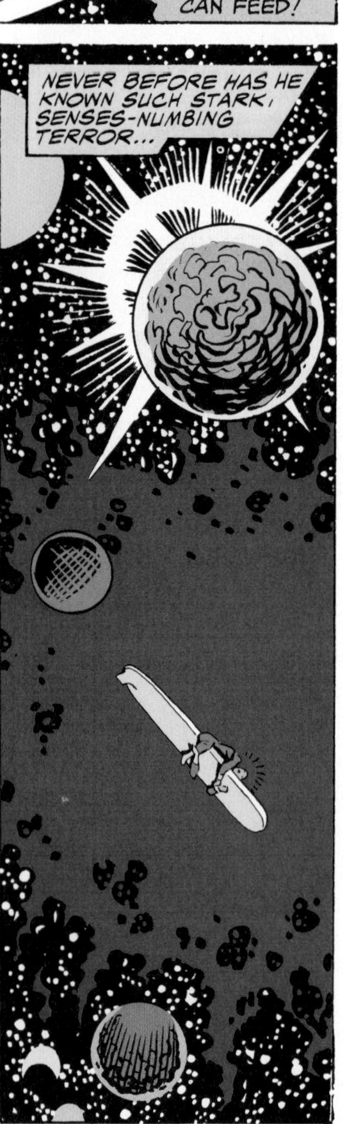
NEVER BEFORE HAS HE KNOWN SUCH STARK, SENSES-NUMBING TERROR...

AND THE FEAR EATER BEGINS TO FEAST!
SO BIG... SO VAST ...THE ENDLESS STARS... I-I'M SO SMALL COMPARED... A MOTE... A NOTHING...

AH, HOW RICH! A BEING AFRAID OF HIS OWN MORTAL BEING, IN TERROR OF HIS OWN HUMANITY! NEVER HAVE I TASTED SUCH A DELICACY!

IF... IF I HAD BEEN LOWLY NORRIN RADD... I... I COULD NEVER HAVE SAVED MY HOME PLANET ZENN-LA...
BECOMING GALACTUS'S HERALD... HE SPARED MY WORLD... AND WITH THE COSMIC POWER HE GRANTED ME... I... I SAVED EARTH MANY TIMES OVER... DID UNTOLD GOOD... IN THE UNIVERSE...

WHAT'S THIS?! THE FEAR FLOW IS SLOWING!
NO! I WANT MORE! MORE!

TO END... THOSE GOOD WORKS IS... UNTHINKABLE... EVEN MORE SO THAN BEING UNABLE TO SOAR THE SPACEWAYS ANYMORE...
SOAR ON MY... SILVER BOARD ...THE SILVER BOARD WHICH STILL EXISTS BENEATH ME... AND IF IT STILL EXISTS...

NONONO! HE HAS COME TO GRIPS WITH HIS DEEPEST FEARS! AND FACING THEM, HE CAN THINK RATIONALLY ONCE AGAIN!
HE WILL REALIZE THAT IF HIS BOARD EXISTS, THEN DEEP WITHIN HIM, SO DOES THE POWER COSMIC...

I SENSE SOMEHOW THAT THE ASSAULTS ON ME ARE ENDED. I KNOW NOT WHAT PRECIPITATED THE CHAIN OF EVENTS WHICH JUST TRANSPIRED--

--I ONLY KNOW THAT ONCE AGAIN I AM FREE! FREE TO TRAVERSE THE UNIVERSE AND RIGHT WRONGS WHERE I FIND THEM!

AND THAT IS ENOUGH! FAREWELL PLANET EARTH!

AH, YESSS. EARTH. HOME OF MANY OTHER UNIQUE BEINGS WITH UNIQUE FEARS.

AND IF THEY DO NOT POSSESS THE AWESOME COSMIC POWER OF THE SILVER SURFER--

--THAT'S ALL THE BETTER FOR ME, ISN'T IT?

THE END?

Writer & Artist: **Al Milgrom** • Colorist: **Gregory Wright** • Letterer: **Jim Novak**
Assistant Editor: **Mike Rockwitz** • Editors: **Terry Kavanagh & Michael Higgins**

THE CAPTAIN
COLD WAR
HEY! GET DOWN, MAN! ARE YOU CRAZY?!
TAKE COVER, MISTER, OR YOU'RE GONNA GET YOUR BACKSIDE FLASH FROZEN!

THAT'S MORE LIKE ...SAY--I KNOW YOU! YOU'RE CAPTAIN AMERICA, AREN'TCHA?
WHAT'S WITH THE WEIRD COSTUME, CAP?
LONG STORY! FOR NOW, JUST CALL ME... THE CAPTAIN! AND FILL ME IN--WHAT'S WITH THE COLD WAVE?

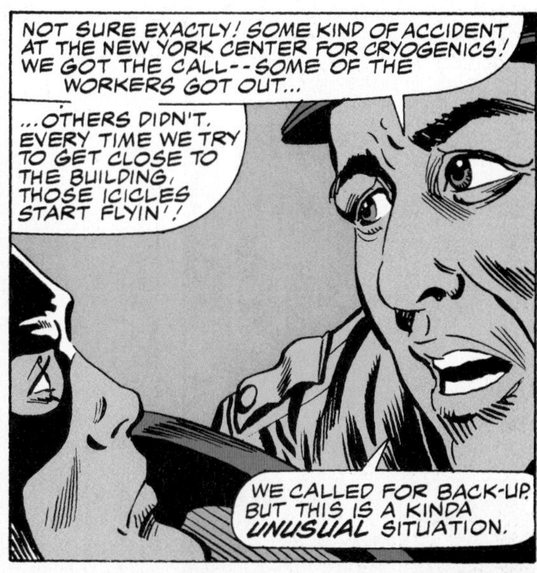
NOT SURE EXACTLY! SOME KIND OF ACCIDENT AT THE NEW YORK CENTER FOR CRYOGENICS! WE GOT THE CALL--SOME OF THE WORKERS GOT OUT...
...OTHERS DIDN'T. EVERY TIME WE TRY TO GET CLOSE TO THE BUILDING, THOSE ICICLES START FLYIN'!
WE CALLED FOR BACK-UP, BUT THIS IS A KINDA UNUSUAL SITUATION.

SO I SEE. AND YOU WEREN'T SURE IF THIS IS JUST SOME MALFUNCTION OF THE EQUIPMENT ...OR IF SOMEONE MALICIOUS IS BEHIND IT.
IN EITHER CASE, I FEAR FOR THE EMPLOYEES!
AND WHERE THERE IS THE EMOTION OF FEAR--

--THERE IS THE FEAR EATER!
NYPD
AHHH! I CAN FEEL THE TERROR EMANATING FROM WITHIN THE BUILDING... AND WITHOUT!
SURELY I SHALL FEAST WELL THIS DAY!

RECENTLY I INVADED THE BEING OF THE SILVER SURFER IN SEARCH OF UNIQUE FORMS OF FEAR TO QUELL MY HUNGER.
BUT HE CONQUERED HIS FEAR AND THUS DROVE ME OFF!
ALTHOUGH NOT BEFORE I LEARNED OF THE BEINGS OF EARTH WITH THEIR RARE FORMS OF COURAGE--AND RARE TYPES OF FEAR!

THIS HUMANOID IS ONE SUCH BEING! UNSEEN, UNFELT, I WILL ENTER HIM--EXPLOIT HIS FEARS...
...AND DEVOUR THEM!
THAT HE WILL DIE IN THE PROCESS IS NO CONCERN OF MINE!

I-I FEEL THIS **CHILL** ALL OF A SUDDEN!

JUST NOW? IT'S LIKE THE DEAD OF WINTER OUT HERE!

NO! IT'S A DIFFERENT **KIND** OF COLD... LIKE A SENSE OF DREAD!

AND SAFELY SETTLED WITHIN THE BODY OF ITS PREY, THE FEAR EATER **"READS"** THE MAN KNOWN AS THE CAPTAIN!

YESSSS! THIS IS ONE OF THOSE 'MEN' THE SURFER HAS ENCOUNTERED!

THOUGH HE HAS NOT EXPERIENCED AS MUCH STAR-SPANNING ADVENTURE AS THE SILVER ONE, STILL... HE HAS HAD A FULL AND VARIED LIFE EXPERIENCE.

CAP, WAIT! OUR BACK-UP...
MAY GET HERE TOO LATE TO HELP WHOEVER'S INSIDE! I'M GOING IN!

TWISTING, DODGING, THE SENTINEL OF LIBERTY USES THE SKILLS LEARNED IN A THOUSAND BATTLES--

--TO CHARGE THE BELEAGURED BUILDING!
CRYOGENIC CENTER OF NEW YORK

ONCE INSIDE HE IS GREETED BY A SCENE EERIE ENOUGH TO MAKE ANY MAN'S BLOOD RUN COLD!
IT IS LIKE AN ICY KINGDOM OF A FAERIE DREAM, ONLY THIS IS NO DREAM--

--IT'S A NIGHTMARE!
THESE SCULPTURES AREN'T SCULPTURES AT ALL!
THEY'RE PEOPLE FROZEN IN BLOCKS OF ICE. THE EMPLOYEES, NO DOUBT. BUT HOW...?

ONCE AGAIN HE SHIVERS--AND NOT JUST FROM THE COLD!
IT IS THE FEAR EATER BURROWING DEEP WITHIN HIM--STIRRING THE ASHES OF MEMORIES GROWN COLD...

I-- I REMEMBER SO CLEARLY... IT WAS DURING WORLD WAR II... BARON ZEMO HAD LAUNCHED HIS DRONE BOMB...
...BUCKY AND I WERE TRYING TO STOP IT...

...BUCKY BARNES... MY PARTNER... MY FRIEND... HE CLUNG TO THE FUSELAGE... TRYING TO DE-FUSE IT...
...I YELLED FOR HIM TO JUMP...

...BUT HE NEVER... GOT THE CHANCE...
BA-KOOM!!

...I KNEW... EVEN AS I HIT THE ICY WATER... HE WAS DEAD...

...I... I REMEMBER THE COLD... IT HURT FOR A MINUTE... THEN I SLEPT...
...THEY TELL ME I WAS FROZEN ALIVE... THAT I DRIFTED...

...WAS WORSHIPPED... BY ESKIMOS... AN ICE GOD... TILL SUB-MARINER INAD-VERTENTLY FREED ME...

...HIT WARMER WATERS... THAWED ME... AND ULTIMATELY WAS RESCUED BY... THE AVENGERS!
THEY BECAME MY NEW ALLIES... COMRADES-IN-ARMS ...FRIENDS...

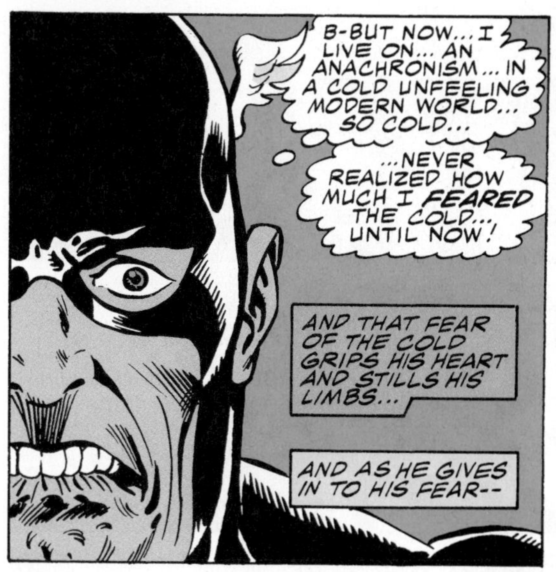
B-BUT NOW... I LIVE ON... AN ANACHRONISM... IN A COLD UNFEELING MODERN WORLD... SO COLD...
...NEVER REALIZED HOW MUCH I *FEARED* THE COLD... UNTIL NOW!
AND THAT FEAR OF THE COLD GRIPS HIS HEART AND STILLS HIS LIMBS...
AND AS HE GIVES IN TO HIS FEAR--

--THE FEAR EATER FEASTS!
AH--SO GOOD! BUT HE IS NOT YET IN TOTAL ROUT! THIS ICY ENVIRON IS BUT THE RESULT OF A MECHANICAL MISHAP--
--BUT USING MY POWERS I CAN *ANIMATE* ONE OF THE FROZEN HUMANS ...MAKE HIM THE LIVING EMBODIMENT OF CAPTAIN AMERICA'S FEAR--
--THUS DRIVE HIM OVER THE EDGE!

SO, CAPTAIN--YOU DARE CHALLENGE THE CHILLING POWER OF *COLD WAR*?!
WHA-?!
SOME NEW VILLAIN--LOOKS LIKE A CROSS BETWEEN IRON MAN'S OLD FOE, JACK FROST, AND THE ICEMAN!

AH, BUT I AM FAR *DEADLIER* THAN EITHER!
ZWAP!

TWIST AND TURN ALL YOU LIKE, CAPTAIN! SOONER OR LATER, I'LL FREEZE YOU SOLID!
THUNNG!
AND ONCE I DO, YOUR BODY WILL BECOME THE DECORATIVE CENTERPIECE OF MY KINGDOM--

--A FROZEN KINGDOM THAT WILL SWELL TO ENCOMPASS THE ENTIRE PLANET, WITH PEOPLE LIVING... AND DYING... AT MY WHIM!

HAH! GOT YOU!
N-NO! I-IT'S HAPPENING AGAIN! I'LL BE ENCASED IN ICE --LOSE THIS NEW WORLD-- THIS SECOND LIFE...

BUT THEN I'LL HAVE LOST MY NEW ALLIES... NEW FRIENDS...

AND WITHIN...
WHAT'S THIS?! INSTEAD OF SUCCUMBING... THE ARRIVAL OF THIS NEW THREAT IS MAKING HIM RESIST... FIGHT BACK!

AND I'D LOSE AN OLD FRIEND AS WELL... THE CAUSE OF FREEDOM... THE CAUSE THAT BUCKY DIED FOR--

I WON'T LET HIM HAVE DIED IN VAIN!
I WON'T!!
SKRAASH

YOU'VE FREED YOURSELF?! IMPOSSIBLE!
IF YOU SAY SO!
I-I'LL TRAP YOU AGAIN!

NOT LIKELY!
NOW--AS MY PAL, THE FALCON WOULD SAY...
CHILL OUT!
SPANG

AND IN OVERCOMING HIS FEAR, THE CAPTAIN OVERCOMES THE FEAR EATER AS WELL!
AAAAAAAA! ONCE AGAIN MY PREY HAS MASTERED HIS FEARS AND DRIVEN ME OUT! THE SWEET TASTE OF TERROR MADE BITTER AND INEDIBLE!
HE WAS NOT AFRAID OF THE COLD PER SE, BUT RATHER BY THE FEAR THAT OTHER INNOCENTS--

--AND THIS "FREEDOM" HE HOLDS SO DEAR, WOULD SUFFER BY HIS FAILURE.
TO CONQUER THAT FEAR HE HAD BUT TO ACT AS HE HAS ALWAYS TAKEN ACTION!

THINGS ARE UNDER CONTROL NOW, OFFICER! YOUR MEN CAN GO IN!
GET THAT, EDDIE! AN ARMY OF COPS HELPLESS HERE, AND ONE GUY GOES IN, COOL AS A CUCUMBER, AND DOES THE JOB!
YEAH! THAT SUPER HERO MUST HAVE ICE WATER IN HIS VEINS!
EH?
AND TICKLED BY THE IRONY OF THESE COMMENTS, THE CAPTAIN FIRST SMILES --THEN LAUGHS...

...A DEEP, CLEANSING LAUGH WHICH BANISHES ALL FEAR...
...AND DRIVES THE STILL UNSATIATED FEAR EATER OFF IN SEARCH OF EASIER PREY!
THE END.

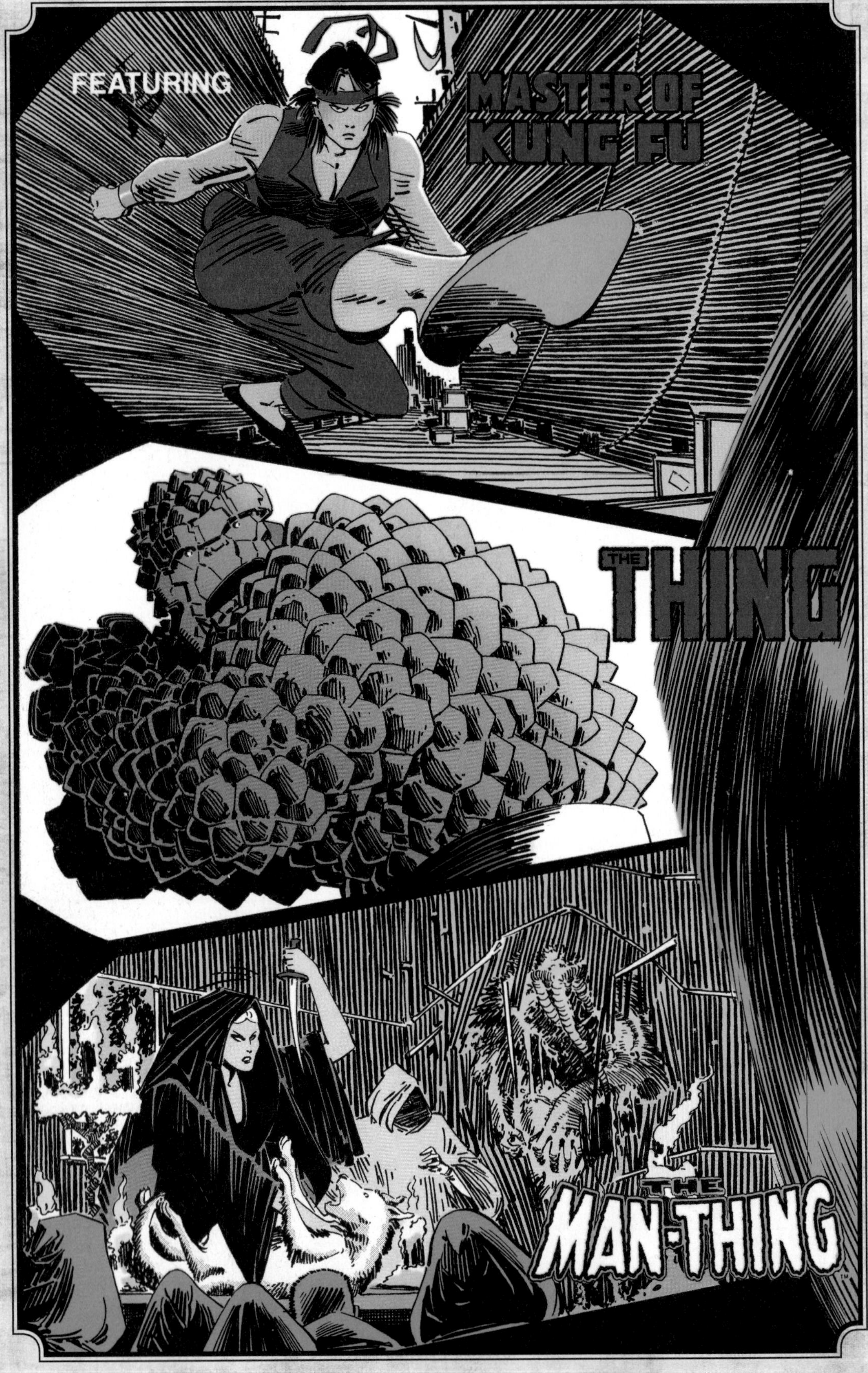

Writer & Artist: **Al Milgrom** • Colorist: **Gregory Wright** • Letterer: **Jim Novak**
Assistant Editor: **Mike Rockwitz** • Editor: **Terry Kavanagh**

THE THING™
THE MEASURE OF A MAN!
LOOK OUT, TIMMY!
WH-WHAT IS IT, MA?
SHEESH! USEDTA BE I COULD GET AWAY WITH TH' HAT AN' OVERCOAT. BUT SINCE I TOOK THAT EXTRA DOSE OF COSMIC RAYS--
--I'MA EVEN UGLIER "THING" THAN I WAS BEFORE!
EVEN BEIN' LEADER OF TH' FANTASTIC FOUR DON'T MAKE UP FOR THAT!
UGH!
I--I SEEN HIS PITCHER IN THE PAPERS BUT I NEVER KNEW HE WAS THAT HORRIBLE!

YA WANNA LOOK AT TH' FREAK? OKAY THEN, HERE! TAKE A GOOD LOOK!
RRRIIIPP!
RUN! HE'S GOING BERSERK!

FEAR! I CAN SENSE IT! AND THERE IS THE CAUSE OF IT-- THAT ORANGE-SKINNED CREATURE!
PERHAPS THE FEAR-EATER HAS FOUND HIS MEAL AT LAST!

MY PREVIOUS ENCOUNTERS WITH THESE UNIQUE TYPES OF BEINGS ENDED ONLY IN FRUSTRATION! CAPTAIN AMERICA... THE SILVER SURFER...
I TASTED OF THEIR FEARS, BUT THEY OVER-CAME THOSE FEARS AND DROVE ME OFF!

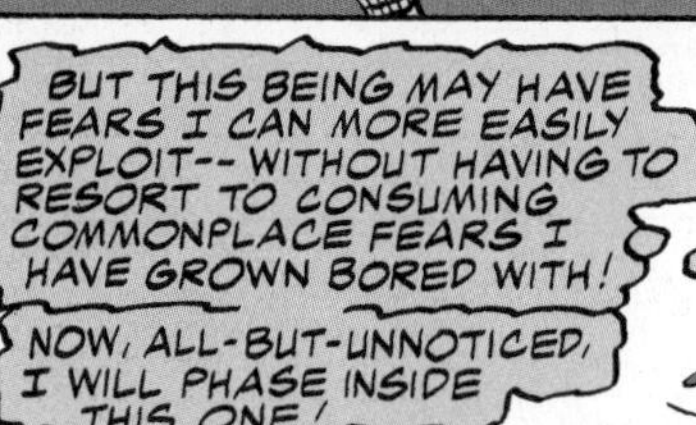
BUT THIS BEING MAY HAVE FEARS I CAN MORE EASILY EXPLOIT-- WITHOUT HAVING TO RESORT TO CONSUMING COMMONPLACE FEARS I HAVE GROWN BORED WITH!
NOW, ALL-BUT-UNNOTICED, I WILL PHASE INSIDE THIS ONE!

AHHHH, I READ HIM WELL! A COSMIC ACCIDENT TRANSFORMED HIM INTO THE INHUMAN BEAST HE IS! AND THOUGH COURAGE ABOUNDS WITHIN HIM--
--HIS FEARS ARE GREAT AS WELL! HAH! IRONIC! WHILE THE SILVER SURFER FEARED BEING RETURNED TO HIS MORTAL IDENTITY ABOVE ALL ELSE--
--BEN GRIMM, CALLED THE THING, IS MOST AFRAID THAT HE WILL NEVER REGAIN HIS HUMAN FORM!

LET ME USE MY POWERS TO PLAY UPON THAT FEAR-- FIRST BY OFFERING HIM HOPE...
LOOK! LOOK! WHAT'S HAPPENING TO HIM NOW?!
I DON'T KNOW, BUT I AIN'T GONNA STAY AROUND TO WATCH!
HUH?

WHAT ARE THOSE YAHOOS JABBERIN' ABOUT?
HEY! THOSE SPIKEY LUMPS-- THEY'RE FADIN'--
DAILY BUGLE

--I'M CHANGIN' BACK TO MY OLD ROCKY SELF! M-MAYBE I'LL KEEP RIGHT ON CHANGIN' BACK TO NORMAL... BACK TO BEN GRIMM!
AND NOW I'LL SNATCH THAT HOPE AWAY...

NO! IT STOPPED! BLAST IT, IT STOPPED!

AHHH--DESPAIR SETS IN! AND WITH IT THE GROWING CERTAINTY--THE GROWING FEAR--THAT HE WILL NEVER BE HUMAN AGAIN!
MUST STRIKE WHILE HE IS VULNERABLE...USE MY POWER ON THE CROWD...

THAT'S IT, AIN'T IT? I'LL NEVER... NEVER BE... HUMAN... AGAIN...
SO, WHAT'S SO GREAT ABOUT BEING HUMAN?

HUMANS ARE WEAK!
HUMANS ARE FOOLS!
COME WITH US! BE OUR KING!
YES, YOU ARE ONE OF US! BE THE KING OF THE MONSTERS!
N-NO... NO!

NO! I AIN'T A MONSTER!

I AIN'T!
GRUNNCHH

HE'S LASHING OUT--FIGHTING BACK--DRIVING HIS FEAR AWAY!
MUST SWITCH TACTICS AT ONCE...

C'MON, YA DANG REJECTS FROM TH' STAR WARS CANTINA SCENE! I SEEN UGLIER MUGS'N YOURS DOWN ON...

...YANCY STREET?

WHAT HAPPENED? THEY'RE ALL GORGEOUS ALL OF A SUDDEN!
GET BACK, GET AWAY!
IT'S HIDEOUS! A MONSTER!

WHAT'S GOIN' ON HERE? AM I FINALLY CRACKIN' UP? LOSIN' IT? I NEVER MEANT TO HURT NOBODY...
LOOK, HE'S TURNING AWAY!
HA! THE UGLY BRUTE IS AFRAID!
LET'S GET IT!

KILL IT!
CAN'T BE HAPPENIN'! MY WORST NIGHTMARE--
SOMETHING THIS UGLY SHOULDN'T BE ALLOWED TO LIVE!

--I'M ALONE! TH' ONLY MONSTER IN A WORLD OF BEAUTY!
AN' I'LL NEVER BE HUMAN AGAIN!

AT LAST! HE'S GIVING IN TO HIS FEARS-- NOW I CAN DEVOUR THEM!
AHHHH-- SO MUCH SPICIER THAN MERE FEAR OF DEATH. IT'S ALMOST A SHAME THAT WHEN I FINISH MY FEAST MY HOST WILL DIE!

WAITAMINNIT!

:GULP!: THE FEAR FLOW IS EBBING--BUT THERE WAS SO MUCH MORE...
HOW CAN HE BE FIGHTING BACK NOW? HOW?!

GET OFFA ME, YOU CREEPS!
IS THIS TH' WAY YOU TREAT SOMEONE WHO'S HAD A RAW DEAL--BEEN DISFIGURED?

THERE AIN'T A DROP OF HUMAN COMPASSION OR DIGNITY IN TH' LOT OF YA!
YER TH' MONSTERS, NOT ME! FER ALL MY UGLY ORANGE HIDE, BENEATH IT ALL I'M STILL A MAN...

A MAN, Y'HEAR ME?!
AN I'D RATHER LOOK LIKE A MONSTER THAN ACT LIKE ONE!
OH, NO! HE'S STAVED OFF HIS FEAR...
HERE I GO AGAIN!
NOW WHAT? I'M LUMPIN' UP AGAIN! AND ALL THESE "BEAUTIFUL PEOPLE" ARE TURNIN' BACK INTO REG'LAR LOOKIN' FOLKS!
OOGH!
WHAT HIT ME?
LUCKY THING NO SERIOUS DAMAGE WAS DONE! WONDER WHAT HAPPENED HERE?
I HEARD ABOUT A BUNCHA PEOPLE TURNIN' INTA MONSTERS DOWN IN WASHINGTON DC*--MAYBE SOMEONE DUMPED SOME'A THAT DRUG INTA TH' LOCAL WATER.
I'D BEST HEAD BACK TO FF HEADQUARTERS AN' TRY TA DOPE THIS OUT...
*SEE CAPTAIN AMERICA #344 --TERRY.
THIS FAILURE WAS... TOO MUCH. IF I DON'T FIND SOME FEAR TO FEAST ON SOON--
--I SHALL SURELY STARVE TO DEATH!
THE END.

Writer & Artist: **Al Milgrom** • Colorist: **Gregory Wright** • Letterer: **Jim Novak**
Assistant Editor: **Mike Rockwitz** • Editor: **Terry Kavanagh**

the MIGHTY THOR
SILENT THUNDER!
BACK, VILE MISCREANTS, BACK I SAY! THE LIKES OF THEE SHALL NEVER THREATEN NEW YORK WHILE THE SON OF ODIN LIVES!
THAT'S WHAT YOU THINK, THUNDER GOD!
YEAH! THESE EXOSKELETONS OF OURS WERE BUILT TO TAKE ON EVEN YOU, THOR!

INVISIBLE TO THE PANIC-STRICKEN CROWD, THE ALIEN FEAR EATER IS DRAWN BY THE FEAR IT SENSES...
SO... ANOTHER OF EARTH'S COSTUMED DEFENDERS! DO I DARE TRY TO FEAST ON THIS ONE'S FEARS?

CHANCING UPON THE SILVER SURFER IN DEEP SPACE, I LEARNED OF THESE BEINGS WHOSE COURAGE... AND FEARS... TRANSCENDED THOSE OF ORDINARY MORTALS. THE PROSPECT OF SUCH FEAR-LADENED DELICACIES SPURRED ME TO RAVENOUS HUNGER.
BUT THE SURFER, CAPTAIN AMERICA, THE THING--

--EACH OVERCAME HIS DEEPEST FEARS, UNKNOWINGLY REPULSING ME IN THE PROCESS!
NOW, THOUGH THE THOUGHT OF RETURNING TO MY FORMER BLAND FARE-- ORDINARY FEAR OF DEATH OR INJURY--LEAVES ME COLD, I AM NEAR TO STARVING!

BETTER TO GO FOR MY FEAR BASIC FOOD GROUPS! ONCE FORTIFIED, I CAN AGAIN SEEK OUT THE MORE DELECTABLE FORMS OF FEAR.

AND YET...
THE POWER IN YON FORCE BEAM COULD INDEED CRIPPLE E'EN A GOD OF ASGARD--
--BUT MY MYSTIC MALLET DEFLECTS YOUR THRUST--

THE FEAR-EATER "READS" HIS PREY...

THIS BEING IS NO MERE MORTAL! HE HAS LIVED UNTOLD EONS AND EXPERIENCED THINGS THAT WOULD DRIVE A HUMAN TO THE FEAR-FILLED BRINK OF TERROR AND BEYOND! HE IS A **GOD**, AN ***IMMORTAL***, AND AS SUCH, ***DEATH*** HOLDS NO FEAR FOR HIM!

HMMMM... NO FEAR, PER SE!

BUT IF I USE THE LAST OF MY POWER, TRANSFORM HIS SURROUNDINGS...

WHAT MADNESS IS THIS?! BALDER...?!

THE FINAL MADNESS, GOOD FRIEND! **RAGNAROK!** THE ULTIMATE BATTLE BETWEEN THE GODS OF ASGARD AND THE FORCES OF EVIL!

THERE! DESTROY MY HALF-BROTHER AND THE FORCES OF ASGARD WILL FALL LIKE DOMINOES! HEED THE WORDS OF LOKI, GOD OF EVIL!

I SAW NO BLOW STRIKE HIM!
NO MATTER! THOUGH IT PAINS VALIANT VOLSTAGG TO LEAVE THE FRAY, NO ARMS BUT MINE OWN HAVE THE MIGHT TO BEAR MIGHTY THOR TO SAFETY!

WHAT SAY YOU, APOTHECARY? WHAT AILS ODIN'S SON?
I CANNOT EXPLAIN IT, VOLSTAGG! HE IS STRICKEN WITH SOME ILLNESS I KNOW NOT! IT COULD WELL PROVE FATAL!
NO!

THIS IS NO FIT ENDING FOR A GOD OF ASGARD! I SHOULD BE DOWN THERE, LEADING MY LEGIONS IN THE FINAL CONFRONTATION WITH THE EVIL ONES!

DEATH EARNED WHILE FIGHTING FOR A NOBLE CAUSE WOULD I WELCOME AND GLADLY!
BUT TO LIE HERE, STRICKEN, ENFEEBLED WHILE MY COMRADES FIGHT THE GOOD FIGHT...

'TIS TOO MUCH TO BEAR!

YES! FOR YOU IT IS, THOR! IT'S YOUR ULTIMATE FEAR! TO BE FORCED TO ACCEPT A PEACEFUL DEATH WHILE YOUR FRIENDS BATTLE TO SAVE THE UNIVERSE!
AND OH-- WHAT A LOVELY, RARE, DELICIOUS FEAR IT IS!

NO! I SHALL NOT ACCEPT THIS! I MUST NOT!

OOLP! H-HE'S STRUGGLING TO RISE, FIGHTING OFF HIS FEAR!
AM I TO BE THWARTED YET AGAIN?! NO! NO! OH...

NO! TRY THOUGH I MIGHT, I CANNOT JOIN THE FRAY!

YES! THE FEAR FEAST WILL CONTINUE! I'VE BEATEN ONE OF THEM AT LAST!
BUT, WAIT...

VERY WELL THEN, I MUST NEEDS ACCEPT MY FATE! I KNOW THAT THE ARMIES OF ASGARD AND MY BOON COMPANIONS, THE HEROES OF EARTH, WILL RISE TO THE CHALLENGE!

I HAVE LEARNED MUCH IN RECENT YEARS AS I LIVED THE LIFE OF A MORTAL ON MIDGARD, NOT LEAST OF WHICH IS THE MORTAL DESIRE TO DIE A PEACEFUL, PAINLESS DEATH!
THOUGH IT RANKLES ME TO BE ABSENT FROM THIS CONFLICT--

--STILL IS IT SOMETHING I CAN LIVE... OR DIE WITH!

AND WITH THE PASSING OF HIS FEAR, THOR UNWITTINGLY DRIVES THE FEAR EATER FROM HIM AS WELL!
NOOOOOOOOOO!

EH?! I AM BACK IN THE CONCRETE CANYONS OF MIDGARD! WHAT DEVILMENT WAS THIS?
IT MUST HAVE BEEN A FEVER DREAM BROUGHT ON BY THE FORCE BEAMS I DEFLECTED!

NO MATTER! THESE NE'ER-DO-WELLS ARE STILL UNCONSCIOUS, THUS THOR BRINGS THEM TO THE LOCAL AUTHORITIES!

THAT WAS TOO MUCH! I MUST EAT AT ONCE, OR I'LL SURELY STARVE TO DEATH!
NO TIME TO BE FUSSY! I'LL JUST GRAB THE FIRST MORTAL MORSEL THAT COMES ALONG-- BUT THEY'VE ALL FLED FROM THE SITE OF THE BATTLE...

WAIT! HA! THERE'S ONE CURIOSITY SEEKER STILL IN THE VICINITY!
GOOD! ONCE I'M RESTORED, I'LL RETURN TO MY QUEST TO DEVOUR THE FEARS OF EARTH'S SUPER HEROES!
I'VE LEARNED FROM MY FAILURES, THE NEXT TIME I SHALL WIN! AND TOO BAD MY VICTIMS WILL DIE IN THE PROCESS!

BUT NOW, TO ENTER THIS MORTAL...
AND "READ" HIM...

I-I CAN'T READ HIM!

I-IT'S IMPOSSIBLE! HE HAS NO FEAR! NONE!
AND IF HE HAS NO FEAR, THEN WEAKENED AS I AM... I WILL DIEEEEEEEEEEE

FOR A BRIEF INSTANT, THE FEAR EATER, WHO HAS BROUGHT FEAR TO SO MANY, KNOWS THE CLUTCHING TERROR OF FEAR HIMSELF--
--AND THEN IS GONE!

WELL, LOOKS LIKE THOR HANDLED THINGS HERE, GUESS I'M NOT NEEDED AFTER ALL!
I SHOULD HAVE KNOWN, REALLY. AFTER ALL, WHAT COULD BLIND LAWYER, MATT MURDOCK, DO THAT THE GOD OF THUNDER COULDN'T?
EVEN IF WITH MY ENHANCED OTHER SENSES I'M BETTER KNOWN AS:
DAREDEVIL
THE MAN WITHOUT FEAR!
THE END

The BOOK of The VISHANTI
A GATHERING OF FEAR
PART ONE
OF ALL THE MYRIAD GODS AND DEMONS WHO INHABIT THE POCKET UNIVERSES SURROUNDING MAN'S WORLD--AND WHO, LIKE SHARKS CIRCLING A LIFE-RAFT, PREY UPON HUMANITY'S PSYCHIC FLOTSAM--THERE ARE SEVEN WHO, TAKEN TOGETHER, MAY BE CALLED THE FEAR LORDS.
THREE QUALITIES ARE POSSESSSD BY EACH OF THESE ENTITIES.
FIRST: A FEAR LORD IS NO LOWLY DEMON, SUCH AS THE DENIZENS OF DENAK, BUT A MIGHTY BEING WHOSE POWER IS MEASURED ON A COSMIC SCALE.
SECOND: FEAR LORDS ARE NOT MOTIVATED BY BASE CRAVINGS FOR HUMAN WORSHIP OR FOR DOMINION OVER LOWLIER CREATURES; BUT BY DESIRE FOR THE GREATEST, PUREST FEAR--WHICH IS SUSTENANCE AND LIFE ITSELF TO THEM.
ROY THOMAS & JEAN-MARC LOFFICIER WRITERS / LARRY ALEXANDER PENCILER / TONY DeZUNIGA INKER / CLEM ROBINS LETTERS / GEORGE ROUSSOS COLORIST
THIRD: EACH FEAR LORD IS A MYSTERY--HIS ORIGINS, OFTEN HIS VERY EXISTENCE , KNOWN TO FEW.
HOWEVER, IN AN HISTORICAL CONCLAVE HELD IN THE HALLS OF FEAR, CITADEL OF HIM WHO IS CALLED THE DWELLER IN THE DARK, THE SEVEN MET OF LATE...
...HAVING FIRST PASSED DOWN THE LONG, SOMBER CORRIDOR WHOSE NICHES ARE OCCUPIED BY THE SHADE-THRALLS WHO SERVE THE DWELLER.

AROUND A TABLE OF OBSIDIAN, AMID AN IMPOSSIBLY VAST AND SHADOW-BLACKENED HALL, SAT THE FEAR LORDS, IN UTTER DARKNESS.
GRUDGINGLY ACKNOWLEDGING EACH OTHER AS PEERS, THEY HAD COME TO DEFINE AND PERHAPS DEFEND THEIR VARIOUS UNHOLY SPHERES OF INTEREST...
WELL.
WE HAVE SAT HERE FOR DAYS ALREADY... NONE OF US DEIGNING EVEN TO SPEAK, TILL NOW, LEST WE GIVE SOME ADVANTAGE TO THE OTHERS.
STILL, SOMEONE MUST BEGIN...AND AS YOUR HOST, IT WOULD ILL BEHOOVE ME TO BE SO PRESUMPTUOUS.
THEN I SHALL GO FIRST, DWELLER--I, WHOSE PRESENCE IS DREADED THROUGH-OUT THE MULTI-VERSE!
BUT SEEK NOT TO KNOW MY SECRET GENESIS--FOR NONE KNOWS WHENCE I COME OR WHAT I AM--
--WHICH IS AS IT SHOULD BE--
--FOR FEAR, THAT ETERNAL MEAT UPON WHICH WE ALL DO FEAST, MUST ALWAYS REMAIN AS I AM--
--THE LURKING UNKNOWN!*
MANY ARE THE WORLDS I HAVE BROUGHT TO THEIR KNEES, SO I MIGHT FEED UPON THEIR FEARS.
THE ONLY DEFEAT I HAVE EVER MET WAS IN THE TIMELESS PLACE CALLED ASGARD--
--WHERE I WAS SUMMONED BY ODIN HIMSELF, TO DEAL WITH A HUMAN FEMALE KNOWN AS JANE FOSTER.
*SEE LETTERS PAGE FOR SOURCES.--Mike
"FOR REASONS OF HIS OWN, ODIN DID NOT WISH HIS SON TO MATE WITH A MORTAL.

"I CARED NOT. I REVELED IN THE FEAR I CAUSED WITHIN THE WOMAN'S BREAST, AND WOULD HAVE CONSUMED HER--
"--HAD NOT THE THUNDER GOD THOR INTERVENED, THE GODDESS SIF AT HIS SIDE.
"AGAINST TWO SO FEARLESS, I WAS AT A TEMPORARY DISADVANTAGE...
...SO I FLED, THAT I MIGHT TRIUMPH ANOTHER DAY.
MY KIND, TOO, HAS TASTED DEFEAT AT THE HANDS OF THE SO-CALLED 'EARTH GODS.'
I AM KKALLAKKU, HATCH LORD OF THE KKALLAKKI...KNOWN THROUGHOUT THE COSMOS AS THE FEAR EATERS.
"MY SPECIES, EVEN MORE THAN SOME OF YOU SIX, MUST FEED UPON THE FEARS OF SENTIENT CREATURES, SIMPLY TO GO ON EXISTING.
"THAT IS NOT ONLY OUR NEED, HOWEVER--BUT ALSO OUR ULTIMATE GRATIFICATION.
"WE KKALLAKKI TAKE GREAT PLEASURE BOTH IN CREATING--AND THEN IN EXTRACTING--THE DELECTABLE EMOTION OF FEAR FROM THE LOWER ORDERS, WHICH WE ALWAYS CONSIDERED NOTHING MORE THAN DEFENSELESS CATTLE...
"--UNTIL ONE OF OUR NUMBER ENCOUNTERED THE SO-CALLED SILVER SURFER.
"THE FORMER HERALD OF WORLD-DEVOURING GALACTUS RESISTED ALL OUR COUSIN'S PSYCHIC EFFORTS TO PLANT THE SEEDS OF TERROR WITHIN HIM...
"...YET INADVERTENTLY TOOK HIM BACK TO THE PLANET EARTH.

"THERE, ASTONISHINGLY, HE FAILED TWICE MORE TO DRIVE MAD WITH FEAR THE TWO EARTHLINGS KNOWN UNAPPETIZINGLY AS THE CAPTAIN AND THE THING.
"FOR, WHEN HE WAS FINALLY CAST OUT BY A FOURTH INTENDED VICTIM--THE SELFSAME THOR JUST SPOKEN OF--
"I ASK YOU--WHAT SORT OF NAMES ARE THESE, COMPARED WITH THE MAGNIFICENT MULTISYLLABISM OF OUR OWN?
"--OUR COUSIN PERISHED, AFTER TRYING IN DESPERATION TO ENTER A BLIND HUMAN WHO WAS TRULY A MAN WITHOUT FEAR.
"AND WHAT NOURISHMENT, I WONDER, NURTURES CERTAIN HUMANS, THAT THEY COULD SURVIVE OUR MENTAL ONSLAUGHT?
SINCE THEN, WE KKALLAKKI HAVE STAYED AWAY FROM THE EARTH.
BUT WE WOULD WELCOME ANY ALLIANCE WHICH MIGHT DESTROY IT--BEFORE IT CONTAMINATES OTHER WORLDS WE COVET.
IS THAT WHAT I WAS SUMMONED HERE TO CONSIDER?
UNLIKE YOU OTHERS, I--THE SCARECROW--HAVE LONG RESIDED UPON THE EARTH.
I CONSIDER IT MY WORLD, IN A SENSE.
"I EVEN FOUGHT ALONGSIDE THAT SAME MAN-CREATURE WHOM THIS GOAT-FACED SLUG CALLED THE THING, AGAINST A FLAMING DEMON WHO MENACED IT.
GANGWAY, STRAW MAN! IT'S CLOBBERIN' TIME!
"THE DEMON, HOWEVER, WAS MERELY A LACKEY...

"...THE SERVITOR OF THE DEMON-KING KALUMAI.
"THOUGH HE THOUGHT HIMSELF A GOD, KALUMAI ACTED THROUGH SUCH MINOR DEVILS--AND ONCE EVEN TOOK OVER THE BODY OF A HUMAN--
"BUT, IN THE END, I MYSELF DESTROYED HIM.
KNOW YOU THIS, MY FELLOW FEAR LORDS--
I AM NO MERE MAD MORTAL, LIKE THIS SO-CALLED "SCARECROW" WHO HAS LATELY BATTLED THE VENGEFUL GHOST RIDER.
YOU DO NOT KNOW WHO I AM--WHAT I AM--YET I KNOW YOU CAN SENSE THE STARK FEAR I COMMAND.
I WARN YOU--I WARN YOU ALL--
--STAY AWAY FROM THE EARTH!
AND NOW--I TAKE MY LEAVE OF YOU.
THE LAUGHTER OF THE SCARECROW ECHOES IN THE GREAT HALL, LONG AFTER ITS HUMAN INITIATOR IS GONE.
BUT THE FEAR LORDS HAVE GATHERED HERE FOR A GRIM PURPOSE...
...AND IT WILL TAKE FAR MORE THAN A THING OF LIVING CLOTH AND STRAW TO DETER THEM.
HEE HEE HEE HEE HEE HEE HEE HEE HEE HE
NEXT: THE HOPES AND FEARS...

The BOOK OF The VISHANTI
A GATHERING OF FEAR
PART TWO
...AND AFTER THE DEPARTURE OF THE MOCKING SCARECROW, ONLY SIX OF THE FABLED FEAR LORDS REMAINED IN THE HALLS OF FEAR:
THEIR HOST, THE DWELLER IN THE DARK... THE LURKING UNKNOWN... KKALLAKU THE FEAR-EATER... NIGHTMARE... D'SPAYRE...
THOMAS * LOFFICIER * ALEXANDER * DZON * ROBINS * ROUSSOS
...AND THE DARK-CLAD WOMAN CALLED NOX.
WE HAVE HEARD THE TALES OF THE LURKING UNKNOWN...AND OF THE FEAR-EATER...AND RECEIVED NAUGHT BUT INSULTS FROM THE SO-CALLED SCARECROW.
PERHAPS YOU, WHO ARE LITTLE KNOWN TO ANY OF US, WILL HONOR US WITH YOUR STORY, NOX.
IN MANY WAYS, YOU ARE THE MOST MYSTERIOUS OF US ALL.
FEW IN ALL THE MULTIVERSE HAVE EVEN HEARD OF YOU.
EVEN I KNEW NOT FOR CERTAIN WHETHER YOU TRULY EXISTED...LET ALONE WHETHER YOU WOULD ANSWER MY SUMMONS.
I ANSWERED YOUR...INVITATION... BECAUSE IT AMUSED ME, DWELLER.
FOR ME, FEAR IS NOT A WEAPON...NOR EVEN A SOURCE OF NOURISHMENT...
...BUT RATHER, A MATTER OF AESTHETIC PLEASURE.
IT GIVES ME INEFFABLE JOY TO CREATE THE MOST INTRICATE FEAR PATTERNS AMONG THE "HELPLESS ONES".
YOU MEAN...AMONG MORTALS.
WHO ELSE SHOULD I MEAN?
STILL, EVEN IN MY MOST INDIRECT MACHINATIONS, I HAVE COME INTO CONTACT WITH SOME OF THE SAME EARTHLINGS WHO HAVE THWARTED YOU, MY FELLOW FEAR LORDS.
PERHAPS MY EXPERIENCE WILL PROVE ENLIGHTENING TO YOU...

"MY NAME, OF COURSE, MEANS NIGHT IN THE GRECIAN TONGUE...
"...THOUGH I AM OLDER, EVEN, THAN THOSE OLYMPIANS WHOM SOME OF THE 'HELPLESS ONES' WORSHIPPED AS GODS, ONLY ONE OR TWO MILLENNIA AGO.
"ONCE, POSING AS THE LOVE-GODDESS APHRODITE, I MADE LOVE TO THE WAR-GOD ARES.
"HE REVOLTED ME...BUT MY PURPOSE WAS TO BEAR TWO CHILDREN...
"PHOBOS AND DEIMOS...'FEAR' AND 'TERROR'... WHOSE EXISTENCE WOULD SHAKE THE HEAVENS.
"MY CHILDREN, ALAS, WERE LATER SLAIN BY HERCULES AND HIS ASGARDIAN ALLY, THOR.
"I SHALL NEVER FORGIVE EITHER OF THEM FOR THAT ACT.
"SOMEWHAT LATER, I SOUGHT TO UNLEASH FEAR BY ANOTHER METHOD.
"UNKNOWN TO HIM, I SECRETLY GUIDED A RENEGADE SCIENTIST'S EFFORTS TO UNLOCK THE ENIGMA OF FEAR.
"AFTERWARD, HE CALLED HIMSELF PSYCHO-MAN.
FEAR
DOUBT
HATE
"BUT HE, TOO, MET DEFEAT ...AT THE HANDS OF INTER-FERING MORTALS KNOWN AS THE FANTASTIC FOUR.
"BY NOW, EARTH HAD PIQUED MY CURIOSITY.
"THOUGH ONLY A BACKWATER WORLD, IT HAD PRODUCED SEVERAL BEINGS WHO STRONGLY RESISTED THE URGINGS OF FEAR.

"NOT LONG AFTERWARD, I CHANCED UPON A CERTAIN DEMON MAKING HIS WAY THROUGH THE COSMOS.
"HE WAS THOG, THE NETHERSPAWN, WHO HAD JUST ESCAPED FROM THE WORLD OF THEREA.
"WITHOUT HIS KNOWLEDGE, I ARRANGED FOR HIM TO OBTAIN A CONSTRUCT HE DUBBED THE 'NIGHTMARE BOX.'
"THIS HE USED TO ERECT A PYRAMID, WHOSE SHEER FEAR-FORCE, WHEN RELEASED, WOULD HAVE PLUNGED ALL MANKIND OVER THE SHEER CLIFFS OF MADNESS.
"ALAS, THOG'S DESIGNS WERE THWARTED BY AN ENCHANTER NAMED DAKHIM--
"--WITH THE HELP OF HIS ALLY, A LOATHSOME MIRE-BEAST KNOWN AS THE MAN-THING--
"--WHO DESTROYED THOG, IN A WEIRDLING DISPLAY OF POWER.
EEE
YAAH
I AM STILL NOT ENTIRELY SURE HOW--
YES, D'SPAYRE?
PLEASE FORGIVE MY INTERRUPTION, LADY NOX--BUT I, TOO, HAVE ENCOUNTERED THAT MUCK-MONSTER...
OH?

BUT, OF COURSE, I AM SUCH A MINOR GODLING, COMPARED TO YOU OTHERS GATHERED ABOUT THIS TABLE...
YOU ARE HERE BECAUSE YOU, TOO, ARE A FEAR LORD, D'SPAYRE.
WE WOULD HEAR WHAT YOU HAVE TO SAY.
THEN, WITH YOUR KIND PERMISSION...
"AS YOU KNOW, I WAS SERVING YOUR CAUSE, GREAT DWELLER, AGAINST THE SELFSAME DAKHIM AND HIS YOUNG DISCIPLE, JENNIFER KALE.
"I SUCCEEDED IN TAKING THEM CAPTIVE...
"...BUT THEN I, TOO, WAS DEFEATED BY THE MAN-THING... IN THE COMPANY OF ANOTHER OF EARTH'S COSTUMED MORTALS, SPIDER-MAN.
"I HAVE SINCE COME TO REALIZE THE TRUTH OF THINGS...
THE MAN-THING WAS CREATED NOT MERELY TO PROTECT THE NEXUS OF REALITY...BUT ALSO AS A WEAPON AGAINST US, THE FEAR LORDS!
HOW ELSE EXPLAIN ITS UNCANNY ABILITY TO MYSTICALLY DESTROY FEAR ITSELF--BY MEANS OF ITS FIERY TOUCH?
FOOLS! COWARDS!
WHAT?
FOR ALL YOUR POSTURING, D'SPAYRE, YOU ARE A MERE SHADOW OF YOUR MASTER...
...WHILE THE LOVELY NOX'S GOALS ARE TOO ARCANE, HER METHODS FAR TOO DEVIOUS.
AND YOU CAN SHOW US HOW TO TEACH MANKIND THE TRUE MEANING OF FEAR, NIGHTMARE?
YOU, WHO CAN ATTACK THEM ONLY WHEN THEY SLEEP?

WHO COULD POSSIBLY KNOW MORTALS BETTER THAN ONE WHO COMES TO THEM WHEN THEY ARE MOST VULNERABLE?
THE FEAR-EATERS? THEY WILL EVENTUALLY BE BETRAYED BY THEIR OWN UNCONTROLLED APPETITES... OR ELSE RUN OUT OF VICTIMS.
AND THE LURKING UNKNOWN'S OBSESSION WITH MYSTERY IS POINTLESS, HIS METHODS MUCH TOO CRUDE!
YOU DARE--?
I DARE, BECAUSE I AM SLY!
I STRIKE IN THE DEPTHS OF SLUMBER.
I CAREFULLY NURTURE MY HUMAN HERD, TAKING ONLY WHAT SUSTENANCE I NEED--ALLOWING THEM TO REPLENISH THEMSELVES, FOR ANOTHER NIGHT'S FEAR-FEEDING.
YOU BOAST --BUT YOU HAVE BEEN DEFEATED AGAIN AND AGAIN BY THE SORCERER, STEPHEN STRANGE...
...AMONG OTHERS.
AND WEREN'T YOU, NIGHTMARE, ONCE SWATTED LIKE A MERE FLY BY THE ENTITY ETERNITY?
YET YOU WOULD GIVE LESSONS TO US!?
IN MY OWN WAY, YES.
BUT YOU HAVE KEPT SILENT TILL THE LAST, MINE HOST.
SURELY IT IS TIME YOU ENLIGHTENED US WITH THE TALE OF YOUR OWN FAILURE AGAINST THE MORTAL HEROES...
I HAVE FAILED ONLY IN TACTICS, NIGHTMARE--NEVER IN MY BROADER STRATEGY.
AND THAT, MY FELLOW FEAR LORDS, IS PRECISELY WHY YOU WERE SUMMONED HERE...!
NEXT: THE PLOT!

RECENTLY, IN HIS DIMENSIONAL DOMAIN, THE DWELLER IN THE DARK MET WITH HIS SIX FELLOW FEAR LORDS...
...BEINGS WHO THRIVE, IN ONE WAY OR ANOTHER, UPON THE FEARS WHICH LURK IN THE HEARTS OF LESSER BEINGS.
SLOWLY, GUARDEDLY, THEY ARE MAKING THEMSELVES KNOWN TO EACH OTHER...
The BOOK of The VISHANTI
A GATHERING OF FEAR
PART III
ROY THOMAS & JEAN-MARC LOFFICIER - WRITERS
LARRY ALEXANDER - PENCILS
TIM DZON -- INKS
PAT BROSSEAU -- LETTERS
GEORGE ROUSSOS - COLORS
...AFTER THEIR FASHION.
NIGHTMARE, D'SPAYRE, NOX, KKALLAKKU, AND THE LURKING UNKNOWN HAVE RELATED THEIR HATRED OF THE HUMAN RACE...
...AND THE SNEERING SCARECROW IS GONE, AFTER DARING TO WARN US TO STAY AWAY FROM THE EARTH PLANE...
THUS, IT NOW BEHOOVES ME TO TELL YOU WHY WE MUST ACT TOGETHER AGAINST DESPISED MANKIND.
IN A SENSE, NIGHTMARE, YOU AND I ARE COUSINS OF A SORT.
WE BOTH COME FROM EVERINNYE, A UNIVERSE HIGHER THAN THE SIXTH DIMENSION--
--THOUGH YOU MAY NOT RELISH BEING REMINDED OF IT.
I AM NO ONE'S "COUSIN" --LEAST OF ALL YOURS, DWELLER!
YOU RENOUNCED ANY POSSIBLE KINSHIP BETWEEN US WHEN YOU CHOSE THE WAY OF THE SHAMBLU--
--THUS BECOMING UNSPEAKABLY FOUL AND UNCLEAN BY THE STANDARDS WHICH ARE THE ONLY THING WE FEAR LORDS HAVE IN COMMON!
MY ESTEEMED COUSIN, I NEED HARDLY REMIND HIM, HAS INSTEAD CHOSEN TO DEGRADE HIMSELF BY ADOPTING HIS PRESENT SHAPE-- AND BY LIVING IN EXILE AMONG THE LOWER UNIVERSES.
DO NOT CRITICIZE MY WAYS, COUSIN-- AND I SHALL NOT CRITICIZE YOURS!

"SINCE I FIRST LAID EYES UPON THE EARTH, IT HAS CIRCLED ITS STAR SOME 20,000 TIMES.
"ATLANTIS WAS PROMINENT AMONG ITS KINGDOMS THEN, RULED OVER BY KING KAMUU AND QUEEN ZARTRA--
"--WHILE THE DEVILISH DEVIANTS RULED LEMURIA.
"THERE WAS MUCH FEAR I COULD HARVEST AND DEVOUR, DURING THE CONSTANT WARFARE BETWEEN MAN AND DEVIANT...
"BUT NOW, A NEW FACTOR THRUST ITSELF INTO THE EQUATION.
"THE ATLANTEAN SORCERESS ZHERED-NA HAD JUST BEEN EXILED BY KAMUU TO THE LANDS WHICH WOULD BE ONE DAY KNOWN AS THE AMERICAS.
"HELPED BY VALKA, AND BY AGAMOTTO THE ALL-SEEING, ZHERED-NA DETECTED MY PRESENCE AND MY PURPOSE.
"IN WORLDS BETWEEN WORLDS, SHE DID CONTEST WITH ME FOR HER NEWFOUND HOME.
"SHE BESTED ME, BUT EVEN AGAMOTTO'S POWER WAS NOT ENOUGH TO DESTROY ME.
"SHE COULD ONLY PLUNGE ME INTO A STATE OF MYSTICAL SLUMBER--
"--AWARE, BUT IMMOBILIZED, IN AN INTER-STITIAL UNIVERSE, ADJACENT TO THAT OF THE EARTH.

"EVEN SO, I WAS ABLE TO SIPHON OFF SOME OF THEIR GREAT FEAR--
"--A RESIDUE OF INCREDIBLE FORCE AND POWER WHICH HAD BEEN BIRTHED IN THE CATA-CLYSM BROUGHT ABOUT BY THE SKY-BORN CELESTIALS--
"--AND THERE-BY TO IMBUE A PORTION OF MY CONSCIOUSNESS WITH INDEPEN-DENT LIFE.
"I NAMED THE ENTITY... D'SPAYRE.
"AYE, THAT SAME D'SPAYRE WHO SITS, EVEN NOW, AT THIS TABLE.
"THIS DONE, IT WAS CHILD'S PLAY FOR D'SPAYRE TO USE THE PANIC CAUSED BY THE GREAT CATACLYSM TO MANIPULATE A HAPLESS CULTIST INTO KILLING ZHERED-NA.
"THUS, EVEN UNMOVING, I HAD MY REVENGE.
"HOWEVER, GUIDED BY KEEN-EYED AGAMOTTO, ZHERED-NA HAD ALREADY PREPARED ONE OF HER DISCIPLES, DAKIHM--
"--ENDOWING HIM WITH IMMORTALITY, TO CARRY ON HER FIGHT.
"MANY A BATTLE, OVER ENSUING CENTURIES, DID D'SPAYRE AND DAKIHM JOIN.
"NEITHER COULD EVER QUITE GAIN THE UPPER HAND OVER THE OTHER...
"YET, EACH TIME, I MYSELF, ABSORBED A BIT MORE PRECIOUS FEAR--
"--BRINGING ME CLOSER, EVER CLOSER, TO THE DAY OF MY RE-LEASE!

"FROM TIME TO TIME, OVER THE AGES, I CREATED OTHER PUPPETS TO HELP ME SPREAD MY GREAT FEAR IN THE REALMS OF MEN.
"ONE RECENT PAWN, INFLUENCED BY DREAMS I SENT FROM AFAR, WAS A SCULPTOR NAMED ZOLTAN DRAGO...
"...WHO, RECHRISTENING HIMSELF 'MR. FEAR,' UNKNOWINGLY FASHIONED HIS MASK TO RESEMBLE MY OWN FACE.
"MY SHADE-THRALLS FOUGHT SUCH GODLINGS AS THOR AND HERCULES IN THE SEWERS BENEATH ONE OF MEN'S GREATEST CITIES...
"...AND LATER, EVEN DR. STRANGE AND HIS PARAMOUR, THE LOVELY IF MIS-ALLIED CLEA.
"IT WAS THE LATTER ENCOUNTER, AND THE PRETERNATURAL FEAR I ABSORBED FROM CLEA, WHICH FINALLY ENABLED ME TO FREE MYSELF FROM MY PARALYSIS OF MILLENNIA.

"INTRIGUED BY THIS SORCERER STRANGE, I SENT NEW PAWNS TO SEE HOW THEY FARED AGAINST HIM:
"FIRST, THE BEAUTIFUL DREAM WEAVER...
"...THE TWIN DEMONS KNOWN AS LUDI...
"...AND FEARSOME NINGAL."
I--AND YOU OTHER FEAR LORDS, IF YOU DEIGN TO ADD YOUR POWERS TO MINE AND REAP THE REWARDS THERE-FOR--
--SHALL NOW SEE EARTH, AND PERHAPS ALL THE COSMOS, ENGULFED AT LONG LAST BY-- THE GREAT FEAR!
AT LEAST, CERTAIN LONG-LAID PLANS OF MINE HAVE SLOWLY REACHED MATURITY.
YET, THE END RESULT, DWELLER, IS THAT, THUS FAR, YOU HAVE FARED NO BETTER THAN WE AGAINST THE LOATHSOME MORTALS AND THEIR VARIOUS GUARDIANS.
THAT, NIGHTMARE, IS PRECISELY WHERE YOU ARE WRONG.
FOR, STILL OTHER PAWNS HAVE I PLACED IN POSITION...
AND SO THEY SHALL--A FEW SHORT ISSUES FROM NOW.

MARVEL COMICS
THE GREAT FEAR PART 1 OF 3
DR. STRANGE
SORCERER SUPREME
1.75 US
$2.15 CAN
38
FEB
UK 95p
APPROVED BY THE COMICS CODE AUTHORITY
30TH ANNIVERSARY
THE FANTASTIC FOUR
1961-1991
THE FURY OF THE FEAR LORDS!

HE WAS ONCE A SURGEON—AN ARROGANT MAN-OF-THE-WORLD SEDUCED BY MATERIAL WEALTH. THEN, WHEN A TRAGIC ACCIDENT DEPRIVED HIM OF HIS SURGICAL SKILLS, **STEPHEN STRANGE** DISCOVERED A SEPARATE REALITY, A HIGHER PLANE OF OCCULT FORCES IN ETERNAL CONFLICT. VOWING TO BE EARTH'S FIRST LINE OF DEFENSE AGAINST MAGICAL MENACE, THE ERSTWHILE PHYSICIAN BECAME EARTH'S FOREMOST MASTER OF THE MYSTIC ARTS! STAN LEE PRESENTS . . .

DOCTOR STRANGE, SORCERER SUPREME!

OR, TO DISPENSE WITH THE ROLE-PLAYING MELODRAMA, RINTRAH--
--READY OR NOT, HERE I COME!
UH-- MASTER, ARE YOU CERTAIN THIS IS THE PROPER WAY TO PURSUE MY THAUMATURGICAL TRAINING?
I SWORE I'D TURN YOU INTO A REAL SORCERER--
WHOOOFF--!
--OR ELSE ONE OF US WAS GOING TO DIE TRYING!
I-- DID NOT SUSPECT-- I WAS INTENDED--
--TO TAKE YOUR OATH QUITE SO LITERALLY!
SURRENDER--
--AND I'LL LEVITATE DOWN AND CATCH YOU!
WHAT? RINTRAH-- SURRENDER?!
THE MOST PROMISING MANOTAUR-CUM-MAGICIAN ON ALL R'VALL--
--ENITHARMON THE WEAVER'S MOST TALENTED SPELL-SPINNING APPRENTICE--
--BOW HIS BROAD NECK TO THE YOKE?!
I SAY THEE NAY!
BY HOGGOTH!

HAVE I HARMED YOU IN A RARE MOMENT OF REVERSION TO A GENETICALLY-DETERMINED BESTIAL INTEMPERANCE?
IF I DID-- I SHALL NEVER FORGIVE MYSELF.
M-MASTER--?

BUT SURELY MY BOLT OF BEDEVILMENT DID NOT WHOLLY D-DESTROY YOU?
ARE YOU ALIVE, BEHIND THESE CLOUDS OF OCCULT OBFUSCATION?
SPEAK TO ME, MASTER!

WHAT
DO
YOU
WANT ME
TO SAY?
MASTER! THANK THE VISHANTI BUT WHICH ONE OF YOU IS--?

"THERE ONCE WAS AN AMBITIOUS MAN-BULL..."
"...WHOSE TALES OF PROWESS WERE MOSTLY COCK-AND-BULL."
"WHEN HE CHALLENGED HIS SUPERIOR..."
"...HE GOT KNOCKED ON HIS POSTERIOR..."
"...FROM HYPER-SPACE CLEAR TO ISTANBUL!"
TH-THAT DOES IT!

BY ALL THE WOVEN WORLDS-- I'LL NOT BE MOCKED!
HAH! I KNEW I COULD FORCE THE REAL DR. STRANGE OUT INTO THE OPEN--

--WHERE WE SHALL SEE PRECISELY WHO SHALL HURL WHOM--
--TO THE HISTORICALLY SIGNIFICANT PORT FORMERLY KNOWN AS CONSTANTINOPLE!
STEPHEN!

RINTRAH--HOLD UP!
SOMEONE'S CALLING--

THWAMM!
ARRRHH--!

OH, NO! I'VE DONE IT AGAIN!
I CHARGED RIGHT THROUGH HIS HALF-FORMED SERAPHIMIC SHIELD!
MY BULLISH TEMPER WILL YET BE THE DEATH OF ME!

FUNNY--I THOUGHT--IT WAS GOING TO BE--MINE!
MASTER! THANK THE VISHANTI YOU'RE--
YES, YES... WE'VE BEEN... ALL THROUGH THAT.
YOU SEE HOW IT IS, SARA...

BOYS WILL BE BOYS...

...EVEN WHEN THEY'RE GROWN MEN AND EXTRA-TER-RESTRIALS.
I SWEAR TO YOU, MISTRESS CLEA-- IT WAS MERELY--
SHE'S JUST PULLING YOUR HOOF, DISCIPLE.
SO, SARA-- HOW DID THE DARK DIMEN-SION'S FORMER PROM QUEEN DO, HER FIRST DAY ON THE JOB AT THE METAPHYSICAL INSTITUTE?
ARE THERE ANY SPOONS LEFT UNBENT?
I THINK I'LL LET HER TELL YOU...
I'M GOING TO LIKE WORKING THERE, STEPHEN...
...INVESTIGATING WHAT PASSES FOR PSI-POWERS IN THIS RELATIVELY MUNDANE SPHERE.
BUT SARA WAS SHOW-ING ME THE ROPES...
"...WHEN ONE OF HER 'REGULARS' SUDDENLY CAME STAGGERING IN..."
YOU'VE GOT TO HELP ME!
THE MIND
HAS YOURS REACHED IT'S FULL POTENTIAL?
MEMORIAL METAPHYSICAL INSTITUTE
NOW, JOANNE, WHAT CARD AM I HOL--
MR. BARRIE? YOUR APPOINT-MENT'S NOT UNTIL--
I--I'M AFRAID, MS. WOLFE! YOU'VE GOT TO HELP ME--RIGHT NOW!
I'M HAVING NIGHT-MARES!

BUT, SIR, EVERYONE HAS NIGHT-MARES...
WHEN THEY'RE WIDE AWAKE ?!
L-LOOK! THERE IT IS AGAIN!

I DON'T SEE ANY-THING.
YOU DON'T? IT'S A DIMENSIONAL APERTURE-- RIGHT HERE IN THIS ROOM!
THEN-- IT'S REAL?!
THAT'S EVEN WORSE!

I CAN'T TAKE THIS ANY-MORE!

DON'T WORRY, SARA--I HAVE HIM.
MEMORIAL METAPHYSICAL INSTITUTE PARKING

AND IF HE HADN'T FAINTED-- AND JOANNE RUN SCREAMING OUT OF THE CUBICLE --YOU'D ALSO HAVE THE BIGGEST MEDIA HEADACHE SINCE MORGANA BLESSING WROTE HER BOOK ABOUT STEPHEN!
UH-- WHAT DO YOU SEE NOW?
ACTUALLY...

NOTHING...
...NOW.

BUT, ON THE WAY, WE ENCOUNTERED TWO MORE PEOPLE HAVING THE EXACT SAME "DAYMARE"!
EACH TIME, I COULD SEE IT-- BUT SARA COULDN'T--
--AND NEITHER COULD ANY-ONE ELSE, EXCEPT THE PERSON HAVING IT.
SOUNDS LIKE A PHENOMENON VISIBLE ONLY TO THOSE WITH INNATE SUPER-NATURAL POWERS.
RINTRAH, I'M AFRAID OUR SORCERY LESSON WILL HAVE TO BE POSTPONED...

THAT'S QUITE ALL RIGHT, MASTER. I'M RATHER USED TO IT.
THERE! AT LEAST I'VE SUFFICIENT MAGIC TO REPAIR THE DAMAGE TO THE WALL.

I MUST FIND OUT HOW WIDESPREAD THIS EPIDEMIC IS.
GOING UPSTAIRS TO CHECK OUT THE ORB OF AGAMOTTO, EH, DOC?
WELL, ACTUALLY, I THOUGHT I'D DO WHAT MOST FOLKS DO IN A SITUATION LIKE THIS...

...AND GO DOWN-STAIRS TO SEE IF THERE'S ANY NEWS OF IT ON CNN!
KLIK
BUT SARA'S RIGHT. THE ORB GENERALLY SUMMONS ME, LIKE A DOCTOR'S BEEPER, WHEN SOMETHING MYS-TICAL HAPPENS.
IN A MOMENT, I'LL TRY TO FIND OUT WHY IT DIDN'T.

FIRST, THOUGH, WE'LL--
HI out there, all you little hitchikers on the highway to hel...
HOLY HOGGOTH! THAT'S NOT DAVE GOODENOW!

This is your old buddy ROADKILL, and his flat cat SPLATT, telling you how we got this way--namely DEAD.

It was a HIT-AND-RUN DRIVER who put these TIRE TREADS on my chest, right, Splatt?

YOU'RE RIGHT, ROADIE.

Now we're doomed to wander the highways and byways until we FIND that socially irresponsible driver, and teach him/her a much-needed lesson concerning common courtesy on the road...

RINTRAH--DO YOU KNOW WHAT THIS IS?

IT'S A CABLE ANTHOLOGY SHOW I OFTEN WATCH, MASTER.

I CHANGED THE CHANNEL EARLIER...

Anyway, tonight's story is about an ARCTIC EXPLORER who's devoured by a GIANT PREHISTORIC CATERPILLAR.

IT'S CALLED, "THE EARLY WORM GETS THE BYRD."

So light up a cigarette, swig down a beer, UNfasten that silly old seat belt--

Not SICK, Doc-- DEAD!
MATTER OF FACT, YOU DON'T LOOK SO GOOD YOURSELF!
KRASH

Come, Splatt. We'll try our luck on THIS side of the fourth wall!
OHHHH
MASTER--!
RINTRAH-- WE'VE GOT TO STOP HIM!

My, we ARE in an assertive mood, aren't we?
Well, until we meet AGAIN--

--Keep on TRUCKIN'!
HE GOT AWAY!
SARA--HOW'S STEPHEN?

HE'S ONLY STUNNED, BUT-- CAN'T YOU FOLLOW THAT CREEP?
CLEA? RINTRAH? WHY DON'T YOU ANSWER ME?
PERHAPS, MY DEAR WOMAN, IT'S BECAUSE--

--THEY HAVE MORE URGENT THINGS TO CONCERN THEM JUST NOW.
IS IT NOT FIT-TING THAT I SHOULD INVITE A FEW OF YOU INTO MY HOME? AFTER ALL--
--HAVE I NOT BEEN INTRUDING, EVER SO SLIGHTLY, INTO THE WAKING WORLD?
I SUSPECTED YOU, THE MOMENT I HEARD ABOUT THOSE "DAYMARES"--AND I'M SURE CLEA DID, AS WELL.
WHY ARE YOU DOING--WHATEVER IT IS YOU ARE DOING?
I--I KNOW THAT GUY--FROM MORGANA'S BOOK!
HIS NAME IS NIGHT-MARE.
THE MANSION IS GONE--AND WE'RE IN HIS DREAM DI-MENSION!
THAT IS NONE OF YOUR AFFAIR, STRANGE. BE WARNED!
WE FEAR LORDS HAVE AN AGEN-DA--
--AND IF YOU AND YOUR LITTLE FRIENDS TRY TO THWART US, YOU WILL REGRET IT!
STEPHEN'S "LITTLE FRIENDS" DON'T STEP ASIDE FOR ANYONE!
COME ON, RINTRAH!
INDEED! EVEN WITH THE MASTER STILL CATCHING HIS BREATH, WE STILL OUTWEIGH AND OUTNUMBER THIS BRINGER OF BAD DREAMS!

YOU--HAD TO SAY THAT-- DIDN'T YOU?
I WOULD ASK NIGHTMARE FROM WHERE HE SUMMONED THIS DIRESOME DROVE OF DEMONS--
--BUT I SUPPOSE HE MERELY--DREAMED THEM UP.
YOU ALL RIGHT, DOC?
YES. STRIKING MY HEAD MADE ME RECALL--I READ OF THE "FEAR LORDS" RECENTLY, IN THE BOOK OF THE VISHANTI.
THEY MUST HAVE REPRESSED MY MEMORY SOMEHOW--AND HIDDEN THEMSELVES FROM THE ORB, TO BOOT.
NOW THAT I REMEMBER--I'VE GOT TO GET RID OF ALL THESE DISTRACTIONS!
AND I'D BETTER HURRY--
--BEFORE THOSE GARGOYLES DRAG CLEA AND RINTRAH OFF INTO REGIONS WHERE I CAN'T EASILY FOLLOW!
BY THE WARP AND WOOF OF THE WOVEN WORLDS--THEY'RE GONE!
WE'VE FRIGHTENED THEM AWAY, LADY CLEA.
WELL, WE WERE HOLDING OUR OWN, ANYWAY--
--THOUGH I SUSPECT THAT MYSTICAL WHIRLWIND OF STEPHEN'S MIGHT BE WHAT TURNED THE TIDE.
OH.
BY THE AWESOME POWER OF OMNIPOTENT OSHTUR--BE YOU GONE!

I HOPE YOU ARE SUFFICIENTLY PROUD OF YOURSELF -- DRIVING OFF A FEW PITIFUL PHANTOMS.
I DON'T FIGHT TO SALVE MY PRIDE -- ANY MORE THAN I'D BOAST ABOUT SCARING PEOPLE HALF TO DEATH WITH DAY-DREAMS.
WHAT ARE YOU AND YOUR FELLOW FEAR LORDS UP TO, NIGHTMARE?
I AM A CREATURE OF THE NIGHT, STRANGE.
IT IS HARDLY MY MISSION TO ENLIGHTEN.
AS THE DWELLER REQUESTED, I HAVE ADMONISHED YOU NOT TO OPPOSE US.
I TOLD HIM YOU WOULD NOT LISTEN--BUT HE WOULD INSIST ON GIVING YOU FAIR WARN-ING.
IT NOW SEEMS WE WILL BE FORCED TO DESTROY YOU--
--AND I, FOR ONE, WOULD NOT HAVE IT ANY OTHER WAYYYY!
HE'S GONE--
--AND THAT MEANS THIS MANIFESTATION OF HIS DREAM DIMENSION WON'T LONG SURVIVE HIS PASSING!
IT DOESN'T...

...BUT **WE** DO, THANKS TO A PROTECTIVE SPHERE.
ARE YOU ALL RIGHT, SARA?
YOU ARE NOT AS ACCUSTOMED AS WE ARE TO SUCH MULTIVERSAL MACHINATIONS...
I'LL... LIVE, RINTRAH.

IF I WANTED A QUIET, **MAGIC-FREE** LIFE, I'D HAVE FLIPPED THE CHANNEL ON "*DR. STRANGE'S NEIGHBORHOOD*" A LONG, **LONG** TIME AGO.
BUT-- STEPHEN, IF I'M NOT BEING NOSY-- WHO ARE THOSE **"FEAR LORDS"** NIGHTMARE MENTIONED?

HIMSELF-- SOME **OLD FOES** OF MINE--AND AN ENTITY OR TWO EVEN I'D NEVER HEARD OF.*
WHICH REMINDS ME--I'D BETTER CHECK THE ***BOOK OF THE VISHANTI***AGAIN--
--AND FIND OUT WHY THE **ORB OF AGAMOTTO** DIDN'T ALERT ME EARLIER ABOUT THOSE **DAYMARES.**

*SEE DOC #31-33. --MIKE.

HELLO. SINCE OUR HOST, **ROADKILL**, IS TEMPORARILY INDISPOSED--THIS IS **SKIRRA CORVUS,** OWNER OF THE **HORROR NETWORK**--
--WITH AN OPEN CHALLENGE TO **DR. STEPHEN STRANGE!**
WHAT--!?!
WE AT **HORROR-TV** WISH TO **DEBATE** THE CONTROVERSIAL SUBJECT OF MORGANA BLESSING'S RECENT BESTSELLER--

--BUT THUS FAR HE HAS REFUSED TO **RESPOND** TO OUR LETTERS AND TELEPHONE CALLS.
HERE AND NOW, WE PUBLICLY **REPEAT** OUR CHALLENGE TO THE SO-CALLED "WIZARD OF BLEECKER STREET"--
--TO APPEAR ON **HORROR-TV** TO DISCUSS THE REALITY AND FALSENESS OF **MAGIC.**

FRANKENSTEN
THE TV-MOVIE
I NEVER GOT ANY MESSAGES FROM--
AND NOW, THE REALLY AUTHENTIC, ACCURATE, NO-LIE VERSION--ACTUALLY BASED ON MARY SHELLEY'S NOVEL, FOR ONCE...
I'M AFRAID THAT ONE'S NOT GOING TO LEAP OUT OF THE TV, STEPHEN...

THEN I'M GOING TO GO SEE HIM, RIGHT NOW!
EVEN BEFORE YOU CHECK YOUR TALISMANS?
YES. CARE TO COME ALONG?
OF COURSE I WANT TO COME.

RINTRAH, I WON'T INSIST--BUT IF YOU COULD STAY, TO MAKE SURE SARA DOESN'T SUFFER ANY DE-LAYED TRAUMAS--
I SHALL NOT FAIL IN MY DUTY, MASTER.
I'M SURE YOU WON'T.

NOW, A SIMPLE SPELL OF INVISI-BILITY, AND WE'RE OFF.
I KNOW YOU, STEPHEN. YOU THINK THERE'S MORE TO THIS TV MOGUL'S CHAL-LENGE THAN MEETS THE EYE--
--OR WE WOULDN'T BE GIVING IT TOP PRIORITY.
YES. CALL IT "WIZARD'S INTUITION," IF YOU WILL.
EVEN SO, I'M SURPRISED THAT YOU KNOW OFF-HAND WHERE TO FIND THIS NEW CABLE OPERA-TION.
I PASSED THE BUILDING ONCE BEFORE...

...AND IT'S NOT *TOO* HARD TO FIND.

DON'T TURN *VISIBLE,* TILL THAT *SECRETARY* TURNS HER HEAD.

EXCUSE ME, MISS, WE--

MS. MARMELSTEIN, WILL YOU PLEASE SEND *DR. AND MRS. STRANGE* RIGHT IN?

UH... YOU *HEARD* HIM.

"DR. AND MRS. STRANGE"?

THANK YOU. THAT WILL SAVE CONSIDERABLE *TIME.*

ALL RIGHT, MR. CORVUS...

SINCE YOU KNOW SO MUCH ABOUT CLEA AND MYSELF, WE'LL LET *YOU* DO THE TALKING--*FIRST.* .

YOU MAY ALREADY KNOW THAT *HORROR-TV* EMERGED VIRTUALLY *OVERNIGHT*--OFFERING ITS SERVICES TO SUBSCRIBERS AT LUDICROUSLY LOW RATES.

ACTUALLY, WE'VE BEEN A LITTLE *BUSY...*

I BEGAN THIS CABLE NETWORK TO QUICKLY *UP THE ANTE,* SO TO SPEAK, ON *HUMAN TOLERATION OF FEAR.*
MANKIND IS GOING TO *NEED* ALL THAT TYPE OF ENDURANCE IT CAN ATTAIN-- AND *SOON.*
SO WHAT'S YOUR CONNECTION TO *NIGHTMARE* AND THE *FEAR LORDS?*
PLEASE, MRS. STRANGE --I'D LIKE TO TELL THIS *MY OWN WAY.*

THERE'S SOMETHING *WRONG* WITH THIS MAN, STEPHEN--
--AND MY *SPELL* WILL SOON GET TO THE *BOTTOM* OF IT!
CLEA...
NO, DON'T *DISCOURAGE* HER, MAGICIAN...

...PERHAPS IT *IS* BETTER TO GET THIS *OVER* WITH!
BY MY FOREBEARS, THE *FALTINE*--!

ALLOW ME TO RE-INTRODUCE MYSELF, VIA MY ***THOUGHTS***.
I HAVE BEEN CALLED THE ***SCARE-CROW***--
--BUT I PREFER THE APPELLATION ***"STRAW MAN,"*** TO AVOID CONFUSION WITH A CERTAIN ***MORTAL PSYCHOTIC***.

IF YOU WANTED TO FOOL ***ME***, YOU'D HAVE AVOIDED A PHONY NAME LIKE *"SKIRRA CORVUS"*--OLD ICELANDIC FOR *"SCARE,"* AND LATIN FOR *"CROW."*
I WISHED TO PIQUE YOUR ***CURIOSITY***, NOT DECEIVE YOU.
I HARDLY NEEDED THAT, AFTER TODAY'S ENCOUNTERS WITH ***NIGHT-MARE***, ONE OF YOUR FELLOW ***FEAR LORDS***...
FORMER FELLOWS, YOU MEAN.

"TRUE! I KNOW YOU ***WALKED OUT*** ON THE CONCLAVE CALLED BY THE ***DWELLER IN THE DARKNESS***...*
"...EVEN ADMONISHING THEM TO KEEP THEIR FEAR-INSPIRING HANDS ***OFF*** THE EARTH.
"BUT WHAT ABOUT ***D'SPAYRE***, THE ***FEAR-EATER***, THE ***LURKING UNKNOWN***, AND THAT MYSTERY-WOMAN ***NOX***?
*DOC #31-33.-MIKE.

I KNOW ***YOU'VE*** FOUGHT ON THE SIDE OF ***RIGHT*** IN THE PAST...
BUT THE ***DWELLER*** MANAGED TO KEEP HIS EXACT ***PLANS*** A SECRET EVEN FROM MY TALISMANS.
AND I, IN TURN, REGRET LEAVING BEFORE I LEARNED THEM. PERHAPS ***TO-GETHER*** WE CAN--
STEPHEN--

--I FEEL SOMETHING ***MATERIALIZING*** IN THIS VERY ROOM!
YOUR POWERS ARE STILL ***ACUTE***, CLEA.
OVER THERE--

--THE LURKING UNKNOWN!
IS THIS SOME TRAP THE STRAW MAN LAID FOR US?
YOU WRONG ME, WOMAN--AND TO PROVE IT--

HE SACRIFICED HIMSELF--AN ENTITY WE HARDLY KNEW--YET I FEEL SUCH DESPAIR AT HIS LOSS--!
OF COURSE! THAT CAN ONLY MEAN THAT STILL A THIRD FEAR LORD MUST BE PRESENT.
SHOW YOURSELF--
--D'SPAYRE!
YOUR HUMBLE SERVANT, MY DEAR DOCTOR.

WHAT ARE YOU DOING HERE, SKULL-FACED ONE?
THE DWELLER IN THE DARKNESS SENT ME TO DEAL WITH THE TRAITOR--AND WITH ANY WHO DARED DE-FEND HIM.
UNWORTHY AS I AM OF BEING A FEAR LORD, I MERELY WISHED TO HELP, BY INDUCING FEELINGS OF DEPRESSION AND HOPELESS-NESS, AS IS MY WONT.
BUT IF YOU DO NOT WANT MY "WONT"--

--I SHALL MOST MODESTLY TAKE MY LEAVE.
TAKE IT--AND GET OUT--

--SO I CAN DEAL WITH DR. STRANGE!
GOOD! THIS PLACE WAS GETTING ALL CLUTTERED UP WITH FEAR LORDS!

MR. CORVUS? I THOUGHT I HEARD SOMETHI--

YEEEK--!

I THINK I'LL TAKE MY COFFEE BREAK NOW.

EXCELLENT, CLEA! YOUR SPELL'S BLINDED THE LURKER!

YOU TOLD ME MOST OF THIS CONCLAVE FEED ON FEAR.

SINCE OUR FEAR OF THEM IS LESS THAN MOST PEOPLE'S WOULD BE, AT LEAST HE WON'T BE GAINING STRENGTH AS WE DO BATTLE.

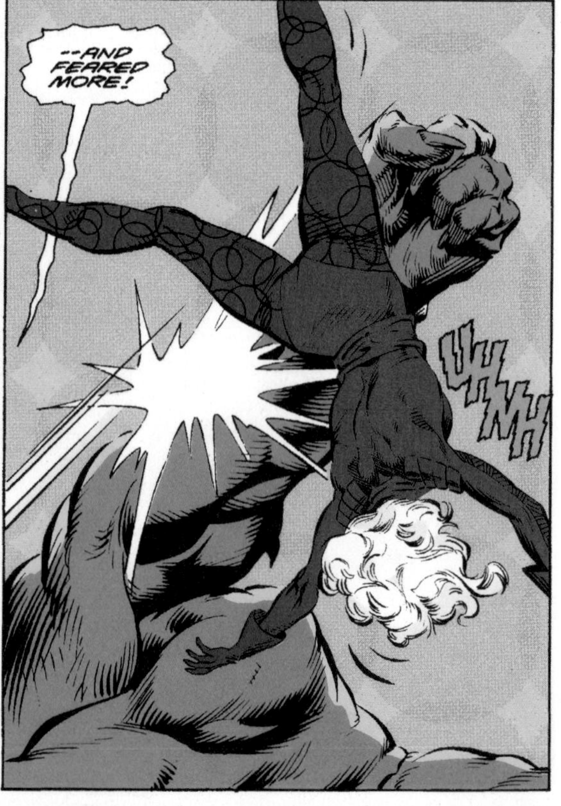

YOU'LL PAY FOR THIS, FIEND!
HAH! IT TOOK TWO ASGARD-IANS--THOR AND SIF--TO HAND ME MY SOLE DEFEAT!
WHAT MAKES YOU THINK YOU, ALONE, CAN DO AS WELL AS THEY?

BECAUSE I SENSE THAT YOU'RE A FRAUD--
--ONE THAT THE HOARY HANDS OF HOGGOTH CAN DEFEAT--THUS--
YAARRGG--!

YOU HAVE HURLED YOUR MAGICAL MIGHT AGAINST ME, MAGE--
--AND YOU HAVE FAILED!
NOW, YOU SHALL SEE WHY THE NAME OF THE LURK-ING UNKNOWN IS FEARED ACROSS THE COSMOS!

YOU CALL "LURKING UNKNOWN" A NAME?
IT SOUNDS MORE LIKE SOME SORT OF TRANS-DIMENSIONAL DISEASE!
LET'S TAKE HIM, STEPHEN!

HE HAS NO CHANCE--NOW!
SOMETHING'S--HAPPENING TO HIM--!
HE WAS BEATEN, THE MOMENT WE STOPPED FEARING HIM--
--AND GOT ANGRY, INSTEAD!
FOR, A FEAR NOT FEARED--IS NO FEAR, AT ALL--
NOOOOOOOO
--AND DIMINISHES TO THE POINT OF NOTHING-NESS!
HE WAS THE CRUDEST OF THE FEAR LORDS--WITH POWER OF COSMIC OR MINUSCULE PROPORTIONS, DE-PENDING UPON THE EMOTIONS HE COULD STIR WITHIN HIS PREY.
BUT WHAT DO HE AND THE OTHER FEAR LORDS WANT, STEPHEN?
WHAT'S THIS "GREAT FEAR" THE LURKER SPOKE OF?
EVEN WITH OUR MYSTIC POWERS, CLEA, WE CAN ONLY GUESS. BUT--
HEAR ME, DWELLER--NIGHTMARE--D'SPAYRE--ALL YOU SKULKERS WHO FEED OFF THE FEARS THAT DWELL IN THE BENIGHTED CORNERS OF MANKIND'S SOUL!
WE WILL NOT PASSIVELY AWAIT YOUR COWARDLY ATTACK.
WE SHALL SEEK YOU OUT--AND SMASH YOU--THE VISHANTI BE OUR WITNESS!
I LIKE THE WAY YOU PUT THAT, STEPHEN.
WHAT?
"WE."

SO, D'SPAYRE...
...YOU DARE RETURN TO MY HALLS OF FEAR, DESPITE HAVING SUFFERED ABJECT DEFEAT.
I AM MORTIFIED, O DWELLER IN DARK-NESS...
TRULY, COMPARED TO ALL THE FEAR LORDS SAVE THE DISGRACED LURKER, I AM AN INSIGNIFICANT WORM.
IN THAT, AT LEAST, YOU ARE CORRECT, COUSIN.
AND YET-- FORGIVE ME, COUSIN--YOUR OWN ENCOUNTER WITH STRANGE WAS SOMETHING LESS THAN AN UNABASHED VICTORY.
A DRAW IS NOT A FAILURE!
ENOUGH! I JOINED A CABAL OF SEVEN, AND NOW--
--ONE FEAR LORD HAS DESTROYED ANOTHER, TO BE BESTED IN TURN-- AND WE OTHERS SQUABBLE AMONG OURSELVES.
I, WATCH LORD OF THE FIRE-EATERS, FEEL AS DOES THE LADY NOX.
THE LURKER'S SACRIFICE SHALL NOT BE IN VAIN, KKALLAKKA.
WE WHO FEAST ON FEAR HAVE NOW PLEDGED OURSELVES TO CREATE IT IN UNBRIDLED ABUNDANCE--
--TO REDUCE ALL HUMANITY TO A STATE OF QUIVERING, UNREASONING, UN-CEASING TERROR!
AND IF THE SELF-STYLED SORCERER SUPREME STANDS ATHWART OUR FIVE-STRONG PATH--
--HE SHALL BE SWIFTLY REDUCED TO THE MOST PITIABLE, FEAR-FILLED WRETCH OF ALL--
--BY THE GREAT FEAR!
NEXT: FEAR AND TREMBLING...

MARVEL COMICS
THE GREAT FEAR PART 2 OF 3
DR. STRANGE
SORCERER SUPREME
1.75 US
$2.15 CAN
39
MAR
UK95p
APPROVED BY THE COMICS CODE AUTHORITY
SHERWOOD '91
30TH ANNIVERSARY
1962 1992
THE AMAZING SPIDER-MAN

...AND NOW THERE ARE FIVE.
FIVE MASTERS OF COSMIC DREAD-- FIVE HARBINGERS OF THE ULTIMATE HORROR THAT LURKS GIBBERING AT THE DARK CENTER OF HUMAN EXISTENCE.
FEAR IS ALL.
AND THUS, WE ARE ALL.
FOR WE ARE THE FEAR LORDS!
A MOST INSPIRATIONAL SPEECH, DWELLER IN DARKNESS.
YOU'VE NOT ENDURED AS MANY OF THEM AS I HAVE, KKALLAKKU.
YET SURELY IT DOES NOT BODE WELL FOR THE "GREAT FEAR" WE MEAN TO SPREAD ON EARTH--
--THAT THE LURKING UNKNOWN WAS DEFEATED BY DR. STRANGE.
IT WAS OUR TRAITOROUS FELLOW FEAR LORD, THE SCARECROW, WHO WAS AT FAULT THERE, D'SPAYRE.
AYE, NOX! IT WAS HE WHO UNDID OUR SPELL OF OBVIATION, WHICH HAD WIPED ALL KNOWLEDGE OF US FROM STRANGE'S MIND.
I STAND MOST HUMBLY CORRECTED, ONE AND ALL.
STILL, IT IS UNFORTUNATE THAT DR. STRANGE LIKEWISE ESCAPED THE CLUTCHES OF MYSELF AND NIGHTMARE.
YOURS, ONLY! I WAS SENT MERELY TO WARN HIM AWAY.
IF HE NOW RESISTS OUR ATTEMPT TO REDUCE MANKIND TO SHIMMERING BLOBS OF SENTIENT FEAR, ON WHICH WE ALL MAY FEED-- HE IS DOOMED.
THEN-- TO YOUR APPOINTED TASKS, MILORDS!
AND WHEN YOU FOUR FOOLS-- GORGED ON MEN'S TERRORS-- BECOME A MERE FEAR-FEAST FOR THE DWELLER IN DARKNESS--
--ALL THE MULTIVERSE SHALL LEARN THE TRUTH ONCE SPOKEN BY A ROMAN HUMAN CALLED STADIUS:
"IT WAS FEAR THAT FIRST MADE GODS IN THE WORLD!"

THE FEAR THAT KILLS! *

* WILLIAM WORDSWORTH.

I STILL DON'T *UNDERSTAND*, STEPHEN.

WHY ARE YOU HANGING A PORTRAIT OF THAT *STRAW MAN* WHO WAS KILLED AT THE *HORROR-TV* OFFICE?

BECAUSE IT'S THE *ONLY THING* THERE THAT *SURVIVED* OUR BATTLE WITH THE *LURKING UNKNOWN*, SARA.*

I WONDER-- HOW CAN YOU TELL A *"REAL"* SCARECROW--WHEN A REAL SCARECROW IS ONLY AN *IMITATION HUMAN?*

*LAST ISSUE.--MIKE.

ROY & DANN THOMAS -- WRITERS
GEOF ISHERWOOD - PENCILER
JIM SANDERS III -- INKER
PAT BROSSEAU - LETTERER
GEORGE ROUSSOS - COLORIST
MIKE ROCKWITZ -- EDITOR
TOM DeFALCO - EDITOR IN CHIEF
WITH SPECIAL THANKS TO R.J.M. LOFFICIER

BACK IN THE DARK DIMENSION, I'M BETTING.
AM I THAT TRANSPARENT? DEALING WITH COSMIC ENTITIES ALWAYS REMINDS ME THAT, DESPITE BEING MARRIED TO STEPHEN, MY PLACE ISN'T REALLY ON EARTH, AT ALL.
I'M HARD PRESSED TO RESIST RETURNING TO MY FORMER REALM, TO SEE HOW MY MOTHER AND HER NEW CONSORT ARE RUNNING THINGS.
I'D THINK THAT MIGHT INTEREST YOU, TOO, SARA.
NOT PARTICULARLY.

WE SHOULD LOOK IN ON UMAR AND MORDO-- AND WE WILL-- AS SOON AS WE'VE DEALT WITH THE FEAR LORDS.
BUT, YOU KNOW, THIS STRAW MAN'S ALWAYS BEEN A MYSTERY, EVEN TO ME...
YES, WONG?

IMEI AND I WERE SHOPPING FOR OUR COMING WEDDING, MASTER, WHEN--
WELL, PERHAPS YOU'D BEST LOOK OUTSIDE.
OUTSIDE?

DO YOU HAVE ANY OPINION ON THE MASTER'S PHILOSOPHICAL PARADOX, CLEA?
WHAT? SORRY, RINTRAH. MY MIND WAS...ELSEWHERE.
HE WAS ONCE A SURGEON—AN ARROGANT MAN-OF-THE-WORLD SEDUCED BY MATERIAL WEALTH. THEN, WHEN A TRAGIC ACCIDENT DEPRIVED HIM OF HIS SURGICAL SKILLS, STEPHEN STRANGE DISCOVERED A SEPARATE REALITY, A HIGHER PLANE OF OCCULT FORCES IN ETERNAL CONFLICT. VOWING TO BE EARTH'S FIRST LINE OF DEFENSE AGAINST MAGICAL MENACE, THE ERSTWHILE PHYSICIAN BECAME EARTH'S FOREMOST MASTER OF THE MYSTIC ARTS! STAN LEE PRESENTS . . . DR. STRANGE, SORCERER SUPREME!
BY THE HOARY HOSTS OF HOGGOTH!
IT'S PITCH BLACK OUT THERE--
--IN THE MIDDLE OF THE MORNING!
KRUNK!
EVEN FLASH-LIGHTS--CAR LIGHTS--CAN BARELY PENETRATE THE DARK-NESS!
CLEA--RINTRAH--LET'S GO!
THOSE PEOPLE NEED HELP!

INTERESTING. *MY* ALIEN EYES SEEM TO UTILIZE THE MINIMAL AMOUNT OF LIGHT AVAILABLE RATHER BETTER THAN--

MORTY'S CARPET WORLD

KRASH

WHA--?

LOOK OUT, GAUDILY-ATTIRED FEMALE!

TH-*THANKS,* MAN! YOU SAVED MY--

HEY! WHAT'S WRONG WITH YOU, ANYWAY? YOU FEEL LIKE A *WALKING HAIRBALL!*

I AM MERELY A PUBLIC-SPIRITED *CITIZEN,* DOING HIS DUTY, AND--

HE'S GOT *HORNS!* FOR CRYIN' OUT LOUD--

MORTY'S

THE GUY'S GOT HORNS!

--WITH ALL-REVEALING LIGHT!!
MORTY'S
MORTY'S
YOU'VE PUSHED THE BLACKNESS BACK, STEPHEN--
--THE WAY I ONCE DID, IN THE DARK DIMENSION!
DO NOT GIVE YOUR MYSTIC MATE UNDUE CREDIT, WOMAN.
I HAVE NOT YET TRULY BEGUN TO TEST HIS METTLE.
WHO'S THAT--STEPPING THROUGH A HOLE IN THE GLOOM?
I AM NOX--SHE WHOSE VERY NAME MEANS "NIGHT"!
NOX--YOU'RE A FEAR LORD, AND I CAN'T ALLOW YOU ONTO THIS ASTRAL PLANE!
BUT I KNOW YOU'RE NOT LIKE THE OTHERS.
THEY MUST EITHER CREATE OR DEVOUR FEAR SIMPLY TO LIVE--WHILE, WITH YOU, IT'S MORE A MATTER OF PERSONAL AESTHETICS.
SHALL WE ATTEMPT TO SMITE HER, MASTER?
NOT JUST YET.
YOU HAVE LEARNED MORE ABOUT US THAN IT IS SAFE FOR YOU TO KNOW, MORTAL.
THEN YOU MUST ALSO BE AWARE THAT I HAD TWO SONS, WHOM I LOVED...
...PHOBOS AND DEIMOS.

PHOBOS AND DEIMOS.
FEAR AND TERROR!
I WAS PROUD OF THEM, IN AN AGE GONE BY--BUT THEY WERE BASELY SLAIN, BY THE EARTH-GODS THOR AND HERCULES.*
IN NIGHT WERE THEY CONCEIVED AND BIRTHED--
NO, MAGE, I DO NOT NEED FEAR TO SURVIVE, OR EVEN TO THRIVE--BUT MY SONS DO.
I JOINED THE DWELLER'S NEBULOUS GROUPING BECAUSE, AS THEY SPREAD FEAR AND TERROR IN THIS DIMENSION, THE CONDITIONS WOULD BE BETTER THAN EVER BEFORE FOR THE REINCARNATION OF MY BELOVED CHILDREN.
*AS REVEALED IN D.S. #32. --MIKE.
DON'T LOOK NOW, BUT I THINK THE GOOD MOTHER NOX JUST UPPED THE ANTE ON US!
THE "ANTI" -WHAT, MASTER?
ANTI-US, RINTRAH.
--IN NIGHT SHALL THEY BE BORN ANEW!
GREETINGS FROM OBLIVION--
--MOTHER DEAREST!

LOOK INTO OUR FACES, MAGE! DO WE NOT INSPIRE FEAR?
DO WE NOT FILL YOUR HEART WITH TERROR?
NOTHING THE DIVINE POWER OF THE SERAPHIM CAN'T SHIELD ME FROM!
AT LEAST THERE ARE BUT TWO OF THEM.
RIGHT! RINTRAH, YOU CHARGE THEM FROM THE REAR, WHILE STEPHEN AND I--
NNOOO
WHAT'S WRONG, MY LOVE? I DON'T SEE-- BY MY GREAT ANCESTOR KAN!
WH-WHAT ARE THEY, WONG?
I THINK DR. STRANGE TOLD ME THEY ARE CALLED--
--FEAR-EATERS!
THE SKY, ALREADY BLACK, SEEMS DARKER YET AS A MULTITUDE OF THE DREAD KKALLAKKI POUR FORTH THROUGH A SPACE WARP.
CONSIDERABLY SMALLER NOW THAN THEIR HATCH LORD KKALLAKKU, THEY, TOO, WILL GROW LARGER BY DRINKING IN THE FEAR THEY ENGENDER--
AAAAA
--AND THERE'S LIKELY TO BE PLENTY OF THAT!
EEEE SOMEBODY G-GET THEM OFF ME!
CLEA-- RINTRAH-- CAN YOU HOLD OFF THE TERROR TWINS FOR A FEW MOMENTS?
NO PROB-LEM.
GOOD, BECAUSE THEN--

--I CAN DEAL WITH THE *FEAR-EATERS!*

CLEA--ARE YOU TRULY CERTAIN WE ARE THE *EQUAL* OF THIS PAIR?

NO. BUT IF I HADN'T *SAID* WE WERE--

--HE WOULDN'T HAVE *LEFT!*

HOW *NOBLE*--FOR WITH HIS DEPARTURE, YOUR *FEAR* INCREASES, DESPITE YOUR BEST EFFORTS--

--AND WE BECOME *STRONGER*, WITH EACH TREMULOUS QUIVER!

MAY THE HOARY HAND OF *HOGGOTH* MY CLOISTERED MIND *UNCHAIN*--THAT THE *FEARS* WHICH MEN BESET--

--NOW FLOW INTO *MY BRAIN!*

IT *WORKS!* I CAN *FEEL* IT WORKING.

IN AN INSTANT, THE SUM OF ALL THE *FEARS* GENERATED BY THE KKALLAKKI FLOWS FROM *HUMAN* MINDS INTO *MINE*.

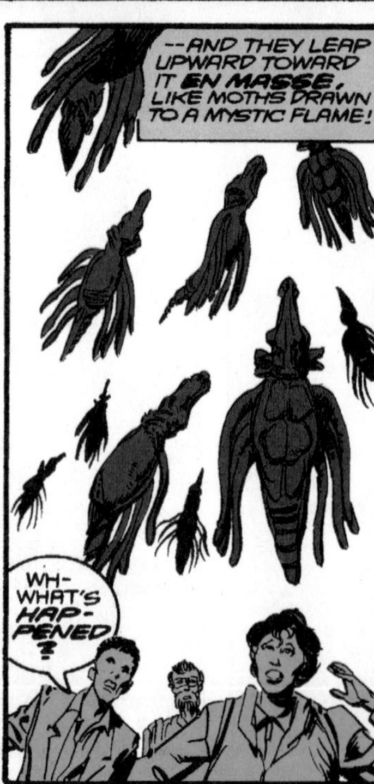

ALL THEY CAN SEE AND SMELL AND TASTE IS THE MIASMA OF FEARS WHICH SWIRLS ABOUT ME LIKE AN ARO-MATIC FOG.
THE FEAR THEY SENSE IS NOT FEIGNED.
NOT SINCE I WAS A CHILD HAVE I BEEN SO TERRIBLY, IRRATIONALLY AFRAID.
I LEVITATE HIGH INTO THE AIR, FOR I KNOW THAT IS MY ONLY POSSI-BLE ESCAPE...
BUT THE KKALLAKKI FOLLOW, LIKE PIRANHAS SCENT-ING BLOOD.
EVEN THE HATCH LORD JOINS IN, SUCCUMB-ING TO THE HUNGER RISING WITH-IN HIM.
AND I REALLY THINK I MIGHT JUST DIE OF FRIGHT, ANY SECOND NOW.
NOR HAVE I ANY PITY TO SPARE, AT THE MOMENT, FOR WHAT IS HAPPENING BELOW...
WELL DONE, MY LOVING SONS!
YOU MAKE YOUR MOTHER PROUD!
WE HAVE FAILED, MISTRESS CLEA!
WE-- DID ALL WE COULD!
HIGH ABOVE, ALL I CAN THINK OF-- THE THOUGHT THAT FILLS MY MIND TO OVER-FLOWING--
--IS THAT I MUST FLEE STILL FURTHER, IF I'M TO RID MYSELF OF THE FEAR-EATERS...

...AND THAT THOUGHT, TOO, IS FATHER TO A DEED.
A FEW CHOICE WORDS TO THE FALTINE, AND A GATE-WAY OF FLAME OPENS BEFORE ME.
DESPERATELY, I PLUNGE THROUGH IT--
--INTO THE DI-MENSION BEYOND.
LOCUSTS WITH NO WILLS OF THEIR OWN, THE FEAR-EATERS SWARM IN AFTER ME...
BUT THEN, TO THEIR ALIEN ASTONISHMENT, THEY CAN NO LONGER DETECT MY PRESENCE.
IT IS AS IF I HAVE VANISHED FROM SIGHT AND SENSES.
I REALLY HAVEN'T, OF COURSE...
IT'S JUST THAT THE SIZE-DISTORTION ON THIS ASTRAL PLANE HAS SHRUNK BOTH MY PHYSICAL SELF--
--AND WITH IT, MY MAGICALLY-ABSORBED FEARS--
--TO THE POINT WHERE THE KKALLAKKI CAN NO LONGER PERCEIVE ME.
THE URGE TO SELF-PRESER-VATION DOES THE REST.
I DIVE BACK THROUGH THE DIMENSIONAL APERTURE--
--TO FIND THAT SPATIAL DISPLACE-MENT HAS CAUSED ME TO ERUPT INTO THE SKY SOME WHERE ABOVE THE ATLANTIC.
I WONDER FEAR-FULLY IF THERE'S BEEN TEMPORAL DISPLACEMENT, AS WELL.
IF SO, I MAY HAVE COME OUT IN SOME FAR-FLUNG FUTURE, OR IN THE AGE OF PRE-MAMMALIAN MOLLUSKS.

YET, IN THIS MOMENT, IT'S THE KKALLAKKI THAT I'M REALLY AFRAID OF--
--SO MY SPELL SHRINKS THE FIERY FALTINIAN GATEWAY TO NOTHINGNESS, TRAPPING THEM IN ANOTHER REALITY.
...AND NOW THERE ARE FOUR.
YOU DO MY WORK WELL, STEPHEN STRANGE...ALL UNSUSPECTING.
AND WHAT, PRECISELY, IS YOUR WORK, DWELLER IN DARKNESS?
BUT THEN, YOU CAN HEAR ME NO MORE THAN STRANGE CAN HEAR YOU.
AND YET I AM HUMBLED BY HOW PRESCIENT YOU WERE CONCERNING OUR FELLOW FEAR LORDS, DEAR NIGHTMARE.
YOU PREDICTED* THAT THE LURKING UNKNOWN WAS FAR TOO CRUDE TO BEST DR. STRANGE--
--WHILE THE FEAR-EATERS WOULD BE BETRAYED BY THEIR OWN UNCONTROLLED APPETITES.
I ALWAYS SENSED YOU HAD NO REAL INTEREST IN THE GROUPING OF FEAR LORDS YOU SUMMONED.
D'SPAYRE! SO YOU MISTRUSTED THE DWELLER ALL ALONG, AS WELL?
YOU ARE MERELY USING US--
--FOR SOME SECRET PURPOSE I ONLY NOW BEGIN TO FATHOM.
* IN DOC #32--MIKE.

YOU HAVE BECOME A **GROVELER!**

YOU AND I KNOW HIM SO MUCH **BETTER** THAN THE OTHERS DO.

AS ONE OF **LESSER** POWER THAN EITHER OF YOU--

--I SIMPLY WISH TO AVOID BEING OBLITERATED IN THE **CROSSFIRE.**

YOU WERE NOT **ALWAYS** SO SELF-EFFACING.

IT IS BECAUSE I WAS MENTALLY **CREATED** BY THE DWELLER, TO DO HIS BIDDING WHILE HE LAY DREAMING.

YOU CAN AFFORD TO **DESPISE** HIM BECAUSE HE CHOSE THE **WAY OF THE SHAMBLU,** THUS BECOMING UNSPEAKABLY **FOUL** BY YOUR STANDARDS.

I MUST TREAD A **MIDDLE** PATH BETWEEN YOU TWO ENTITIES FROM THE DIMENSION **EVERINNYE,** ABOVE THE SIXTH DIMENSION.

AND NOW I TAKE MY LEAVE, BUT REMEMBER, PLEASE--

--BE **GENTLE** WITH US LOWLIER FORMS.

GOOD RIDDANCE!

IT IS THE LADY **NOX** WHO INTERESTS ME NOW.

IT IS ***TIME...***

...TIME THESE TWO WERE **EXECUTED,** BY THE **SWORD OF NIGHT** WHICH STEALS SOULS EVEN AS IT SLAYS!

AS IF A MERE **BEHEADING** WERE NOT **FINALITY** ENOUGH?

AT LEAST SPARE MISTRESS **CLEA,** I PRAY YOU...

DON'T ASK FOR FAVORS FOR ME, RINTRAH!

I WAS ONCE A **QUEEN**-- AND I'LL MEET MY FATE AS I FIND IT.

WONG-- SHE MEANS TO **KILL** THEM!

CAN'T WE GET THROUGH THAT **MYSTIC FIELD** AROUND THEM?

NO...

YOU WERE THE BANE OF LIGHT, CLEA, IN A DIMENSION OF BLESSED DARK-NESS.
FOR THAT REASON ALONE, IF FOR NO OTHER, I SHALL SLAY YOU FIRST.
I'D SPIT IN YOUR EYE--
--IF YOUR OFFSPRING DIDN'T FILL ME WITH SUCH FEAR.
EH?
A SCINTILLA OF BRIGHT-NESS AMID THE NIGHT!
THEN I MUST STRIKE QUICKLY, BEFORE--
WHAT'S THIS? SHIELDS FORM AROUND THEM--
--AND MYSTIC TALONS GRASP ME, FROM OUT OF NOWHERE!
PHOBOS! DEIMOS! SHATTER THE SHIELDS AND SLAY OUR CAPTIVES!
CAPTIVES NO LONGER, LADY NOX!
THAK
AH! BLUSH THOUGH I DO TO ADMIT IT, IT IS GOOD TO KNOW THERE IS STILL A PLACE IN THE COSMOS FOR SHEER BRUTE STRENGTH.

LOOK AT THEM!
THESE TWO AREN'T EVEN BLACK AS NIGHT ANY LONGER--BUT FADING TO GREY!
MOTHER--
--HELP US!
NOW EVEN MY WEAVE-SPELLS OVERCOME THEM.
I NO LONGER FEEL AFRAID OF THESE TWO--
BECAUSE, DISCIPLE--
--WHEN I TRIUMPHED OVER MY FEARS, I WAS FREE TO DRAIN SOME FROM YOU AND CLEA, AS WELL!
SO THAT IS WHY I SUDDENLY FELT EMBOLDENED TO LASH OUT AGAINST THESE SECOND-GENERATION GODLINGS!
STEPHEN! THANK THE FALTINE YOU'RE ALL RIGHT!
AND THE TERROR TWINS ARE REVERTING TO NOTHING!
THEY ARE, YES-- BUT NOT SO NOX!
YOU HAVE ROBBED ME A SECOND TIME OF MY SONS, STRANGE.
IN RETURN, I SHALL ROB YOU OF THOSE BELOVED BY YOU!
WATCH OUT, RINTRAH!
THE TENDRILS OF NIGHT CAN STRANGLE THE VERY SOUL--!

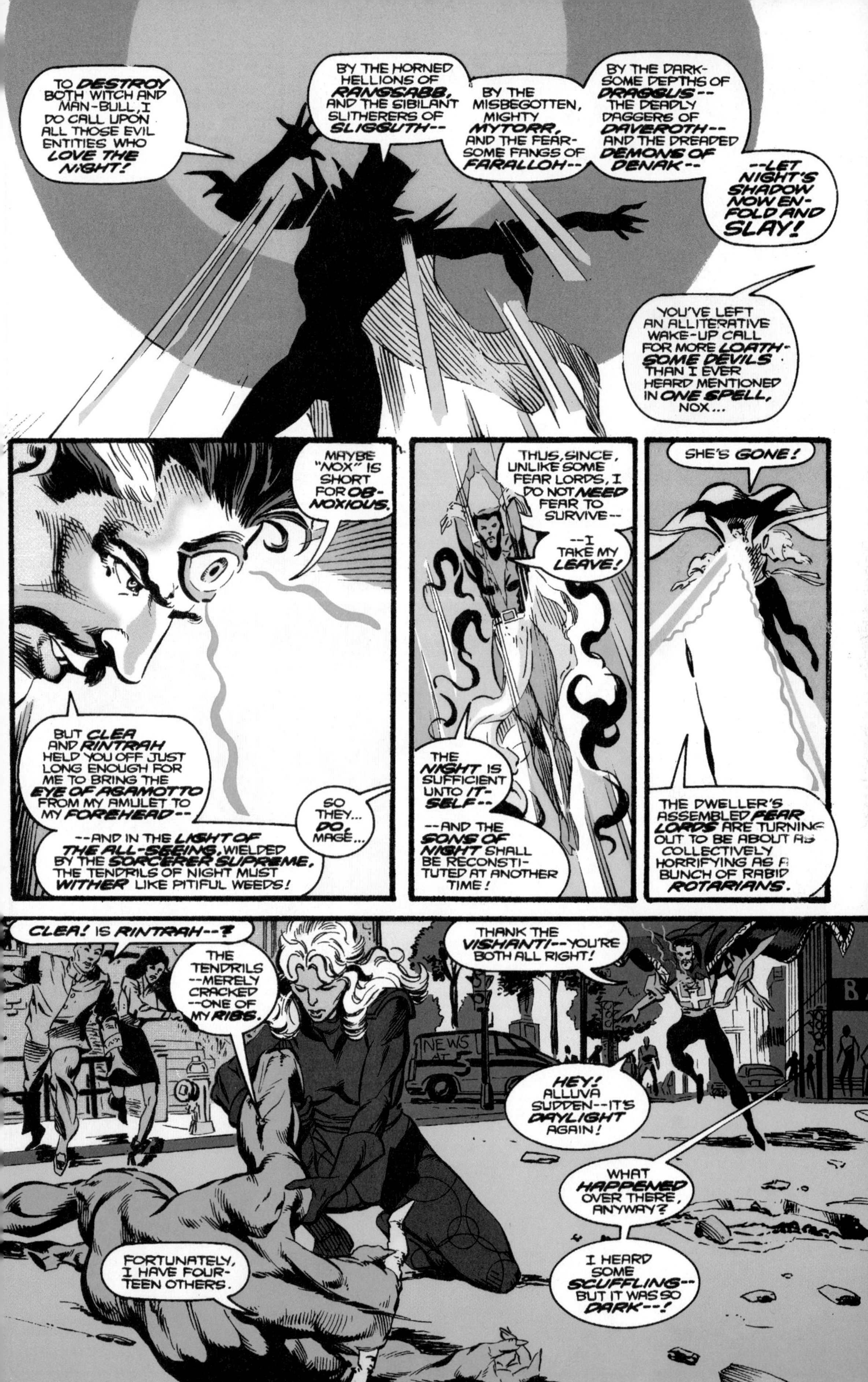
TO DESTROY BOTH WITCH AND MAN-BULL, I DO CALL UPON ALL THOSE EVIL ENTITIES WHO LOVE THE NIGHT!
BY THE HORNED HELLIONS OF RANGSABB, AND THE SIBILANT SLITHERERS OF SLIGGUTH--
BY THE MISBEGOTTEN, MIGHTY MYTORR, AND THE FEAR-SOME FANGS OF FARALLOH--
BY THE DARK-SOME DEPTHS OF DRAGGUS-- THE DEADLY DAGGERS OF DAVEROTH-- AND THE DREADED DEMONS OF DENAK--
--LET NIGHT'S SHADOW NOW ENFOLD AND SLAY!
YOU'VE LEFT AN ALLITERATIVE WAKE-UP CALL FOR MORE LOATHSOME DEVILS THAN I EVER HEARD MENTIONED IN ONE SPELL, NOX...
MAYBE "NOX" IS SHORT FOR OBNOXIOUS.
BUT CLEA AND RINTRAH HELD YOU OFF JUST LONG ENOUGH FOR ME TO BRING THE EYE OF AGAMOTTO FROM MY AMULET TO MY FOREHEAD--
SO THEY... DO, MAGE...
--AND IN THE LIGHT OF THE ALL-SEEING, WIELDED BY THE SORCERER SUPREME, THE TENDRILS OF NIGHT MUST WITHER LIKE PITIFUL WEEDS!
THUS, SINCE, UNLIKE SOME FEAR LORDS, I DO NOT NEED FEAR TO SURVIVE--
--I TAKE MY LEAVE!
THE NIGHT IS SUFFICIENT UNTO ITSELF--
--AND THE SONS OF NIGHT SHALL BE RECONSTITUTED AT ANOTHER TIME!
SHE'S GONE!
THE DWELLER'S ASSEMBLED FEAR LORDS ARE TURNING OUT TO BE ABOUT AS COLLECTIVELY HORRIFYING AS A BUNCH OF RABID ROTARIANS.
CLEA! IS RINTRAH--?
THE TENDRILS --MERELY CRACKED --ONE OF MY RIBS.
THANK THE VISHANTI--YOU'RE BOTH ALL RIGHT!
NEWS AT 5
HEY! ALLUVA SUDDEN--IT'S DAYLIGHT AGAIN!
WHAT HAPPENED OVER THERE, ANYWAY?
I HEARD SOME SCUFFLING-- BUT IT WAS SO DARK--!
FORTUNATELY, I HAVE FOURTEEN OTHERS.

WHAT!? I'M STARTLED TO IMAGINE THAT YOU COULD ACTUALLY CREDIT ANY OF THOSE--

I DON'T. I MERELY ASKED IF YOU DID.

THEN THE ANSWER IS NO.

BELIEVE ME--I WAS AS MUCH IN THE DARK AS ANYBODY ELSE!

0:12

YOU SAW AND HEARD IT HERE FIRST, FOLKS!

DR. STRANGE, TOUTED BY ONE WELL-KNOWN AUTHOR AS EARTH'S "SORCERER SUPREME," ALL BUT PUBLICLY ADMITTED HE'S AS PHONY AS A THREE-DOLLAR BILL.

LEAVING AUTHOR MORGANA BLESSING PRECISELY WHERE?

RUMORS ABOUND THAT HER PUBLISHER IS THREATENING TO SUE MS. BLESSING FOR FALSE--

PARDON ME, MY FINE YOUNG SPECIMEN OF FEMININE PULCHRITUDE, BUT IF YOU WISH SOMEONE TO UTTER AN APT AND SALUBRIOUS QUIP TO THE MULTITUDES UPON REQUEST--

--MAY I PROFFER MY OWN NOT INVALUABLE SERVICES?

HUH? SORRY--CELEBRITY IMPERSONATIONS ARE DEFINITELY PASSE!

"CELEBRITY IMPERSONATIONS"? GODFREY DANIELS, WHATEVER DID THE CHILD MEAN?

I AM MOST DEFINITELY THE REAL McGONNIGLE!

THIS IS FELICIA FARROW--FOR CHANNEL 10'S "MATERIAL WITNESS NEWS"!

SO THE GOOD GUYS WON, HUH, DOC?
GOOD THING, TOO.
WONG AND IME! LOOK ALL IN!
OUR WEDDING PLANS... YAWWN! ...KEPT US FROM SLEEPING LAST NIGHT.
ACTUALLY, SARA, ALL WE'VE DEFEATED SO FAR ARE A FEW OF THE LESSER FEAR LORDS...
...AND FRANKLY, I'M NOT SO SURE THAT'S NOT WHAT THE DWELLER IN DARKNESS WANTED, ALL ALONG...!
I SEE, MY SHADE THRALLS, THAT I UNDERESTIMATED STRANGE.
FORTUNATELY, HE CANNOT FIND MY DIMENSION TO ATTACK ME HERE, FOR IT IS CONSTANTLY ON THE MOVE.
THAT GIVES ME A TEMPORARY ADVANTAGE WHICH I MUST EXPLOIT, BEFORE...
...AND SO THERE ARE THREE, EH, COUSIN...
...JUST AS YOU PLANNED, FROM THE VERY BEGINNING!
D'SPAYRE! SUPPOSE YOU EXPLAIN YOUR ACCUSATIONS!
CLEARLY, YOU WANTED THE OTHER FOUR-- AND NIGHTMARE--TO CREATE AN ATMOSPHERE OF FEAR ON EARTH--
--ONE WHICH, IN THE END, WOULD FEED ONLY YOUR DARK APPETITES.
I SUPPOSE I COULD EXEMPT MYSELF, SINCE I TRADE MORE IN DESPAIR THAN FEAR. STILL, THE POINT REMAINS.
WHAT NEXT, THEN, O FOLLOWER OF THE WAY OF SHAMBLU?
AWAY, CRAVEN ONE!
IF I COULD HAVE EVEN THE STRAW MAN DESTROYED WHEN HE CROSSED ME--
--ONE WHO IS MERELY THE CREATION OF MY OWN DREAMING MIND HAD BEST REMEMBER HE EXISTS MERELY TO EAT THE SCRAPS I LEAVE BEHIND!
NO ONE SEEMS TO WANT POOR D'SPAYRE AROUND, THESE DAYS.
PERHAPS IT'S BEST I WATCH THE EVENTS TO COME FROM A FAR SPHERE...!

THIS IS BAD BUSI-NESS!
THERE'S MORE TO THIS THAN MEETS THE EYE OF AGA-MOTTO, CLEA.
IN FACT, THE DWELLER'S SUCCEEDED IN PREVENT-ING THE ORB FROM EVEN DETECTING HIS WHERE-ABOUTS.
THEN--HE MUST WIELD MORE POWER THAN WE EVER IMAGINED!
DOC-- PLEASE! IMEI AND WONG HAVE FINALLY DRIFTED OFF...

OH--SORRY. I'LL TRY TO KEEP IT DOWN.
BUT REALLY, SARA--I DO THINK THAT WHAT STEPHEN'S TRYING TO ACCOMPLISH HERE IS A BIT MORE IMPORTANT THAN--
N-NO... NO...
WONG--IMEI--THEY'RE STIRRING--!

THE GREY MAN--WITH THE TENTACLED HEAD--
HE'S REACH-ING FOR US! HIS TALONED HANDS--!
BY THE POWER OF AGAMOTTO, WHICH IS THE POWER OF THE LIGHT-- I COMMAND YOU BOTH--

--AWAKE!
THAT DREAM-- IT SEEMED AS REAL AS THIS HOUSE!
AND THE TENTACLED HEAD-- IT WAS TERRI-FYING--!
MASTER-- EACH OF THEM HAD THE SAME DREAM!?

YES, RINTRAH. THAT MEANS-- THE DWELLER IN DARKNESS HAS MADE HIS MOVE!
FOR, SIGNIFICANTLY, IT WAS HE THEY DREAMT OF--NOT NIGHT-MARE!
I COULD PULL BACK THESE TWO-- BUT MANY OTHERS ARE IN HIS POWER.
AND THAT SHOULD BE ESPECIALLY ENRAGING TO--

--"NIGHT-MARE!"
THIS IS AN OUT-RAGE!
ALL OVER THE WORLD, MORTALS IN SLUMBER SUDDEN-LY SHUDDER WITH TERROR AT THEIR DREAMS.
ORDINARILY, A MOST SATISFYING SIGHT.
BUT TONIGHT, IT IS NOT THE FACE OF NIGHTMARE THEY SEE--OR ANY OF MY OTHER MYRIAD ASPECTS--
--BUT RATHER, THAT OF THE ACCURSED DWELLER!
HE IS ATTEMPTING TO TAKE OVER MY OWN ASTRAL PLANE!
THE DWELLER HAS BETRAYED ME--JUST AS HE BETRAYED THE OTHER FEAR LORDS--
--JUST AS I MEAN TO BETRAY HIM, GIVEN THE CHANCE!
UP, DREAM-STALKER!
WE SHALL ROOT UP THAT PUTRID PLOTTER, BEFORE HE CAN GAIN A FIRM FOOTHOLD IN THE DIMENSION OF DREAM!
HURRY, STEED! WE MUST--
ARRRHH! WE HAVE--STRUCK AN UNSEEN BARRIER!
YOU ARE ONE STEP BEHIND ME, AS ALWAYS, NIGHT-MARE.
STILL, I HAVE BEEN GENEROUS.
YOU MAY CONTINUE TO LORD IT OVER THE TINY PATCH OF DREAM IN WHICH I HAVE IMPRISON-ED YOU!

DO NOT CONFUSE ME WITH THOSE OTHERS YOU LED AROUND BY THE NOSE, FOUL ONE!
EVEN "IMPRISONED," I STILL WIELD TOTAL CONTROL OVER EVERY IOTA OF MATTER AND ENERGY IN THIS WORLD OF NIGHTMARES--
--AND CAN PEOPLE IT INSTANTLY WITH AN ARMY OF PHANTASMS TO DO MY BIDDING!
DO NOT STOP TILL YOU HAVE BROKEN THROUGH, AND TORN THE DWELLER TOOTH FROM TENTACLE!
HURL YOURSELVES AGAINST YONDER BARRIER, MY PRETTIES!
DID YOU POSSIBLY IMAGINE, YOU PALE SHADOW OF A VAPID SPECTRE--
--THAT I HAD COME ALONE?
ATTACK THEM, MY THRALLS AND THINGS!
I'VE GOT TO GO IN THERE!
BUT, MASTER-- WHY NOT LET THE TWO FEAR LORDS OBLITERATE EACH OTHER?
FOR ONE THING, RINTRAH, THE DWELLER HOLDS MILLIONS OF PEOPLE IN HIS SPELL, AT THIS MOMENT.
IF HE WERE DESTROYED NOW--IT MIGHT WELL BE FATAL TO THEM--

"--AND WHO KNOWS WHAT WILL HAPPEN IF THAT STRUGGLE BETWEEN DREAM-DEMONS SOMEHOW ERUPTS THROUGH THEM INTO THE EARTH-PLANE--RIGHT, STEPHEN?
"STEPHEN?"
BY HOGGOTH! ALREADY, THEIR FORCES OF MINIONS HAVE VIRTUALLY WIPED OUT EACH OTHER AS WELL AS THE BARRIER--
--LEAVING NIGHTMARE AND THE DWELLER IN DARKNESS TO SQUARE OFF, ONE-ON-ONE!
WAS THIS THE AIM OF YOUR PRECIOUS SECRET AGENDA?
WE HAVE DISSIPATED OUR POWERS, YOU--YOU DISCIPLE OF SHAMBLU!
THERE IS NO LONGER ANY PLACE FOR YOU, FOOL, IN THE SPHERES OF EITHER DREAM OR FEAR!
WEAKENED WE BOTH MAY BE, BY OUR PROXY BATTLE--
--BUT STILL IT IS I WHO MUST ULTIMATELY TRIUMPH!
AMAZING! THEY'RE SO CAUGHT UP IN THEIR AMBITIONS--AND IN THEIR HATRED OF EACH OTHER--THEY HAVEN'T EVEN NOTICED ME.
WELL, MRS. STRANGE DIDN'T RAISE ANY CHILDREN STUPID ENOUGH NOT TO TAKE ADVANTAGE OF THAT SALIENT FACT...

...OR AT LEAST TO TRY LIKE THE DEVILS OF DENAK!
NNNGNN--!
IT'S STRANGE! HE HAS-- URRRGK--!
CAN'T QUITE SEE-- THROUGH THE LIGHT OF AGAMOTTO I UNLEASHED ON THEM.
ARE THEY--?
ARRRHH
TRULY A MOST RARE CONVERGENCE OF INTERESTS AND ANALYSES, NIGHTMARE.
AYE. TOGETHER WE STILL RETAINED POWER ENOUGH TO DEFEAT THE SORCERER, WHO IS OUT OF HIS ELEMENT.
WE SHOULD HAVE REALIZED THAT HIS INTERVENTION WOULD BE THE ONE THING THAT COULD UNITE US--MAKE US PUT ASIDE OUR TURGID TERRITORIAL SQUABBLES--
--AT LEAST LONG ENOUGH TO BEST HIM--THEN FEED ON FEARS OF HUMANKIND!
AYE. BUT LET US MAKE SOME CONCESSION TO EARTH'S MYSTIC GUARDIAN, SHALL WE?
FIRST WE GORGE--THEN WE FIGHT, EH?
WHEN WE REDUCE THE EARTH TO A QUIVERING, INSANE MASS OF FRIGHTENED HUMAN FLESH--
--LET US ARRANGE FOR HIM TO WATCH!
NEXT: AND THEN THERE WAS ONE! THE STARTLING CONCLUSION TO THE "FEAR LORDS" EPIC!

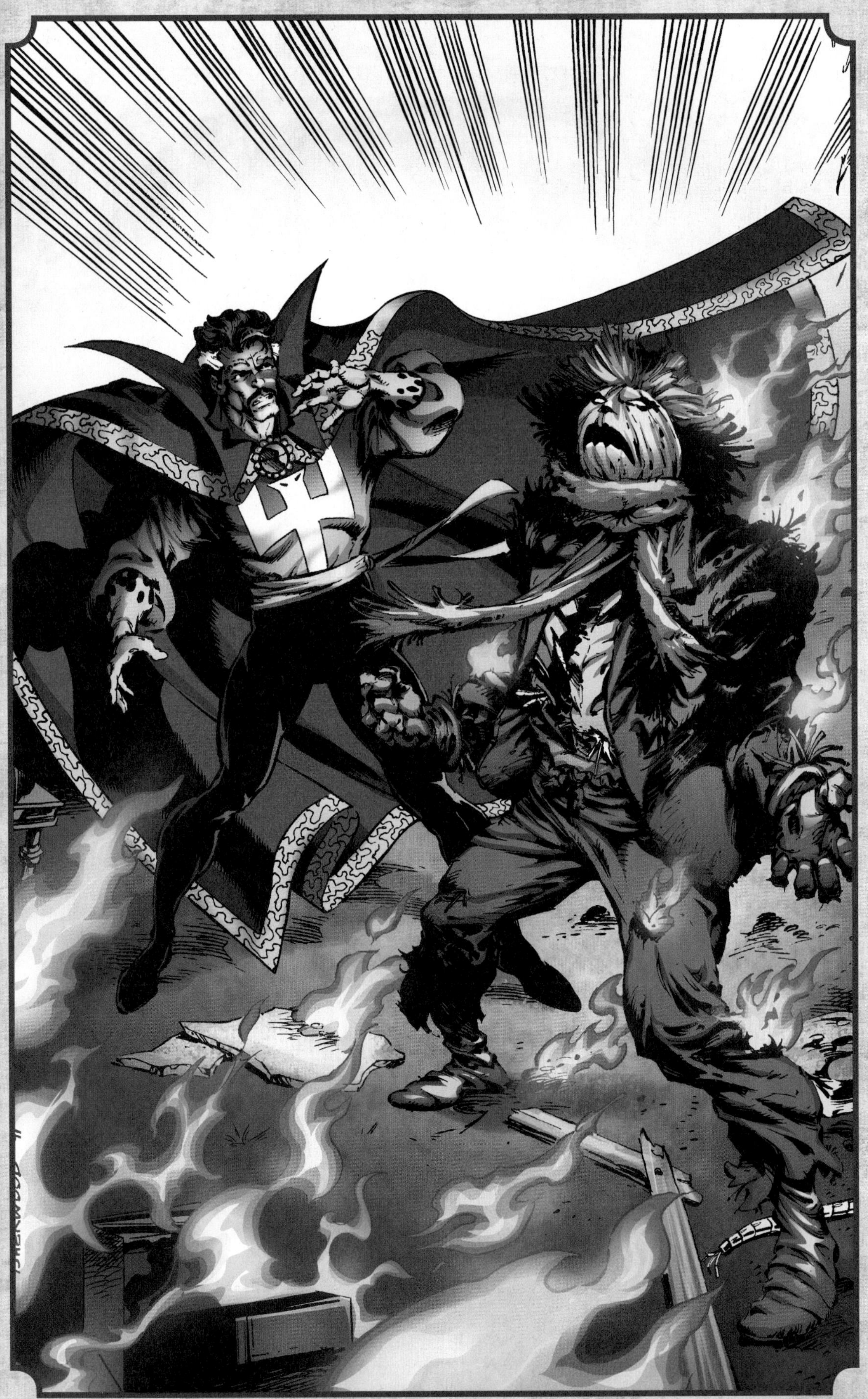

MARVEL COMICS

©1992 MARVEL ENT. GROUP, INC.

1.75 US
$2.15 CAN
40
APR
UK 95p

APPROVED BY THE COMICS CODE AUTHORITY

THE GREAT FEAR PART 3 OF 3

DR. STRANGE®

SORCERER SUPREME™

THE FEARSOME CONCLUSION!

GUEST-STARRING DAREDEVIL THE MAN WITHOUT FEAR!

ISHERWOOD '12

30TH ANNIVERSARY 1962 1992

THE AMAZING SPIDER-MAN

HE WAS ONCE A SURGEON—AN ARROGANT MAN-OF-THE-WORLD SEDUCED BY MATERIAL WEALTH. THEN, WHEN A TRAGIC ACCIDENT DEPRIVED HIM OF HIS SURGICAL SKILLS, STEPHEN STRANGE DISCOVERED A SEPARATE REALITY, A HIGHER PLANE OF OCCULT FORCES IN ETERNAL CONFLICT. VOWING TO BE EARTH'S FIRST LINE OF DEFENSE AGAINST MAGICAL MENACE, THE ERSTWHILE PHYSICIAN BECAME EARTH'S FOREMOST MASTER OF THE MYSTIC ARTS! STAN LEE PRESENTS . . .

DOCTOR STRANGE, SORCERER SUPREME!

...AND NOW THERE ARE THREE, EH, DWELLER IN DARKNESS?
AS EVER, NIGHTMARE, YOU ARE A DREAM LATE AND A DEVIL SHORT.
OUR FELLOW FEAR LORD, D'SPAYRE, UTTERED THOSE SELFSAME WORDS EARLIER TO ME, AS I FEEL CERTAIN HE DID TO YOU.
PLEASE, GREAT ONES-- I DO NOT WISH TO CHOOSE SIDES BETWIXT TWO OH-SO-POWERFUL ENTITIES.
MY OWN ABILITIES ARE SO MUCH MORE MODEST, I COULD SCARCELY FAIL TO BE GROUND TO T.S. ELIOT'S FAR-FAMED "HANDFUL OF DUST" IN SUCH A CLASH OF CHIMERICAL TITANS.
STILL, I DO SUPPOSE THAT, YOU TWAIN BEING SO EVENLY MATCHED AS YOU ARE, EVEN SO HUMBLE A PERSONAGE AS D'SPAYRE MIGHT PERHAPS HOLD THE BALANCE OF POWER BETWEEN YOU.
IF THAT BE SO-- AND MIND YOU, I DO NOT MAINTAIN FOR A MOMENT THAT IT IS--
--PERHAPS EACH OF YOU SHOULD SEEK TO GIVE ME AMPLE REASON WHY I SHOULD TAKE HIS PART, RATHER THAN HIS RIVAL'S, HMM?
AND IF I NEED AN IMPARTIAL SOUL TO HELP ME JUDGE, WHY, I SHALL TURN TO OUR HONORED GUEST...

...THE ESTEEMED DR. STRANGE, SORCERER SUPREME!
HOW COULD YOU FAIL TO MAKE THE CORRECT CHOICE, COUSIN...
...WHEN YOU KNOW FULL WELL THAT THE DWELLER ASSEMBLED US FEAR LORDS ONLY TO FURTHER HIS OWN INSATIABLE APPETITE FOR HUMAN FEAR.
SOMETHING YOU WOULD NEVER HAVE CONSIDERED DOING, I AM CERTAIN, BARON OF BAD DREAMS
DON'T FEEL TOO SORRY FOR ME.
FOR A HELPLESS CAPTIVE PRETENDING TO STILL BE UNCONSCIOUS, I'M ACTUALLY DOING FAIRLY WELL...
FOR, THE THREE REMAINING FEAR LORDS ARE IGNORING ME AS THEY BICKER AMONG THEMSELVES.
AND THAT GIVES ME A CHANCE TO MUTTER A WHISPERED SPELL...
...ONE WHICH RESULTS IN THE CREATION OF THE TINIEST OF SENDINGS...
...WHICH, IN TURN, MAKES ITS EGRESS THROUGH THE TINIEST OF DIMENSIONAL APERTURES...

"FROM HOPE AND FEAR SET FREE..."
THROW YOUR LOT IN WITH ME NOW, MY JOY-LESS CREATION, WITHOUT FURTHER WHEEDLING--
YOU--YOU HYPOCRITICAL HARBINGER OF HOPELESS-NESS!
HOW DARE YOU PERCH THERE, LIKE SOME SCAVENGER BIRD, BETWEEN THE DREAM-SPHERE I HAVE CONQUERED, AND THE TINY REM-NANT STILL HELD BY NIGHTMARE?
--OR IT WILL GO HARD WITH YOU WHEN THE DWELLER IN DARKNESS IS TRIUMPHANT!
...INTO, IF THE GODS ARE KIND, THE SO-CALLED REAL WORLD.
I CANNOT TELL IF IT IS SUCCESS-FUL OR NOT.
ONCE IT LEAVES THE REALM OF DREAMS, I LOSE ALL CONTACT WITH IT.
IT HAS ITS MYSTICALLY-SET MISSION...
...THERE, IN AN ASTRAL PLANE IN THE GROWING GRIP OF THE GREAT FEAR...
DON'T SHOOT-- PLEASE!
TH-THEN DON'T M-MOVE --!
ROY & DANN THOMAS WRITERS
GEOF ISHERWOOD PENCILER
JIM SANDERS III INKER
PAT BROSSEAU LETTERER
GEORGE ROUSSOS COLORIST
MIKE ROCKWITZ EDITOR
TOM DEFALCO EDITOR IN CHIEF | WITH SPECIAL THANKS TO R.J.M. LOFFICIER

...AND I CAN ONLY PRAY TO THE ETERNAL VISHANTI...

...THAT, ON ITS OWN IN A WORLD IT NEVER MADE...
...IT FINDS THAT WHICH IT SEEKS.
WHOOOO
IF IT DOESN'T--

--MOTHER EARTH AND I ARE BOTH IN TROUBLE DEEP.
WAK!
NOW, BOYS--
THOK
--YOU'RE BOTH GOING TO BEHAVE YOURSELVES FROM NOW ON, AREN'T YOU--
--AND TRY NOT TO TAKE THINGS THAT DON'T BELONG TO YOU?
UNNH--!
I'LL TAKE THAT AS A MAYBE.

UH... THANKS, MISTER.
THE POLICE WILL NEED YOU TO I.D. THESE TWO WOULD-BE MUGGERS...
NAME'S DAREDEVIL.

POLICE? OH, I DON'T KNOW ABOUT--
WHAT'S THAT? A GNAT?
A GLOWING GNAT?
I'M AFRAID I DON'T--

--KNOW.

WHAT HAPPENED? YOU LOOK ALL-OVER FUNNY!
I FEEL FUNNY. OR MAYBE I SHOULD SAY--
--STRANGE.
GOT TO GO, MA'AM.
PLEASE DO THE RIGHT THING AND CALL THE COPS, OKAY?
...HE IS AWAKE, OUR SORCERER ONCE-SUPREME, YET HE DOES NOT STRUGGLE.
I WONDER WHY.
FOR ONCE, WE ARE IN AGREEMENT
PERHAPS HE IS UP TO SOME-THING...
DON'T WANT THEM TO FIND OUT ABOUT THE SENDING...
...SO A RED HERRING IS DEFINITELY CALLED FOR:
MAY THE AWESOME MIGHT OF OSHTUR...
WHY, I DO BELIEVE HE'S ACTUALLY TRY-ING TO UTTER A SPELL!
DID NOT YOUR MOTHER TELL YOU, WIZARD--
--NOT TO TRY TO TALK WITH YOUR MOUTH FULL?
MMNNGNN...

A VERY NICE TOUCH, COUSIN NIGHT-MARE...
CAN YOU WONDER WHY SO UNASSUMING AN ENTITY AS MYSELF DOES NOT WISH TO CHOOSE BETWEEN THE TWO OF YOU?
I DESIRE NOTHING MORE THAN PEACE 'TWIXT YOU TWAIN.
STILL, IF YOU WILL CONTEST FOR MY FAVOR, PERHAPS YOU SHOULD PROCEED ON EARTH WITH "THE GREAT FEAR"...
...MYSTIC TENDRILS ACTIVATED BY THE MAGE'S VOICE, AND WITHDRAWING WHEN HE LAPSES INTO RESPECTFUL SILENCE.
...WITH THE LOSER VOWING TO SERVE THE WINNER.
LET ME, INDEED, PRO-POSE A MODEST MU-TATION IN METHOD-OLOGY...
SINCE AT ANY GIVEN MOMENT ALL HUMANS ARE EITHER AWAKE OR ASLEEP-- EACH OF YOU MIGHT WAGE THE ASSAULT IN HIS OWN DOMAIN, TO SEE WHICH CAN CREATE THE GREATER FEAR--
--NIGHTMARE IN DREAMS, THE DWELLER IN THE WAKING WORLD.
I, OF COURSE, WOULD BE DUTY-BOUND TO SIDE WITH THE VICTOR.
DONE-- IF MY TENTACLE-FACED FOE CONCURS!
WHY SHOULD I NOT--
--WHEN MY POWER IS SUCH THAT I AM CERTAIN OF VICTORY?
NEITHER OF THEM INTENDS TO KEEP HIS SIDE OF THE BARGAIN--AND BOTH KNOW IT--

--BUT PITY THE POOR EARTH, WHILE THIS SINISTER CHARADE IS PLAYED OUT BY THE TWO MALEVOLENT BEINGS WHO NOW STREAK EARTH-WARD!
WHILE I--THE SWORN MYSTIC PROTECTOR OF THAT ASTRAL PLANE--CAN ONLY LANGUISH IN THE SPHERE OF DREAMS--
--AND TRY NOT TO IMAGINE THE HAVOC BEING WROUGHT BOTH IN THE "REAL" WORLD--
GOOD LORD!
--AND IN THE WORLD OF BAD DREAMS.
DADDY'S NOT HERE, LITTLE BOY--
--BUT I AM!
D-DADDY?
WHICH WILL WIN, I CAN'T HELP WONDERING:
THE DWELLER, SWOLLEN WITH FEED-ING UPON THE EMOTIONS AROUSED BY OTHER FEAR LORDS--
EEEEEEE
--OR NIGHTMARE, ONCE MORE THE MASTER OF THE SOMNOLENT UNCONSCIOUS?
MANY WILL FIND THE IMAGES SO REAL, THEY'LL WISH THEY COULD ESCAPE THEM IN SLEEP--
--WHILE OTHERS WILL BE STRIVING FIERCELY, BUT IN VAIN, TO AWAKEN.
NEITHER FEAR LORD WILL RELEASE HIS CLAMMY GRIP UPON HUMANITY'S SOFT THROAT.
UNDOUBTEDLY, THE DWELLER IN DARKNESS THINKS HE HAS THE EDGE, BECAUSE AT ANY MOMENT MORE PEOPLE ARE AWAKE THAN ASLEEP...
...BUT HOW MUCH MORE VUL-NERABLE TO TERROR ARE THOSE WHO, SLEEPING, MAY BE ATTACKED ONE BY ONE, AND ALONE?

WHILE I STILL CAN ONLY HOPE AND PRAY THAT MY SENDING FOUND THE MYSTERIOUS MASKED MAN CALLED DAREDEVIL...
...HE WHO IS CALLED "THE MAN WITHOUT FEAR"...
WHA--?
...AND THAT HE LIVES UP TO HIS REPUTATION.
DOC--!?
NOT IN THAT OUT-LANDISH OUT-FIT, SARA.
RED--NEVER MY FAVORITE COLOR!
YOU'RE DAREDEVIL, AREN'T YOU? I BELIEVE WE MET ONCE, AT A PARTY.
I'M CLEA, DR. STRANGE'S--WELL, WIFE, I SUPPOSE.
DO YOU MIND TELLING ME HOW YOU WERE ABLE TO PASS RIGHT THROUGH THIS MANSION'S MYSTIC DEFENSES--NOT TO MENTION THE ROOF?
I CAN ONLY GUESS IT'S GOT SOME-THING TO DO WITH THIS BRIGHT LIGHT THAT FLEW INTO MY HEAD--
--AND SAID IT WAS FROM DR. STRANGE.
STEPHEN'S SENDING MESSAGES?!
THEN HE MUST BE ALIVE, THANK HOGGOTH!
WHAT ELSE DID THE SENDING TELL YOU?

NOT A THING.
I HAD THIS FEELING-- AS IF A PHONE CONNECTION WAS SUDDENLY CUT--THEN NOTHING.
EXCEPT--
EXCEPT?
WELL, THAT PAINTING OF A SCARECROW--IT WAS IN MY HEAD, TOO, FOR A MOMENT, BEFORE--
HUH?
WHATEVER WAS INSIDE YOUR HEAD, DAREDEVIL-- IT'S BEEN RE-ACTIVATED BY SEEING THAT PICTURE!
AND IT, IN TURN--
--HAS BROUGHT ME ANEW IN THE WORLD OF MOR-TALS!
TH-- THE SCARE-CROW'S COME TO LIFE!
I PREFER THE COGNO-MEN "STRAW MAN."
HOLY HANNAH! IF I'VE FREED SOME DEMON--!
BITE YOUR TONGUE-- THOSE OF YOU WHO HAVE TONGUES.
AS YOU KNOW, CLEA, I TURNED AGAINST MY FELLOW FEAR LORDS--BUT WAS FORCED TO RETIRE TO MY OTHERWORLD, BEYOND THE PAINTING, TO REPLENISH MY STRENGTH.
AND HAVE YOU REPLENISHED IT?
AS BEST I COULD, IN THE SCANT TIME ALLOTTED TO ME, SORCERESS.
FOR, UNLESS WE ACT RIGHT NOW, WHETHER WE ARE FULLY IN READI-NESS OR NOT--
--YOUR ADOPTED WORLD WILL BE FRIGHTENED-- TO DEATH!

AAAHHHHHHHH
THE CLEAR, GREEN-FLECKED RADIANCE OF FEAR!
THERE IS NOTHING IN ALL THE MULTIVERSE TO COMPARE WITH IT!
TOO TRUE, OCTOPOID!
I COULD SEND THE USUAL GORILLAS AND DINOSAURS INTO HUMANITY'S DREAMS--
--BUT ON THIS SPECIAL OCCASION, I PREFER THE PERSONAL APPROACH.
WELL, D'SPAYRE? PRONOUNCE THE INEVITABLE!
NIGHTMARE IS WINNING!
THE DECISION IS NOT QUITE AS CLEAR-CUT AS THAT JUST YET, COUSIN.
TRUE, YOUR GRIP ON PEOPLE IS QUITE TENACIOUS--BUT THE DWELLER HAS THE LEAD IN SHEER NUMBERS.
PERHAPS IF THE CONTEST IS CONTINUED JUST A WEE BIT LONGER...
YOU KNOW THAT'S JUST WHAT D'SPAYRE WANTS, DON'T YOU, STRANGE?
AND SO WOULD NIGHTMARE AND THE DWELLER IN DARKNESS, IF THEY COULD TEAR THEMSELVES AWAY FROM THEIR RAMPAGES FOR A FEW MOMENTS.
BUT YOU CAN SAY NOTHING...

FOR ALL THE INTERFERING I CAN DO JUST NOW, I MIGHT AS WELL BE THE WATCHER--
--OBSERVING FROM AFAR, AS WAKING MEN AND WOMEN THE WORLD OVER BEGIN, ONE BY ONE, TO COLLAPSE FROM THE GREAT FEAR THAT HAS GRIPPED THEM--
--MOVING BEYOND FEAR NOW, TO THE NEXT STEP--
--WHICH IS MIND-NUMBING DESPAIR.
THE DWELLER IN DARKNESS SENSES IT FIRST.
I CAN SEE IT IN HIS EYES.
AND, IN THE SPHERE OF DREAMS, NIGHTMARE MUST BE COMING TO THE SAME STARTLING REALI-ZATION.
O DWELLER IN DARK CELLARS!
WHY SHOULD WE TWO HOLD A CONTEST WHICH CAN BENEFIT NONE BUT THAT WEAKLING D'SPAYRE?
I CONCUR, O MANIPULATOR OF UNDIGESTED BEEF--BUT WHAT DO YOU SUGGEST?
WE SHOULD DIVIDE THE FEAR-REALM IN TWO, RATHER THAN FIGHTING OVER ITS HALVES.
BUT FIRST, WE SHOULD SLAY DR. STRANGE, SO THAT HE CAN NEVER AGAIN BE A THREAT TO US!
YOUR WORDS MAKE RARE GOOD SENSE, NIGHTMARE.
AGREED!
THE DEADLINE IS GETTING CLOSE...
...AND THE PAIN IS EXCRUCIATING--MIND-BLASTING!
IF MY SURMISES AND CALCULATIONS ARE WRONG, THE UNIVERSE IS GOING TO NEED A NEW SORCERER SUPREME.
AAAAAA
DO NOT BOTHER WITH THAT HUMAN VER-MIN!
IN FACT, IT MAY, EVEN IF I'M RIGHT.

IT IS NOT DR. STRANGE THAT EVEN YOU FEAR LORDS MUST NOW FEAR--
--BUT D'SPAYRE!
WHAT? YOU--A CREATURE WHO OWES HIS EXISTENCE TO MY DREAMS--DARE TO THREATEN ME?!
YOU FEAR LORDS CREATED TERROR AMONG MAN-KIND--
LOOK AT HIM! THERE IS A NEW AUTHORITY--EVEN ARROGANCE--IN HIS DEMEANOR!
I GOADED YOU INTO PUSHING HUMANITY OVER THE EDGE, INTO SHEER DESPAIR--
--SO THAT I, NOT YOU, WOULD BE THE ULTIMATE BENEFICIARY OF THE SO-CALLED "GREAT FEAR"!
NEVER!
NO? AND JUST HOW WILL YOU PREVENT ME?
BY HURLING OUR COMBINED POWERS AGAINST YOU--NOW!
FOR ONCE, WE ARE IN CONCERT, DWELLER!
BUT--THE TRAITOR WITHSTANDS OUR TWIN ASSAULT--INDEED, SEEMS EVEN TO RELISH IT!
YOU WERE BOTH FOOLS TO BOMBARD THE EARTH WITH UNRELENTING FEAR! FOR, TOO MUCH FEAR LEADS ONLY TO DESPAIR--
--AND WHERE DESPAIR IS, NO ROOM REMAINS FOR FEAR.
BECAUSE, TO FEAR MAY INCLUDE THE HOPE THAT ONE CAN STILL ESCAPE--BUT TO DESPAIR IS TO RELINQUISH ALL HOPE.
OR AM I GETTING TOO FAR AHEAD OF YOU?
I...
WHAT HE'S SAYING IS THAT YOU TWO HAVE BEEN RADIATING FEAR--BUT AS PEOPLE GREW MORE DESPAIRING THAN AFRAID, YOU WEREN'T GETTING ANY FEAR BACK TO FEED ON.
YOU'D HAVE NOTICED IT LONG AGO, IF YOUR GARGANTUAN EGOS HADN'T BLINDED YOU!

I THINK THE DOCTOR HAS SUMMED IT UP NICELY.
BOTH OF YOU HAD YOUR SECRET PLANS-- SO I MERELY DEVELOPED MY OWN TO TAKE ADVANTAGE OF THEM.
NEVER-- HAVE I FELT-- SO REVOLTINGLY WEAK--!
MUST F-FLEE--
--FLEE BACK INTO MY DREAM DIMENSION, AND CLOSE IT UP AFTER ME!
AWAY, DREAM-STALKER!
HIS REALM WAS TOO CLOSE FOR ME TO STOP HIM-- BUT AS FOR YOU, DWELLER--!
HARRY S. TRUMAN ONCE SAID THAT THE ONLY THING NEW UNDER THE SUN IS THE HISTORY YOU DON'T KNOW YET.
AND THIS, IT SEEMS, IS THE DAY I LEARN A BIT ABOUT THE DWELLER'S.
FOR, AS HIS BODY-- HIS UNEXPECTEDLY ANDROID BODY-- BREAKS APART UNDER D'SPARE'S ASSAULT LIKE A FAKE ROLODEX--
--THE DWELLER'S HEAD LEAPS FREE--
--AND FINGER-LIKE TENTACLES ENABLE HIM TO SCUTTLE THROUGH A DIMENSIONAL APERTURE, TO SAFETY.
YOU DIDN'T KNOW THE TRUE DWELLER WAS MERELY THE HEAD, DID YOU, MAGE?
TAKING UP THE WAY OF THE SHAMBLU EONS AGO, HE LEARNED TO CREATE SYNTHETIC BODIES HE COULD WEAR LIKE A PAIR OF SHOES.
STILL, HE'S ESCAPED YOU-- TO RETURN TO HIS SLEEP OF CENTURIES...
AMPLE TIME FOR ME TO HAVE MY WAY WITH YOUR WORLD, DON'T YOU THINK?
I SUPPOSE I COULD PROLONG YOUR AGONY, BY LEAVING YOU ALIVE TO OBSERVE MY TRIUMPH--BUT NO.
BETTER IF I KILL YOU NOW-- SO I NEED NEVER CONCERN MYSELF WITH YOU AGAIN.

YES, I REALLY DO THINK THAT'S BESssSSSS

GOT HIM, PEOPLE!

COME ON IN AND FINISH HIM OFF!

MY SPECIALTY IS HEAVIES LIKE THE KINGPIN.

HOW DO I WIND UP W

WEIRDOS LIKE THIS G

AND BLACKHEART

HOWEVER YOU GOT HERE, HUMAN, YOU'LL NOT LIVE LONG ENOUGH TO LEARN THE ANSWER TO--

WHAT? TWO OF DR. STRANGE'S MINIONS, AND--

--THE STRAW MAN!?

AND CLEA AND I ARE DISCIPLES, VILLAIN, NOT "MINIONS"!

DON'T TELL HIM, RINTRAH. SHOW HIM!

DID YOU THINK AN OAF SUCH AS THE LURKING ONE COULD DESTROY ME, D'SPAYRE?

GREAT! SO WHY'D YOU SEND FOR ME, INSTEAD OF SORCERERS LOCAL #101?
WHO WAS I SUPPOSED TO CALL? GHOST-BUSTERS?
YOU'RE THE "MAN WITHOUT FEAR," AREN'T YOU?
NEITHER DAREDEVIL NOR THE STRAW MAN RESPONDS-- WHICH IS JUST AS WELL.
THEY'VE GOT THEIR HANDS FULL, JUST NOW.
I CAN'T BELIEVE THIS! I'M TRYING TO FIGHT A COSMIC ENTITY --WITH A BILLY CLUB!
I ADMIT, YOU ARE A FORMIDABLE FOEMAN-- NOW THAT YOU HAVE AB-SORBED THE TERROR GENERATED BY FIVE FEAR LORDS.
THEN IMAGINE HOW POWERFUL I SHALL BE-- WHEN I HAVE ASSIMILATED ALL THE FEAR YOU CRE-ATED ON EARTH WITH YOUR SHORT-LIVED TELEVI-SION CHANNEL!
THEY CAN'T STAND UP TO D'SPAYRE FOR LONG.
I TRY TO SAY AN INCANTATION, HOPING NIGHTMARE TOOK HIS GAG-SPELL WITH HIM WHEN HE FLED.
MMMFF--!
NO SUCH LUCK.
I CAN TALK-- BUT I CAN'T INCANT!
AND WHEN OLD SKULL-FACE EASILY SIDE-STEPS THE SCARE-CROW'S HEADLONG LEAP--
--IT GIVES HIM A CHANCE TO CONNECT WITH THE OFF-BALANCE DAREDEVIL!
YOU CAN DO ME NO REAL HARM-- BUT PERHAPS YOUR LIGHT-WEIGHT FRIEND COULD--
--SO I WILL DEAL WITH HIM AS THE LURKING ONE DID, EARLIER!
--AND DEFTLY TOUCHES MY COSMIC CLAMP!
YET, EVEN AS THE MYSTIC FIRES SET HIM AFIRE, THE STRAW MAN WHIRLS--

MORE QUICKLY THAN I COULD REPEAT IT HERE, I SHOUT OUT THE SPELL I'VE BEEN TRYING TO SPEAK FOR SO LONG--
--AND I'M FREE, BY THE TIME MY CLOAK OF LEVITATION CAN FLOAT ONTO MY SHOULDERS.
IT FEELS GOOD.
HOW CAN THIS BE??
THINK ABOUT IT, D'SPAYRE!
THE LURKING UNKNOWN NEVER REALLY DEFEATED THE STRAW MAN--BUT ONLY BURNED UP ONE OF HIS MANY GRAIN-STALK BODIES.
HE PUT ON ANOTHER ONE TO COME HERE--BUT THAT, TOO, WAS ULTIMATELY EXPENDABLE.
HIS CLUMSY LEAP WAS CALCULATED TO GIVE YOU A CHANCE TO "OBLITERATE" HIM--PROBABLY BY MAGICAL FIRE.
PART OF THAT MAGIC CAME FROM NIGHTMARE--SO THE STRAW MAN FUNNELED IT THROUGH HIMSELF, TO CANCEL OUT THE SPELL THAT HELD ME!
WHAT IS THE USE OF EXPLAINING ALL THAT TO HIM, MASTER?
I'M WITH YOU, FERDINAND.
WASTE THIS GUY, STRANGE--WITH THE HOARY HANDS OF WHOEVER!

HAPPY TO OBLIGE, D.D.--THOUGH I DON'T THINK THE HANDS OF HOGGOTH ARE WHAT'S CALLED FOR AT THIS PARTICULAR JUNCTURE.
I THINK, RATHER-- THE BEDEVILING BOLTS OF BALTHAKK!
WE ARE SEEKING OUT OBSCURE SOURCES, AREN'T WE, GOOD DOCTOR?
TRUE--THEY ARE A MOST POTENT, IF LONG NEGLECTED, FORM OF ATTACK--
--BUT YOU HAVE NO HOPE OF DEFEATING ME BY THOSE MEANS, OR BY ANY OTHER!
HE SHAKES THE BOLTS OFF, LIKE A HOUND SHAKING OFF RAIN.
I MENTALLY PREPARE A NEW MYSTIC BOMBARDMENT...
BUT D'SPAYRE STILL HAS THE EDGE-- AND HE TAKES IT.
CAN'T YOU FACE THE FACTS, MAGICIAN?
I HAVE ABSORBED THE FEARS AND TERRORS OF MULTITUDES-- AND I COULD GO ON BATTLING YOU THIS WAY FOR YEARS.
CENTURIES!
I CALL ON THE VISHANTI, AND ON OSHTUR--YES, EVEN ON HOGGOTH--
BUT SOMEHOW, MY HEART ISN'T IN IT--
--AND D'SPAYRE MELTS A HALF-FORMED SET OF RAGGADORR'S RINGS AS IF THEY WERE MADE OF BUTTER.
WHY NOT GIVE IN TO THE INEVITABLE, STRANGE?
NO SINGLE ENTITY COULD BEST ME NOW--
LEAST OF ALL ONE WHO CAME TO HIS OCCULT CAREER AFTER MONTHS AS A DRUNKEN DERELICT!
M-MAYBE--
--YOU'RE RIGHT...!

OF COURSE I'M RIGHT.

DESPAIR IS ALWAYS THE CORRECT RE-ACTION TO AN INSOLUBLE PROBLEM.

EVEN YOUR WIFE AND YOUR BOVINE APPRENTICE COULD TELL YOU THAT.--

THE JOB OF SORCERER SUPREME IS FAR TOO BIG FOR ANY ONE MAN-- LET ALONE YOU.
YOU'VE ALWAYS KNOWN THAT, HAVEN'T YOU?

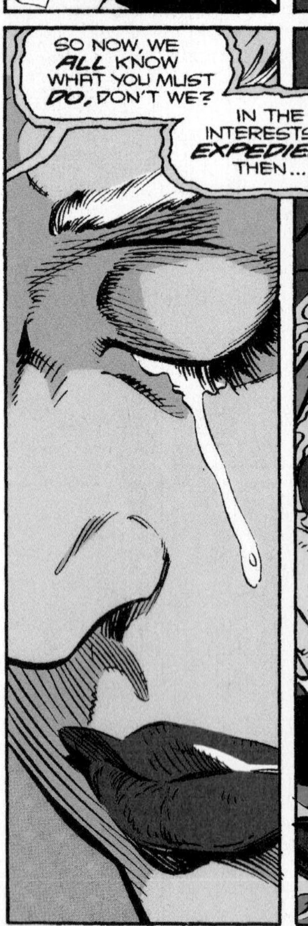
SO NOW, WE ALL KNOW WHAT YOU MUST DO, DON'T WE?

IN THE INTERESTS OF EXPEDIENCY, THEN...
...HERE!

I SINCERELY APOLOGIZE THAT I'M ALL OUT OF "BARE BODKINS," THE METHOD FA-VORED BY YOUR WORLD'S BARD...

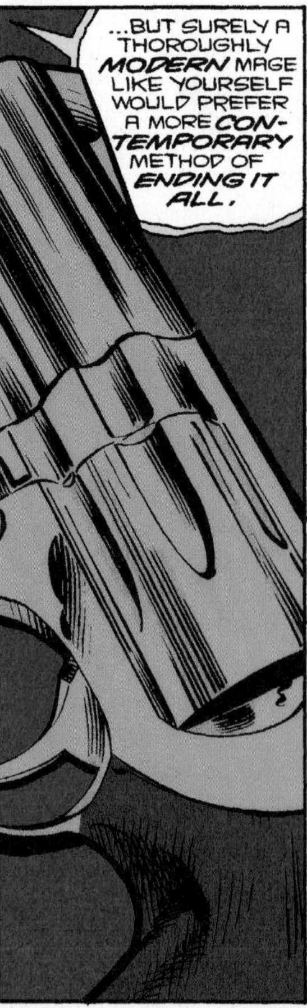
...BUT SURELY A THOROUGHLY MODERN MAGE LIKE YOURSELF WOULD PREFER A MORE CON-TEMPORARY METHOD OF ENDING IT ALL.

YOU SEE, MY DEAR DOCTOR?
EVEN THOSE WHO LOVE YOU BEST CAN SEE NO OTHER HONORABLE WAY OUT FOR YOU, IN YOUR HOUR OF ABYSMAL AND UTTER DEFEAT.
AND WHO ELSE WILL CARE? SINCE MS. BLESSING'S BIOGRAPHY, YOU HAVE BECOME MERELY THE ANSWER TO A QUESTION IN "TRIVIAL PURSUIT"...
...AT MOST, A CATEGORY ON "JEOPARDY."

SO GO ON... PICK IT UP.
THERE'S A GOOD MAN.
BUT... I HAVE... A RESPONSIBILITY... TO H-HUMANITY...

NONSENSE. YOU'VE NOTHING TO LIVE FOR.
THOUSANDS DO, EVERY YEAR, AND NO ONE MISSES THEM, REALLY.
GO AHEAD. OFF YOURSELF, AS THEY SAY.

THAT'S IT! ONE SQUEEZE OF THE TRIGGER... AND YOUR TROUBLES ARE FOREVER AT AN END.
MUST LIVE... FOR THOSE I LOVE...

FOR WHOM? FOR DAREDEVIL?
FOR THAT BARNYARD BEAST?
FOR CLEA, WHO CAN'T EVEN BEAR TO WATCH YOU LAY DOWN YOUR BURDEN?

LIVING IS HARD, MAGICIAN.
DYING IS EASY.
IT'S THE ONLY WAY NOT FRAUGHT WITH YEARS TO COME OF MOURNFUL, MAUDLIN SORROW... SO GO AHEAD...
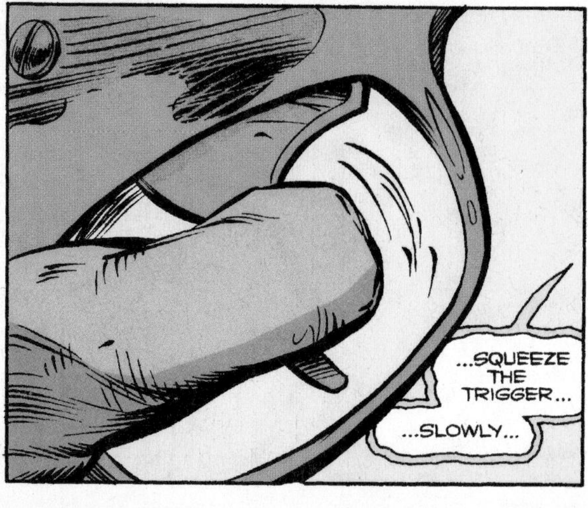
...SQUEEZE THE TRIGGER...
...SLOWLY...

BY HOGGOTH--
YOU'VE **MELTED** A PERFECTLY GOOD **PIS-TOL!?**
BUT-- I WAS SO **CERTAIN--**
NO!
YOU **OVERPLAYED** YOUR HAND, D'SPAYRE.

YOU WERE RIGHT. I **COULDN'T** GO ON LIVING-- AND FIGHTING --FOR **"MANKIND."**
TOO **ABSTRACT** A CONCEPT--TOO **DISTANT**.
BUT I **COULD** LIVE FOR JUST **ONE** PERSON!
NO **ONE** PERSON--
--NOT EVEN **CLEA--**

I MEANT TO, D'SPAYRE-- FOR, IN YOUR OWN WAY, YOU'RE EVEN WORSE THAN NIGHTMARE OR THE DWELLER IN DARKNESS.
YES... YES! I'M NO GOOD!
BUT...YOU MUST SPARE ME...
I'M NOT WORTH KILLING...
I CAN'T LISTEN TO YOU-- OR I'LL WIND UP SETTING YOU FREE!
MAY THE CRIMSON BANDS OF CYTORRAK ENCIRCLE D'SPAYRE AROUND-- TILL HE BE CUT OFF FROM HUMAN SENSE-- FROM SIGHT AND TOUCH AND SOUND!
CLEA... RINTRAH...GLAD TO SEE YOU'VE RECOVERED.
YOU TWO WANT TO JUMP IN HERE?
ONLY TO ADD A FEW FALTINIAN FLAMES TO REINFORCE THE OUTSIDE OF YOUR SPHERE.
AND MY SPELL-WEAVINGS, I HOPE, SHALL TIE THE PACKAGE UP NEATLY... AND STRONGLY.
SORRY I COULDN'T HELP MORE, PEOPLE.
ARE YOU SERIOUS?
WITHOUT YOU AS THE RECEPTABLE FOR MY SENDING-- WELL, FRANKLY, I'D RATHER NOT THINK ABOUT THAT.
YOU'RE THE MAN WITHOUT FEAR, AFTER ALL.
WE COULDN'T EXPECT YOU TO BE IMMUNE TO DESPAIR, TOO.

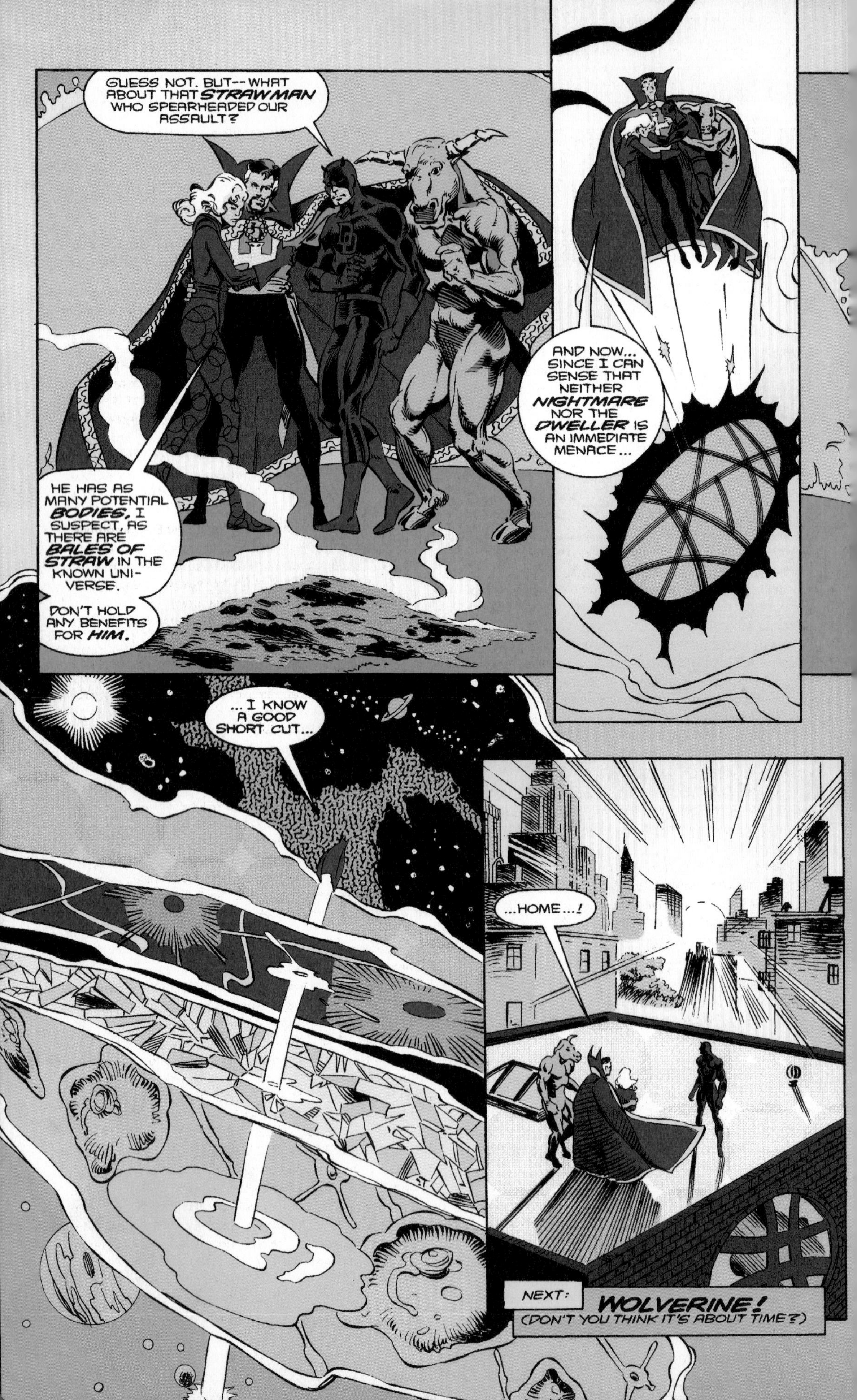
GUESS NOT. BUT--WHAT ABOUT THAT STRAWMAN WHO SPEARHEADED OUR ASSAULT?
HE HAS AS MANY POTENTIAL BODIES, I SUSPECT, AS THERE ARE BALES OF STRAW IN THE KNOWN UNI-VERSE.
DON'T HOLD ANY BENEFITS FOR HIM.
AND NOW... SINCE I CAN SENSE THAT NEITHER NIGHTMARE NOR THE DWELLER IS AN IMMEDIATE MENACE...
...I KNOW A GOOD SHORT CUT...
...HOME...!
NEXT:
WOLVERINE!
(DON'T YOU THINK IT'S ABOUT TIME?)

NIGHTMAIL

c/o MARVEL COMICS GROUP, 575 MADISON AVE. N.Y.C. 10022

A BIT OF RAG AND A CLUMP OF STRAW

by Scott Edelman

It was the Dead of Night.

Roger Slifer had forsaken Morristown, Indiana, for the last time, and Duffy Vohland had "volunteered" me to carry the Roguish One's drawing board, chess set, entire comic book collection, and life-size Raquel Welch blow-up pillow through the New York City subway system. I refused.

No self-proclaimed Twiggy freak wants to be caught stalking Brooklyn's alleys with a life-size Raquel Welch blow-up pillow!

But Duffy dragged me halfway there and we trundled Rog's meagre worldly belongings through the streets till we reached his new abode— Duffy's house. Seems Rog snared a job at Marvel with Duffy's help, and that was Duff's punishment. (You should see the bad karma he got for talking Tony Isabella into getting *me* a job. Sisyphus, watch out!)

As we took the Toonerville Trolley back to Georgetown (a Brooklyn neighborhood noted for its population sparseness, much acreage of which is devoted to empty lots, often bringing to mind post-war Dresden), Rog said, as he dropped an exacto-blade on my foot, "How cum no one's ever done a book with a hero called The Scarecrow before?"

The bus was hushed, mainly because there was no one in the vehicle aside from Roger, Duffy, myself, and the driver who had fallen asleep at the wheel.

I shouted into the still man's hearing aid. He stirred, checked his watch, realized that he'd let the motor idle for three hours, and started directing the bus to the wilds of Georgetown.

Thus was The Scarecrow born.

Little did Len Wein realize when he finally approved the plot for this first story that there had been twelve separate and distinct "first" stories written for the character before he had even *heard* of it.

A few examples:

SCIENTIFIC: The Scarecrow is an actual scarecrow inhabited by one of the microscopic men from Psychoman's home world (See GIANT-SIZE FANTASTIC FOUR #5; purists please see FANTASTIC FOUR ANNUAL #5). He contacts Michael Morbius for help in defeating the villainous Psychoman. Afterwards, upon discovering that he is stuck in the body, and cannot return to his homeworld, he spends the rest of the strip trying to cope with life on the planet earth, and thwarting dastardly doings with emotional powers such as those used by his aforementioned planetary compadre.

INTROSPECTIVE: A young man, testing his own mind and endurance by putting himself in total isolation, enters his own mind and daringly deals with and defeats his own emotions. When brought back to shuffle on the mortal coil once more, he finds himself in complete control of the emotions of others. He dons a scarecrow costume as a symbol of fear, and decides to battle crime for a combination of kicks and egoboo.

ROMANTIC: The Scarecrow is a pulp hero who was killed in the 40's who has been sent back to earth by some mysterious force because the world needs a defender once more.

RELIGIOUS: Our straw man is a messenger of God who has been placed here to keep in balance the eternal scales of good and evil.

But I could go on forever this way. Roger had sparked the beginnings of a fire in my mind, and it took Tony Isabella to feed the flame, and Len Wein to cause it to spring forth into a full blaze.

When I started working for Marvel on her British editions, Tony Isabella was still editing a massive portion of the black and-white magazines, and was looking for some new series ideas to rotate with Tigra and Frankenstein in the pages of MONSTERS UNLEASHED (now defunct).

Wishing to try my hand at scripting, I recommended The Scarecrow.

Little did I dream that Tony would take me out to lunch at BeniHana's (one of my favorite restaurants) and treat me to a meal while we discussed various ideas. It would be set in the 1930's. The Scarecrow would be destroyed once or twice every issue, but would always return. He would use false scarecrow's as decoys. He would not say a word, and never even laugh. He would have a pumpkin head with a leering smile (courtesy of John Byrne, a Canadian fan whose work graces the pages of FOOM, and who did one of the initial sketches for the character, which we'll hopefully be presenting in a future issue of DEAD OF NIGHT).

I wrote up the plot, which dealt with a gang takeover in Chicago, and The Scarecrow's vengeance on behalf of a group of innocent bystanders, gave it to Tony, and sat back, happy and content with the knowledge that The Scarecrow would finally see print.

I was wrong.

The artist who the assignment was given to had since disappeared into the wilds of the city, and Don McGregor, Tony Isabella replacement, who has since been replaced by Archie Goodwin, decided that he wanted to end the series' in the pages of MONSTERS UNLEASHED anyway. Who would have thought that he'd end the continuing series' by getting the book cancelled?

So I began to look for a new home for The Scarecrow.

Len started telling writers that he was looking for back-up features for GIANT-SIZE WEREWOLF BY NIGHT and GIANT-SIZE WEREWOLF BY NIGHT and GIANT-SIZE DRACULA. So I grabbed Len by his lapels (unfortunately he wasn't wearing any that day) and told him that if he didn't use The Scarecrow somewhere I'd let a kindergarden class nest in his office. So he asked me if the stipulation "somewhere" could be fulfilled by his using my script in place of the guest towels in his bathroom.

I told him it couldn't.

After seconds of heated discussion, we decided to place The Scarecrow series in the back of GIANT-SIZE WEREWOLF BY NIGHT (since cancelled). After two more plot revisions, the version you now hold in your hands was formed.

But in-between then and now, word came down from the nebulous Ninth Floor, wherein all economic decisions are made, that two of the reprint books needed a boost in sales. So we decided to place the series in *them.*

Now The Scarecrow stalks THE DEAD OF NIGHT every two months, and BLOODSTONE battles earth's mightiest creatures in the lands WHERE MONSTERS DWELL.

Who said childbirth was easy?

And the moral of the story is— Roger Slifer has already justified his existence... now it's your turn. If you want to be rewarded by the Creator (at least of this comic), send your comments on anything from poker to RUN, BUDDY, RUN (with allowable asides dealing with The Scarecrow) to:

NIGHTMAILS
c/o Marvel Comics Group
575 Madison Avenue
New York, NY
10022

sketches by John Romita.